Managing God's
Higher Learning

ASIAWORLD

Series Editor: Mark Selden

This series charts the frontiers of Asia in global perspective. Central to its concerns are Asian interactions—political, economic, social, cultural, and historical—that are transnational and global, that cross and redefine borders and networks, including those of nation, region, ethnicity, gender, technology, and demography. It looks to multiple methodologies to chart the dynamics of a region that has been the home to major civilizations and is central to global processes of war, peace, and development in the new millennium.

Titles in the Series

Managing God's Higher Learning

U.S.-China Cultural Encounter and Canton Christian College (Lingnan University), 1888–1952

Dong Wang

LEXINGTON BOOKS

A division of
ROWMAN & LITTLEFIELD PUBLISHERS, INC.
Lanham • Boulder • New York • Toronto • Plymouth, UK

To Rose

LEXINGTON BOOKS

A division of Rowman & Littlefield Publishers, Inc.
A wholly owned subsidiary of The Rowman & Littlefield Publishing Group, Inc.
4501 Forbes Boulevard, Suite 200
Lanham, MD 20706

Estover Road
Plymouth PL6 7PY
United Kingdom

British Library Cataloguing in Publication Information Available

Library of Congress Cataloging-in-Publication Data

Wang, Dong.
   Managing god's higher learning : U.S.-China cultural encounter and Canton
Christian College (Lingnan University) 1888-1952 / Dong Wang.
      p.   cm.— (Asiaworld)
   Includes bibliographical references and index.
   ISBN-13: 978-0-7391-1935-8 (cloth : alk. paper)
   ISBN-10: 0-7391-1935-4 (cloth : alk. paper)
   ISBN-13: 978-0-7391-1936-5 (pbk. : alk. paper)
   ISBN-10: 0-7391-1936-2 (pbk. : alk. paper)
      1. Ling nan da xue (Guangzhou, China)—History.   2. Church colleges—
China.   3. Christian education—China.   4. Universities and colleges—
China.   I. Title.
   LG51.C3W36   2007
   378.51'275—dc22

                                                                    2007003554

Printed in the United States of America

∞ ™ The paper used in this publication meets the minimum requirements of
American National Standard for Information Sciences—Permanence of Paper for
Printed Library Materials, ANSI/NISO Z39.48–1992.

Contents

List of Illustrations

Chapter 5

Conclusion

Acknowledgments

In retrospect, choosing Lingnan as the subject of my second monograph in English was providential. First of all, it originated from my year-long visit to Lingnan University in Hong Kong as a Lingnan Foundation Teaching Scholar, where Lily Hu, then a librarian at Lingnan, facilitated my first plunge into a world then unknown to me. My first encounter with Daisy Chia-yaung Hu, another knowledgeable librarian then at the Harvard-Yenching Library, on a United Airlines flight from Boston to Chicago *en route* to Hong Kong in early March 2002, yielded the revelation about the Lingnan records housed at Harvard and has led to a lasting friendship.

Over the past five years, the Lingnan story has absorbed and fascinated me for a number of reasons.

First, it connects with my deep interest in the history of Christianity in China. In the late 1980s, Lu Yao of Shandong University encouraged me to look into missions, missionaries, and anti-missionary incidents in China, a "grey zone" in Chinese academic enquiry at the time. My archival exposure to the subject goes back to my work in 1988 at the Three-Self Patriotic Movement Library in Shanghai. The forays I made in my early years into the topic of Christianity in China planted some important seeds and made it easier for me to understand the role of Canton Christian College in the cultural encounter between China and the United States. My time in Hong Kong from 2001 to 2002 rekindled my interest in Christianity in China.

Second, the Lingnan story and my ongoing experience with Lingnan in an international context have afforded me the opportunity to rethink some larger themes. As the 200th anniversary of the Protestant entry into China draws near, there is much to reflect on in the encounter between ideas, cultures, institutions, and human beings. The rich Lingnan archives deposited at the Harvard-Yenching Library, the Yale Divinity School Library, Guangdong Provincial Archives, Sun Yat-sen University, the

Fong Sum Wood Library at Lingnan University in Hong Kong, and the Honnold/Mudd Library of the Claremont Colleges offer an in-depth view of the encounter between China and the United States. These archives illuminate the nature of Christianity and its actual operations in China, and opened up perspectives that differed from those that I had known.

The publication of the present monograph attests to the extensive assistance I have received from numerous friends and colleagues on both sides of the Pacific and of the Atlantic. I owe grateful thanks to Daniel H. Bays for his enduring support. Our conversations in Hong Kong at the end of 2001, as well as the invitation to the China Christian colleges conference organized by Dan and Ellen Widmer at Wesleyan University in September 2003, motivated me to pursue Lingnan as a research subject. A similar impetus came from Tao Feiya of Shanghai University, who invited me to present my first paper on Lingnan at the international symposium on "Reinterpreting East Asian Christianity" held at Shanghai University in October 2002.

Lingnan's numerous links with the outside world strengthened and expanded my own contacts. There is no word strong enough to express my appreciation to the many scholars who have helped me throughout the preparation of the manuscript. I have had the privilege of working once again with Paul Sorrell and Stein Haugom Olsen, who were instrumental in refining my writing, voicing a second opinion, and seeing the project through to its publication. Special thanks are due to Jessie G. Lutz—who developed China's Christian colleges as a serious academic topic—for reading the manuscript in its entirety. Edward Rhoads gave me detailed feedback, helping me reshape sections of the book and giving me the benefit of his knowledge of China and the Guangzhou area. Mark Selden sharpened my ideas; Terrill E. Lautz of the Henry Luce Foundation was generous in sharing his insights; Gary Tiedemann made useful comments on the manuscript; and Charles Hayford critiqued the manuscript straight from the shoulder. I am also grateful to Paul Cohen, Peter Ng, Jonathan J. Bonk, Kim-kwong Chan, T. Christopher Jespersen, Anthony Cheung, Arthur Rosenbaum, David Pong, Wu Yixiong, John Fitzgerald, Cheng Zhaoqi, Peter C. Perdue, Susan McHone, John Ziemer, Eugenio Menegon, Fukamachi Hideo, Liu Xian, Wang Licheng, and Patty Loo for the exchange of ideas and assistance of various kinds. My students—particularly those in my classes on Christianity in China, history of United States-China relations, and modern China—have taught me a great deal as well.

The groundwork for this study was carried out largely at the Fong Sum Wood Library at Lingnan University in Hong Kong, the Yale Divinity School Library, the Harvard libraries (the Harvard-Yenching Library,

Widener Library, Andover-Harvard Theological Library, Fung Asian Center Library, and Harvard Law School Library), Guangdong Provincial Archives, and the libraries at Sun Yat-sen University and Claremont Colleges. Martha L. Smalley, Xiao Jinghua, Raymond Lum, Grace Chen, Joan R. Duffy, and Carrie Marsh, among others, made my visits pleasurable and productive.

As someone who has benefited from the Lingnan spirit or ethos (*Lingnan jingshen*), I have not yet found a way to repay my debts to scores of Lingnanians (*Lingnan ren*), who never hesitated in giving me invaluable leads and assistance. From its conception, the project received full support from Leslie Stone, executive director of the Lingnan Foundation. Together with the Lingnan Foundation, the Lingnan (University) College Board of Trustees under the leadership of James T. Wu—the driving force behind the Lingnan revival since 1988—gave me a real feel for the multifaceted history of Lingnan. Lee Sui-ming went through the entire manuscript, catching errors and adding supplementary material and photographs of great value. Austin Frank, Mary Chang, Li Xia, Max WY Lue, Vinnie Cheung, and Herdip Singh have also lent a helping hand.

The book is generously funded by the East-West Institute of International Studies at Gordon College, my home institution. I am indebted to Raymond and Priscilla Lee, R. Judson Carlberg, Mark Sargent, Thomas Askew, Janet and Jeff Brice, Shirley Houston, Myron Schirer-Suter, Martha Crain, Alec Li, and my history colleagues for their support of my work.

Finally, it was a delight again to work with the wonderful staff at Lexington Books, Rowman & Littlefield. Sincere thanks go to MacDuff Stewart, Katherine Macdonald, Kim Lyons, and Patrick Dillon for their guidance.

Portions of the book have appeared in the *Journal of American-East Asian Relations* as an article, entitled "Circulating American Higher Education: The Case of Lingnan University (1888–1951)," vol. 9, nos. 3–4 (delayed fall-winter 2000; the back issue published in year 2006): 147–167. Permission to reprint is acknowledged herewith.

The following pages are the result of my venturing into the world of Canton Christian College (Lingnan University) in a bygone era (1888–1952). Should they have any power to impart the charms of the place to the imagination of the reader, I hope that he or she would not repine at lingering with me in the story of Lingnan . . .[1]

NOTE

1. See Washington Irving, *Tales of the Alhambra* (Granada: Ediciones Miguel Sánchez, 1994), p. 31.

Introduction

Themes Driving the Story of Lingnan and Chapter Outline[1]

On March 2, 1922, a testimonial dinner organized by the Institute of International Education (hereafter IIE) was held at Delmonico's in New York City to honor Charles Keyser Edmunds (1876–1949; president of Lingnan University, Canton, China, 1907–1924; president of Pomona College in Claremont, California, 1928–1941) for his contribution to U.S.–China relations. Toastmaster Stephen P. Duggan, director of IIE, began the after-dinner speeches by emphasizing the theme of "bringing America to China and China to America":

> The honor that we are showing to this civilization [China] is shared by a great American educator, a man who left America twenty years ago to go to China, filled with a fine missionary spirit, to bring to China the best of our civilization. He could not do better than bring himself because the best of our civilization is incarnated in Dr. Edmunds. He has come back, bringing from China the fine lessons of life and culture and wisdom that China has to give to the Western World, because, despite our ignorance of China and despite our indifference because of our ignorance, any one who has been there will tell those of us who have not been that there are great lessons of life that China has to teach us.[2]

In the following pages, I present the story of bringing America to China and China to America through an empirical study of a single but transnational institution, Lingnan University (1888–1952), based in Guangzhou (Canton)—the most progressive enclave in China in that period, with longstanding ties with foreign countries. Many aspects of Lingnan—such as its management, governance, and its wide-ranging interactions across the Pacific—have either rarely been made the subject of scholarly discussion or are different from what we think we know about U.S.–China cultural encounter and Christian higher education in China in the past. Across time, space, and human experience, the world of Lingnan not only opens a window on higher education, politics, society, economics, Christianity, and cultural encounters—but also on women and business management, the various factors that favored or threatened the university's success (and even survival), as well as the wider sphere of U.S.–China relations.

Over the centuries, many men and women crossed the bridge from West to East. Jonathan Spence rightly notes that "[t]hey bared their own souls and mirrored their own societies in their action, yet in doing so they highlighted fundamental Chinese values."[3] In a similar manner, Lingnan speaks to us still, across the divides of time, space, and race, from the indefinable plateau where West and East meet. In the course of such an encounter, foreigners and Chinese changed and were changed by locales in variable ways.

THEMES DRIVING THE STORY OF LINGNAN

The Expanding Horizons of Christianity in China: Rethinking Christian Colleges in China

There has been much talk about China's "peaceful" and "un-peaceful" rise and the implications for America.[4] Regardless of the variously optimistic, alarmist, and negative reactions to China's reforms since 1978— often characterized as "a second revolution" in the history of the People's Republic of China[5]—there is little disagreement that China's poorly educated labor force could well "moderate its long term growth potential."[6] What makes higher education tick in China in the age of reform? As the nation demands increased literacy for its adult labor force, it could well draw inspiration from what was achieved in Guangzhou in the not-so-distant past by Lingnan University.

The history of Lingnan University is a complex one, with many changes over the years of name (in both English and Chinese), the conception of education, and the locale of the institution. Established in 1888 in Canton, the college was known successively as the Christian College in China (1888–1903), Canton Christian College (1903–1926), and Lingnan University (1926–1951). Its Chinese names were more numerous: Gezhi shuyuan (1888–1900), Lingnan xuetang (1900–1912), Lingnan xuexiao (1912–1918), Lingnan daxue (1918–1927), and Sili Lingnan daxue (1927–1952). The different levels of study offered included the elementary (primary) school (*gaodeng xiaoxue*), the preparatory (middle school, high school) school (*zhongxue*), the overseas school (*huaqiao xuexiao*), and the college proper.

After the closure of Lingnan University in Guangzhou in 1952, Lingnan College (*Lingnan xueyuan*) was founded in Hong Kong in 1967, and in 1999 the Hong Kong Special Administrative Region government granted it university status with its name changed to Lingnan University (Lingnan daxue). In 1988, the original institution, now known as Lingnan (University) College, was constituted as part of Sun Yat-sen University (*Zhongshan daxue Lingnan xueyuan*) in Guangzhou at the urging of Lingnan alumni.[7] (See photo 1; photo 2.)

In December 1987, thirty-six years after Lingnan's forced merger with Sun Yat-sen University (*Zhongshan daxue*), the Chinese Ministry of Education approved the establishment of Lingnan (University) College as part of Sun Yat-sen University in Guangzhou, where the old Lingnan had been located.[8] The Ministry's decision came on the eve of the celebration of the centenary of Lingnan University, and it also came at the strong request of Lingnan alumni, both overseas and domestic.[9] Since then, Lingnan's loyal

Photo 1. Lingnan (University) College, Guangzhou, Guangdong.
Photograph provided by Li Xia.

Photo 2. *Lingnan University Hong Kong. Photograph provided by Max WY Lue.*

alumni all over the world, particularly those in Hong Kong and the United States, have contributed over U.S.$20 million to the institution (up to 2006). In addition, Guangzhou Lingnan (University) College's teaching and research development fund, registered with the Hong Kong Special Administrative Region government since 1997, has risen to US$1.28 million.[10] Over Thanksgiving 2005, Lingnan alumni organized a grand "2005 Lingnan Global Reunion" (*quanqiu Lingnanren Xianggang da tuanjü*) in Hong Kong and Guangzhou to "raise the profile of Lingnan education" and to "support Lingnan education into the next century."[11]

Despite the lack of an alma mater since 1952, the Lingnan enterprise has "spread around the world, with alumni clubs on almost every continent."[12] Although the Lingnan University that existed from 1888 to 1952 is long gone as an institution, its memory has continued to command so much loyalty that a careful examination of the Lingnan story is necessary to help understand the evolving nature of Sino-American cultural encounter from the late nineteenth through the twenty-first century.

Daniel H. Bays and Ellen Widmer chart the trajectory of English and Chinese historiography on China's Christian colleges by dividing the development of scholarship into three stages.[13] First, the period from the mid-1950s to the early 1960s marked the appearance of a series of celebratory books on the Chinese Christian colleges. The second stage, in the

1970s, witnessed the publication of Jessie G. Lutz's pioneering study, *China and the Christian Colleges 1850–1950* and Philip West's *Yenching University and Sino-Western Relations, 1916–1952*.[14] According to Bays and Widmer, a third stage has taken place mainly within China, where two academic centers have steered the direction of research in the area. They are the Center for Historical Research on the History of the China Christian Colleges (*Zhongguo jiaohui daxue yanjiu zhongxin*) at Central China Normal University (*Huazhong shifan daxue*) in Wuhan, and the Centre for the Study of Religion and Chinese Society of Chung Chi College at the Chinese University of Hong Kong.

Existing studies of the eighteen Christian colleges and universities in modern China[15] have significantly enriched our knowledge of these shared foreign experiments in higher education. However, at the risk of overgeneralization, several historiographical patterns of scholarship can be discerned here.[16] First, attention is often drawn to confrontation, rather than appreciation, negotiation, accommodation, and integration, in the transfer of an American educational model to Chinese soil. This line of thinking understandably reflects a historical perception of the role of mission schools as part of the failed efforts to convert China to Christianity in the past. Second, despite efforts to bridge the gap in recent years,[17] the wide-ranging cultural interactions that occurred across the Pacific and the various links between Christian colleges and their local environments—as compared with their evangelical mission and political participation in successive Chinese revolutions—need to be broached further.[18] Third, the existing literature on the China Christian colleges and universities has not grappled with the problem of how these educational institutions, with their strongly individual histories—such as Yenching University (*Yanjing daxue*) and Lingnan University—differed significantly from one another.

The foundation of Lingnan University as a Western evangelical enterprise takes us back to the initial encounter between China and America. By the end of the nineteenth century, the tempo of intellectual and cultural contacts between Chinese and American elites had increased.[19] As it reached out to South China's elites and well-to-do merchants and raised its academic standards as one of the leading institutions of higher learning in China, Lingnan University, whose founder Andrew Happer had envisioned it as founded on a broader base than a purely proselytizing one, swiftly expanded its role in improving social conditions for the Chinese people. It also sought to build the type of Christian character that involved the whole person, as well as offering training in "citizenship, scientific agriculture, medicine, engineering, and liberal arts."[20]

The case of Lingnan University points us to the following four areas that may be helpful in the rethinking of Christian colleges in China.

First of all, in order to fully assess the dynamics of the China Christian colleges and universities we need to probe into an overlooked topic, i.e., the operational and financial management of each institution.[21] Second, in Lingnan's efforts to provide quality education and teaching excellence, the transplantation of the American educational model was planned as "China-centric," as well as being a service rendered to America, or to the entire humanity.[22] Generations of Lingnanians, both American and Chinese at various levels, were deeply concerned with such issues as solving China's many structural problems, building a nation, and, finally, making China strong. Third, in tackling such problems, the Lingnan story reveals the adaptive nature of U.S.–China cultural interaction. The eclecticism characteristic of Lingnan involved the integration of American imports— people and knowledge—into the geographical and social context of South China. The fourth point centers on the "Lingnan ethos" (*Lingnan jingshen*, Lingnan spirit). In her well-known study, Jessie G. Lutz notes that the development and growth of the Christian colleges in China "took place with little reference to the life and desire of the Chinese people."[23] In a similar vein, Wen-hsin Yeh, in her acclaimed work, *The Alienated Academy: Culture and Politics in Republican China, 1919–1937*, stresses the profound sense of "estrangement" and "alienation" that characterized campus culture during the interwar period.[24] The "Lingnan spirit" offers a counterexample to the findings of Lutz and Yeh. Lingnan's mission of "Education for Service" (*Zuoyü yingcai, fuwu shehui*) exemplified its goal of serving society, and Lingnan made an effort to tailor the education it offered to the needs of the South China region. Furthermore, the careful grading of different levels of study (*yitiaolong jiaoyü*) not only nurtured the loyalty of generations of students, but also sustained the college's very existence, its expansion, and the recent revival of Lingnan (University) College (*Lingnan xueyuan*) of Sun Yat-sen University in Guangzhou, and of Lingnan University (*Lingnan daxue*) in Hong Kong.[25] In sum, the Lingnan experience shows that Christian higher learning institutions should be given fuller consideration in assessing the diverse forces that have shaped Chinese educational history.

Bringing America to China: Adaptation and Eclecticism

In recent years, Chinese scholarship on the history of Christian education in China has been gaining ground over Western production.[26] Some recent Chinese publications, such as Wang Licheng's richly documented book on the University of Shanghai (also known as Shanghai College, *Hujiang daxue*) and Zhang Kaiyuan's foreword to a pictorial book series on the University of Nanking (Nanjing), West China Union University, and Fukien (Fujian) Christian University, devote some space to the issues of adaptation to Chinese society (*shiying Zhongguo shehui*), education *for* society (*jiaoyü shehuihua*) and two-way cultural interaction. This is a sign that the older view of Chinese Christian universities as "tools of imperialist cultural invasion" has been set aside.[27]

In the case of Lingnan, the process of bringing the American educational model to China while incorporating local involvement comprised four major aspects: accepting local conditions; adapting American curricula to the needs of Chinese students; maintaining collegiate integrity in the context of rising nationalism spurred by the advances and retreats of the Chinese revolution; and nurturing relationships with various political movements and with the Chinese authorities at national, provincial, and city levels.

First, the fact that Lingnan was rooted in South China while committed to maintaining international standards meant that "the student has the advantage of keeping in close touch with his own country and of correlating his education with the economic, social and general scientific needs of China."[28] In the case of the university's College of Agriculture, applying undergraduate learning to conditions in China was considered "one of the greatest advantages."[29] In the words of Governor Chen of Guangdong Province in 1922, "Canton Christian College is a powerful factor in the reconstruction of China." The new notion of American higher education in the Chinese context also manifested itself in the establishment of an elementary, a middle, and an overseas Chinese school. By 1925, Lingnan had developed three levels of schools: the Elementary School (offering six years' schooling, it opened in 1906), the Middle School (six years, including the College Preparatory year; formerly known as the Preparatory Department, in 1911 it became the Middle School), and the College of Arts and Sciences and the College of Agriculture (each four years).[30]

Second, the importance of adapting the curricula of American universities to the real needs of Chinese students was emphatically stressed at Lingnan. Contrary to the general belief that missionary schools tended to adopt a "more-like-America" policy, the Lingnan experience reveals flexibility and pragmatism. For instance, Charles Edmunds commented: "It will not do at all to force an American curriculum on the Chinese students of the present generation, if ever."[31]

The question of adaptation and eclecticism in the China context was especially pronounced under three of Lingnan's American presidents—Oscar F. Wisner (Yin Shijia, president 1899–1907), Charles K. Edmunds (Yan Wenshi, president 1908–1924), and James McClure Henry (Xiang Yage, president 1924–1927). The American educators at Lingnan were more eager to promote mutual cultural understanding than to impose American learning patterns.[32] With the advent of the 1911 revolution, Lingnanians welcomed the new opportunities for the modernization of education. Edmunds deemed "the work of the education of the people as the foundation of a permanent reform." In the new "self-realization" movement, Lingnan ought to render service as a "true model" to South China.[33]

On the other hand, while united in their commitment to serving the needs of China, Lingnan's Chinese presidents, Chung Wing Kwong (1866–1942, president 1927–1937), Lee Ying Lam (Li Yinglin, 1892–1954, president 1938–1948), and Ch'en Su-ching (Chen Xüjing, 1903–1967, president 1948–1952) had no desire to retain the Chinese model of education.[34] In 1929, a year after the Chinese takeover of the management of Lingnan University, Lee Ying Lam, then vice-president of Lingnan acting on behalf of Chung Wing Kwong (president), together with Clinton Laird (Liang Jingdun, Lingnan faculty 1905–1942), reformulated the character of Lingnan education (*banxue zhi shixiang*) as private (*sili xing*), Christian (*jidu xing*), international (*guoji xing*), and Chinese (*Zhongguo xing*).[35] Chung and Chen, in particular, took a strong stance on internationalization and Americanization, although their major concern was building a strong China. In a 1936 radio address entitled "International Lingnan University" (*guoji de Lingnan daxue*), Chung noted that "in the most recent hundred years, world transportation has become convenient. With the availability of ships, railways, post offices, telegraphs, and airplanes, our earth is shrinking . . . there will be a day when there are no longer racial lines between black, white, yellow, red, and brown." He continued optimistically: "in my opinion, the dawn of worldly ultimate peace all hinges on academics . . . universities throughout the world gather international scholars. Besides the training of their domestic youth, they take great pride in being able to admit more foreign students." Chung then discussed the spirit of internationalism at Lingnan University:

> Currently, Lingnan University has over twenty foreign professors and thirty-six foreign students. The exchange students live, eat, study, and play sport with the local students. Our university is in the process of being internationalized. I hope all Chinese universities, public and private, can open their doors to hire more foreign faculty and take more foreign students.[36]

In comparison with Chung's internationalism, Ch'en Su-ching believed that China's situation could be remedied only by a thoroughgoing Westernization.[37] An outstanding sociologist and a native of Hainan who had lived in Singapore and Malaysia for 6 years in his youth, Ch'en graduated with a Ph.D. from the University of Berlin,[38] an M.A. from the University of Illinois, and a B.A. in sociology from Fudan University. He had high standing in educational circles, having served on the faculties of Lingnan (1928–1928, 1931–1934) and Nankai University (1934–1937), as dean of the College of Law and Commerce of the National Southwest Associated University (Xinan lianda, 1937–1945), and as dean of Nankai University

(1945–1948) before taking up the presidency at Lingnan.[39] Amid the political uncertainties at the dawn of the Communist domination of China, Chen instilled a sense of calm in the entire staff and student body "which has called forth admiring comment from the observers of the near-panic in some other sectors of the Canton community."[40] In the forefront of the debates on the relative merits of Chinese and Western culture in the 1920s and 1930s, Ch'en Su-ching's stated aim was to find a viable role for Chinese culture (*xunzhao yitiao chulu*). Pondering the future of his native culture, he wrote: "to save China from its present threat of extinction, we have to be thoroughly Westernized (*quanpan xihua*). Wholesale Westernization, however, means completely rejecting the monopoly of Chinese tradition in order to provide individuals with opportunities for fulfilling their potential."[41]

Although operating in a sort of protected domain under special rules, Lingnan found itself embroiled in the unstable Chinese politics and anti-foreign agitation that followed the collapse of the Qing dynasty in 1911. Political instability effervesced into protests and rallies against the imperialist presence in China. Unlike some other foreign institutions as portrayed by scholars, including Hsiang-Ya Medical College (Yale-in-China, in Changsha), Lingnan weathered the storm of anti-foreign agitation, labor disputes, and frequent changes of government in Guangzhou as a result of its fairly even-handed and levelheaded management and the mutual interests that bound Americans and Chinese together during these years. One such example was Lingnan's handling of the labor unrest that began on March 8, 1926, influenced by the labor movements in Guangzhou. The labor organization at Lingnan, *Nanda gongren gongji hui* (the Lingnan Workers' Association of Mutual Assistance), representing some 250 local workmen, put forward an eight-clause document demanding a reduction of work hours from ten to eight hours per day, and a salary increase. The union, assisted by armed workers from Guangzhou, demanded an answer from Lingnan within forty-eight hours and threatened a strike. James M. Henry, then Lingnan's president, had the option of calling on foreign consuls to deal with the agitators, as suggested by some foreigners. However, he invited the Lingnan union to meet together with the Peasants and Workers Bureau (*Nonggong ting*) of Guangdong Province for mediation. On March 17, Lingnan and the union signed an agreement that settled the dispute amicably. Lingnan gave its workers a salary raise and a reduction in working hours from ten hours to nine hours a day. The agreement also legitimatized the Lingnan Workers' Association of Mutual Assistance by designating a place for its office and giving it the right to be consulted on matters of hiring and layoffs of workers.[42]

On the other hand, the constant disorder and revolution that threatened both Canton and China as a whole prevented Lingnan University, and Christian higher education in general, from achieving its full potential. Political instability militated against the great achievements that Lingnan could have accomplished, although Lingnanians managed to sustain a modicum of stability during these turbulent years.

Fourth, maintaining a good relationship with the Chinese authorities and local governments of all complexions through these politically confusing and unstable years in South China made Lingnan unique as a local institution. The university's special contribution was emphasized by Ma Soo, representing the Guangdong provincial government at the testimonial dinner for Charles K. Edmunds held in 1922, at a time when the central government in Beijing was weakened by local warlords:

> I am glad to add my feeble voice to the volume of praise that has been read to you by the toastmaster about Dr. Edmunds' work in South China. The Minister of Education in Peking has sent in his greetings, also the Governor of the Province of Kwangtung. You see, in the republic of letters we don't divide, although in politics we do. . . . The Canton Christian College . . . takes an interest in the work of the community. For example, in the silk industry in South China. [*sic*] Silk, as you know, is the largest item of export from Canton, and the Canton Christian College is helping to improve the silk industry there. It does other things. It tries to help the people to live better, to have better conditions of living . . .[43]

Lingnan became a forum for people of different political aspirations to air their views. Notable examples included Sun Yat-sen's high-profile visits to Lingnan in May 1912;[44] the lecture given by a representative of Feng Yüxiang, the "Christian General," condemning the Nationalist Party (Guomindang) founded by Sun Yat-sen; and the visit of Mr. Norman, Sun Yat-sen's former advisor, hosted by Chung Wing Kwong on the Lingnan campus.[45] Then there was the ten-day recess called for Lingnan students to assist with a census of Canton under the auspices of the city's mayor Wu Chaoshu, and the raising of Guomindang flags over the campus in 1925 while Mayor Wu inspected Lingnan. There were also class field trips to the Whampoa Military Academy headed by the young Jiang Jieshi, and the first-hand interviews conducted by Lingnan students and faculty with labor union delegations in Canton from the United States and Britain.[46]

Increasing appeals to the Chinese government for funds and the growing proportion of government grants in Lingnan's budget indicate the further integration of Lingnan into its Chinese context. While drawing up a budget for US$320,000 for 1927–1928—the Chinese portion was US$190,000 (including tuition), and the American Foundation's US$130,000—during a time of political uncertainty in China, Chung Wing Kwong was even able to appeal to and earn the trust of the Guangdong provincial government. As a result, the Guangdong government granted Lingnan, a private university, 260,000 yuan (about US$100,000). In addition, the city of Guangzhou agreed to take care of security matters on the campus, which saved Lingnan over 10,000 yuan.[47] (I shall deal with this point in detail in chapter 3.)

Bringing China to America: Presenting China and Marketing Lingnan

Lingan also brought China to America through various channels of interaction. First, the significant number of both faculty and students who studied at or visited sister universities and colleges in the United States contributed to American knowledge of China. This partly accounts for the strong presence of Lingnan alumni throughout North America until today. In 1925, the President's Report for 1919–1924 contained the following career statistics for 546 alumni and former college and middle school students: medicine 18, political and military 69, engineering 19, commerce 162, education 102, Christian work 13, agriculture 7, journalism 6, fine arts 3, study in America 132, study in Europe 15.[48] Most striking in this list is the high number of students who went on to study in the United States after graduating from Lingnan.

On returning home to America, some former teaching staff pursued careers in China affairs. Earl Swisher, for instance, received a doctorate in Chinese history from Harvard University and became a recognized specialist on China after spending three years (1925–1928) at Lingnan teaching history as an instructor. He published an important general study of the country in 1964.[49] His knack for vivid analysis and his on the spot observation of events taking place in Guangzhou during the tumultuous years 1925–1928 made Swisher's letters and diaries important supplements to our understanding of that period.[50]

Lingnan and China were also presented to the general public in the United States by foreign exchangers at Lingnan who were part of the university's plan to "strengthen the bonds of international understanding and friendship."[51] Though short, their stay in China left an imprint on their professional and personal lives: they still publish exchanger newsletters many years later.[52] Some even made China the subject of their careers. Examples are Ralph N. Clough, one of the forty exchange students of 1936–1937, a long-time Foreign Service Officer in the U.S. State Department and a prolific author on U.S.–China relations;[53] Hugh Deane, a writer of a different and more left perspective wrote and edited many books more sympathetic to Mao Zedong's revolution;[54] and Mel Jacoby, who became a correspondent for *Life* magazine in the late 1930s. Some alumni even passed on their assigned Chinese name to their sons.[55]

My second major point is that Lingnan, Canton, and China achieved prominence in the United States partly as a result of Lingnan's vigorous marketing tactics in North America. Shared visions imparted meaning, enthusiasm, and direction to Lingnan's fundraising campaigns. Earl Swisher recorded his initial encounter with Lingnan and China. In May 1924, he had graduated in history with honors from the University of Colorado, but was uncertain about his next step:

> While walking across campus to work one day shortly before his graduation, he was caught in a typical Colorado cloudburst. He found shelter in a nearby building being used by Canton Christian College to recruit faculty for the forthcoming year. Waiting for the rain to stop, Swisher expressed a mild interest in a position at the College and left his name and address. He was somewhat surprised several weeks later to be offered a contract. By the end of August, he had arrived in Canton to assume his duties.[56]

In Lingnan's campaign in North America, the university was presented as a window on China, which represented opportunities, mutual benefits, and an outlet for superior talents. As W. Henry Grant said, "There is unbounded opportunity here, but only for a first-class job."[57] Conversely, Lingnan, as presented by Charles K. Edmunds, stood for "the great opportunity that we Americans have to serve our own country in helping China come into her rightful place among the nations of modern times, and to benefit ourselves as well as our friends across the Pacific."[58]

A Two-Way Interaction

As a significant Christian university in China, established by Americans in the late nineteenth century, Lingnan takes us back to the historical encounter between China and the United States. In reflecting upon the nature of history, James Sheehan, in his valedictory column as president of the American Historical Association in 2005, states that "what really matters is not whether history is old or new, but whether it is sensitive to the rich variety of the human experience."[59] Recent research into the regulation, participation, and the Chinese communities in Australia from 1860 to 1940 equally yields a conclusion analogous to what Sheehan stresses: the Chinese-Australian encounters "did not happen only in the abstract realm of White Australia and anti-Chinese movements. They took place in varied locales and through diverse contacts between individuals."[60] The Lingnan story, on the same wavelength, presents a trajectory of interactions between Lingnan University (and Canton, Hong Kong, South China, and ultimately China) and the outside world (the

United States, Britain, South Asia, Oceania, South America, etc.) that can be documented in compelling detail.

The May 30th Incident of 1925 in Shanghai, which was triggered by the death of Gu Zhenghong—a worker at a Japanese cotton mill who had been killed while on strike two weeks before—and the subsequent reactions in other cities including Guangzhou, confronted the college's expatriate community with some rather uncomfortable issues of imperialism, colonialism, nationalism, and justice.[61] On June 6, 1925, acting on their own initiative, the foreign staff addressed a letter to the Chinese staff, alumni, and students of Canton Christian College:[62]

> As citizens of our own countries, also working in a college that seeks to promote the welfare of the Chinese nation and foster international friendship, we wish to say something, however inadequate, about the present situation in China, especially in view of recent events in Shanghai . . .
>
> We are not competent at the present juncture and with the information at our disposal to pass judgment and assign responsibility for these particular actions; we are not present and we do not know the full facts. We do, however, feel that in addition to expressing our sympathy with all those [who] are suffering, the time has come to make clear somewhat more publicly what we have often less formally said to our Chinese friends and among ourselves,—that historically the policies which have led to so many Chinese to lose confidence in our foreign States [sic] have often been aggressive and unfair to China. What happened this week in Shanghai was not produced in a day, it is the result of past years.
>
> We are also convinced that our relations with China will never be satisfactory unless they are based entirely upon the principle of justice, and it seems to us only bare justice that China should be treated now and in the future as a full member of the family of nations . . .
>
> We would also most earnestly hope that the present occasion as it affects both Shanghai and other parts of China, should not be used as an opportunity for foreign interference but rather as an occasion for a serious attempt to satisfy the legitimate aspirations of the Chinese people, and for working out with mutual respect better and more equitable relationships.[63]

This powerful statement, one of many such in Lingnan's history, reflects a genuine humility and some degree of solidarity with Chinese nationalist revolutionaries. It also bears witness to the profound interaction between Canton Christian College and its political, social, and religious environment in the age of imperialism and nationalism. The foreign senior management of Lingnan did not deplore the backwardness of Chinese culture from afar. Rather, they sought to run Lingnan in a way that would benefit both China and America.

In 1946, under the auspices of the Associated Boards for Christian Colleges in China and United Service to China, Inc., Sz-to Wai (Situ Wei), a graduate of Lingnan University and the founder of four Lingnan primary and secondary schools in Canton, Shanghai, and Saigon, organized an exhibition of paintings by Chinese war refugee artists that traveled throughout the United States. Despite its commercial nature and other sensitivities, the exhibition flyer in English offered one view of the U.S.-China cultural encounter in the 1940s.

> Cultural exchange between China and America is a two-way bridge which has many piers, among the strongest of which is the China Colleges.[64] . . . To China these Colleges have taken Western languages, and with these languages, the great literature which has been the product of the noblest minds in the West. Through this literature Western history, philosophy, and science have also been introduced to the Chinese. In taking Western music to China the Christian Colleges have made one of their most significant contributions, for from the choral groups which they have developed have come superior artists for China's first symphony orchestras. . . . The bridge established between the two countries by the flow of professors and students does not carry one-way traffic only. In the United States today are several hundred graduates of the Christian Colleges ranging in importance from famous statesmen, writers, and scholars to young graduate students. Each of these graduates brings an appreciation of China's great culture to his American acquaintances and friends.[65]

CHAPTER OUTLINE

This monograph grew out of my desire for a better understanding of the numerous ties that bind China and the United States. Keen to speak to the China field in the Chinese and English language worlds, I have therefore paid close attention to the most up-to-date scholarship in preparing for the manuscript. A note on my use of the Lingnan archives should be made here. Since 2001, my first exposure to the Lingnan topic, rounds of intensive reading of the archives in different localities across the Pacific—Lingnan University Hong Kong, Lingnan (University) College in Guangzhou, Guangdong Provincial Archives, Harvard University, Yale University, and Claremont Colleges—partly explain the mix of materials either in hard copy or on microfilm. The legibility of the microfilms on pre-1952 Lingnan determined my decision about whether the original archives held at Harvard University should be consulted as well.

This book mainly adopts a topical approach and is not intended to cover all aspects of Lingnan's history and development. Its five chapters are organized around the four major themes singled out above. In chapter 1, in addition to a chronological sketch of the history of Lingnan University, I discuss the geographical, cultural, political, and economic setting in which Canton Christian College operated. This chapter addresses questions such as how the issues of adaptation and integration were configured in a specific geographic location, and the ways in which Lingnan functioned in various contexts over the years. Chapter 2 takes a fresh look at the management of Lingnan University in light of some major themes of cultural migration including changes in curriculum, the discourse on higher education in China, international cooperation, and local contribution and participation in the work of the college. Chapter 3 covers the nuts and bolts of Canton Christian College's campaign strategies in different corners of the world in the early twentieth century. It is a prolegomenon to the study of the financial management of Lingnan, a topic usually overlooked in scholarly discussions of the history of Christian higher education in China.[66] The linking of trans-Pacific Christian higher education and corporate business management in the "Lingnan complex" is addressed here. Chapter 4 focuses on higher education for women at Lingnan University, the first coeducational institution of higher education in China. Lingnan took pride in graduating Miss Leung Tsau Ming (Liang Jiuming) in 1921, the first Chinese woman to receive the Bachelor of Arts degree from a coeducational institution in China. At Lingnan, the proportion of women among collegiate students was 17 percent in 1924, 26.9 percent in 1927, 24.5 percent in 1930, 29.3 percent in 1943, and 34.2 percent in 1946—far above the national average of 2.5 percent in the same years.[67] The Lingnan archives reveal that the management of programs for women at Lingnan confounds the assumptions made by historians of Christian education for women. In discussing and implementing projects for women at Lingnan, the overriding emphasis fell on business concerns, rather than reflecting imperialist sentiments "barking at the moon." The final chapter deals with Charles K. Edmunds, former president of both Lingnan University and Pomona College, and the connection between his Chinese and American experiences interpreted by his liberal arts ideals. Edmunds' Lingnan and Pomona stories illustrate a two-way interaction, in areas such as college governance and curriculum, experienced on both sides of the Pacific. Whereas Lingnan University was part of the westward exportation of higher education from America, which in its turn had been inspired by European models, the impact of his Lingnan experience on Charles K. Edmunds is a striking example of the "reflex influence" on America.[68]

NOTES

1. The archival sources of Lingnan University are scattered across the Pacific. The Harvard-Yenching Library holds part of the pre-1952 Lingnan archives in

paper documents stored in 200 boxes (32cm x 24.4cm x 7.5cm), donated by the Trustees of Lingnan University (now the Lingnan Foundation based at Yale University). This portion of the Lingnan archives is also available on microfilm. (While the pre-1952 Harvard Lingnan Archives are stated to be held in 219 boxes, there are some gaps in the numbering.) The post-1952 materials, in 65 boxes with a total linear footage of 29 inches, are housed under Record Group 14 in the Yale Divinity School Library. The rich collection deposited at the Guangdongsheng dang'an'guang [Guangdong provincial archives] under files # 38-1 and # 38-4 is a mix of the Lingnan records in Chinese and English from 1888 to the 1960s. Sun Yat-sen University (Zhongshan daxue) and Lingnan University in Tuen Mun, Hong Kong, also have substantial archival collections, particularly of Lingnan's publications.

2. *Record of the Testimonial Dinner to [sic] Dr. Charles K. Edmunds*, New York, March 2, 1922. Trustees of Lingnan University, microfilm roll 39. Other speakers included the Minister of Education in Beijing (representing the government of the Republic of China); the Governor of the Province of Guangdong (Chen Jiongming); Alfred Sze, the Chinese Minister to the United States; Wellington Koo, the Chinese Minister to England; Frederick Courtland Penfield, former U.S. ambassador to Austria-Hungary; Frank P. Graves, Commissioner of Education; and Ma Soo, the special representative of the Republic of China for the Government at Canton. Ding Shenzun, et al., eds., *Guangdong minguoshi* [The history of Guangdong in the Republic of China] (Guangzhou: Guangdong renmin chubanshe, 2004), vol. 2, p. 1335.

3. Jonathan D. Spence, *Western Advisers in China: To Change China*, 1st ed. published in 1969 by Little, Brown, New York. Reprint ed. (New York: Penguin Books, 1980), introduction.

4. Robert Sutter, "Asia in the Balance: America and China's 'Peaceful Rise'," *Current History* 103, no. 674 (2004): 284–89.

5. John Wong, "China's Economy," in *Understanding Contemporary China*, ed. 2nd (Boulder, CO: Lynne Rienner Publishers, Inc., 2003).

6. Ibid., p. 135. According to John Wong, in 1999 only 7.5 percent of the relevant age group in China were receiving tertiary education, compared to 71.7 percent in South Korea, 56 percent in Taiwan, and 43.8 percent in Singapore. Wong's figures, however, don't correspond to Robert E. Gamer's in the same volume. Gamer writes: "Fewer than 2 percent of China's youth receive higher education (the government is aggressively expanding the size of university student bodies, but that percentage will rise very slowly) . . ." see Robert E. Gamer, "Chinese Politics," in *Understanding Contemporary China*, ed. Robert E. Gamer (Boulder, CO: Lynne Rienner Publishers, 2003), p. 95.

7. See Charles Hodge Corbett, *Lingnan University: A Short History Based Primarily on The Records of the University's American Trustees* (New York, NY: The Trustees of Lingnan University, 1963). *Lingnan xiaoyou* [Lingnan alumni], Guangzhou, 1988, vol. 16, pp. 7–8.

8. In 2006, Lingnan College at Sun Yat-sen University houses the university's Business School, including the departments of Economics Public Finance & Taxation, Finance, International Business, Risk Management & Insurance, and Busi-

ness Management. The School offers a Ph.D. program in world economy, and masters programs in political economy, Western economics, quantitative economics, world economy, finance, public finance, international trade, population, and resource and environmental economics. It also offers MBA and EMBA programs, and foreign degree programs in the U.S. (Chinese Executive MBA, CHEMBA) and in France (Diplome d'Etudes Superieures Specialisée de Commerce Exterieur, DESS). In the 2001 assessment round, Lingnan (University) College's MBA program ranked first among the twenty-eight universities offering an MBA program in China. According to a survey report of the "Most Valuable Full-time MBA Programs in China" released by *Forbes* China in April 2006, Lingnan's MBA program is ranked third among forty-five universities nationwide. Source from *Lingnan tongxun* [Lingnan Bulletin], published by Zhongshan daxue Lingnan (daxue) xueyuan, no. 17 (April 2006): 1. Also see http://www.forbeschina.com/inc/mba form.asp, accessed on October 7, 2006.

9. According to Wu Zhande (James T. Wu) and Lee Sui-ming, as of 2006 financial contributions from the Board of Trustees of Lingnan (University) College (at Sun Yat-sen University), Lingnan alumni, the Lingnan Foundation in the United States (former Trustees of Lingnan University), and other sources reached HK$1.8 billion (1 US$ = HK$7.8). Over a dozen buildings were constructed during the 1990s and 2000s, including the Computer Center in Lam Woo Hall in 1993, Lingnan Hall (1994), the S. T. Wu Library (1995), the Wong Ming Hin Hall Teaching Building (1993), the Wong Chuen King Lecture Hall (1993), the J. T. Wu Administration Center (1998), the Wing Kwong Hall Guest House (1999), the Lingnan Residential Building (1999), the Po Ting IP Hall MBA Teaching Building (2000), and the MBA Center (2006). In addition, funds for teaching and research were established, and college networking and library resources were upgraded, making teaching and research conditions at Lingnan (University) College first class among Chinese business schools. See *Lingnan (University) College of Sun Yat-sen University*, brochure, Guangzhou, China, January 2003; Wu Zhande (James T. Wu), "Lingnan jiaoyü chongxian Kangle de jingguo" [The process of restoring Lingnan education in the spirit of Honglok], manuscript provided by Lee Sui-ming. (Honglok was the name given to the original Lingnan campus in Guangzhou.)

10. See http://www.lingnan.org/lnrj/lnjy.htm. Accessed on June 10, 2002. Statistical figures updated and supplied by Lee Sui-ming in September 2006.

11. http://www.2005lingnanreunioninhongkong.com/index.htm. Accessed on December 2, 2005.

12. Douglas P. Murray, Preface, Lee Sui-ming, ed. *Lingnan daxue wenxian mulu: Guangzhou Lingnan daxue lishi dang'an ziliao* [Index of the Lingnan University archives] (Hong Kong: Lingnan University, 2000).

13. General introduction, in Daniel H. Bays and Ellen Widmer, eds., *China's Christian Colleges: Transpacific Connections, 1900–1950*, forthcoming.

14. Jessie Gregory Lutz, *China and Christian Colleges, 1850–1950* (Ithaca, NY: Cornell University Press, 1971). Philip West, *Yenching University and Sino-Western Relations, 1916–1952* (Cambridge, MA: Harvard University Press, 1976).

15. The eighteen Christian colleges and universities in China are: (Protestant institutions) Canton Christian College (Lingnan University, Lingnan daxue), Fukien Christian University (Fujian xiehe daxue), Ginling College (Jinling nü

wenli xueyuan), Hangchou University (Zhejiang daxue), Hsiang-Ya Medical College (Xiangya yixueyuan, also Yale-in-China, in Changsha), Huachung University (Huazhong daxue), Hwa Na College (Huanan nü wenli xueyuan), Shangtung University (Qilu daxue), St. John's University (Sheng yuehan daxue), Soochow University (Dongwu daxue), University of Nanking (Jilin daxue), University of Shanghai (Hujiang daxue), Women's Christian Medical College (Shanghai nüzi yixueyuan), West China Union University (Huaxi xiehe daxue Chengdu, founded in 1911), Yenching University (Yanjing daxue). The Catholic institutions are Aurora University (Zhendan daxue), Catholic University (Furen daxue), and Tsinku University (Jingu daxue, in Tianjin). See William Purviance Fenn, *Christian Higher Education in Changing China, 1880–1950* (Grand Rapids, MI: William B. Eerdmans Publishing Co., 1976), p. 11. This listing differs from the sixteen Christian colleges and universities cited by Lutz, *China and Christian Colleges, 1850–1950*, pp. 530–31.

16. Some of the ideas here are drawn from my article written in 2002. See Dong Wang, "Circulating American Higher Education: The Case of Lingnan University (1888–1951)," *Journal of American-East Asian Relations* 9, no. 3–4 (delayed 2000, appeared in 2006): 147–67.

17. In her work, Michelle Renshaw addresses the financing of the American hospital in China while presenting a more complex picture of the interaction between foreign missionaries and Chinese hosts. Michelle Renshaw, *Accommodating the Chinese: The American Hospital in China, 1880–1920* (New York: Routledge, 2005). On religion and society, Tao Feiya, "Taian jiaoqu Mazhuang zhen Beixinzhuang jiaohui de ge'an yanjiu" [A case study of the Beixinzhuang church in the town of Mazhuang in the suburbs of Taian], in Wu Ziming (Peter Ng), et al., *Shengshan jiaoxia de shizijia: Zongjiao yü shehui hudong ge'an yanjiu* [Christianity at the foot of Mount Tai: a study of the interplay between religion and society, *sic*.] (Hong Kong: Hanyü Jidujiao wenhua yanjiusuo, 2005), pp. 97–157. Also relevant is a recent series of pictorial publications on Christian universities in China, edited by Zhang Kaiyuan. Xü Yihua, *Sheng Yuehan daxue: Haishang fanwang du* [St. John's university] (Shijiazhuang: Hebei jiaoyü chubanshe, 2003); Zhang Anming, *Jianghan tanhualing: Huazhong daxue* [Huanchung university] (Shijiazhuang: Hebei jiaoyü chubanshe, 2003); Wang Guoping, *Dongwu daxue: boxi tiancizhuang* [Soochow university] (Shijiazhuang: Hebei jiaoyü chubanshe, 2003.); Sun Banghua, *Furen daxue: Huiyou Beilefu* [Catholic university] (Shijiazhuang: Hebei jiaoyü chubanshe, 2004); Sun Haiying, *Jinling nüzi daxue: Jinling baiwufang* [Ginling college in Nanking] (Shijiazhuang: Hebei jiaoyü chubanshe, 2004); Xie Bizhen, *Fujian xiehe daxue: xiangpiao Weiqi cun* [Fukien Christian University] (Shijiazhuang: Hebei jiaoyü chubanshe, 2004); Zhang Liping, *Huaxi xiehe daxue: Xiangsi Huaxiba* [West China Union University] (Shijiazhuang: Hebei jiaoyü chubanshe, 2004). Cheng Li, ed., *Bridging Minds across the Pacific: U.S.-China Educational Exchange* (Lanham, MD: Lexington Books, 2005). Peter Ng, ed., *Changing Paradigms of Christian Higher Education* (Lewiston, NY: The Edwin Mellen Press, 2002).

18. Karen Minden, *Bamboo Stone: The Evolution of A Chinese Medical Elite*, (Toronto: University of Toronto Press, 1994.) Ruth Hayhoe, *China's University, 1895–1995: A Century of Cultural Conflict* (New York: Garland Publishing, Inc.

1996), p. 39. On political involvement by the colleges and its impact on students, see Ryan Dunch's "Mission Schools and Modernity: The Anglo-Chinese College, Fuzhou," in Glen Peterson, et al., eds., *Education, Culture, and Identity in Twentieth-Century China* (Hong Kong: Hong Kong University Press, 2001). See also Xiao Chaoran, *Beijing Daxue yü jindai Zhongguo* [Peking University and modern China, *sic*] (Beijing: Zhongguo shehui kexue chubanshe, 2005).

19. Focusing on Shanghai College (Hujiang daxue), Wang Licheng notes that reaching the Chinese upper class by way of higher learning was a compromise rather than a challenge to the traditional Chinese social structure. Wang Licheng, *Meiguo wenhua shentou yü jindai Zhouguo jiaoyü: Hujiang daxue de lishi* [American cultural penetration and the modern education of China: a history of the University of Shanghai, *sic*] (Shanghai: Fudan daxue chubanshe, 2001), p. 19.

20. "Minutes of Advisory Committee Meeting (Session 28)" held on November 9, 1949 at President S. C. Chen's residence. Present were S. C. Chen, Feng Ping Chuan, Wong Li, Henry Frank, and Paul Wu. Guangdongsheng dang'an'guan, file # 38-4-59.

21. Renshaw, *Accommodating the Chinese: The American Hospital in China, 1880–1920.*

22. Viewing Lingnan as a worthwhile cause, Charles K. Edmunds wrote to Wm. Summer Appleton in Boston, MA, in a letter dated June 28, 1927: "Even assuming, as we do, that you are already interested in certain most worth-while causes, yet as Lingnan University is rendering such a service to both China and America . . . [m]ay one of our officers call upon you at your convenience to give you additional information with regard to the opportunities of extending your good-will to China through Lingnan?" "Memorandum re.: Lingnan University," Office of the Trustees, 150 Fifth Avenue, New York City, Yale Divinity School Library.

23. Jessie Gregory Lutz, *China and the Christian Colleges, 1850–1950* (Ithaca, New York: Cornell University Press, 1971), p. 50.

24. Wen-hsin Yeh, *The Alienated Academy: Culture and Politics in Republican China, 1919–1937* (Cambridge, MA: Harvard University, 1990).

25. Sui-ming Lee, ed., *Nanguo Fenghuang: Zhongshan Daxue Lingnan Xueyuan [a Phoenix of South China: The Story of Lingnan (University) College, Sun Yat-Sen University]* (Hong Kong: The Commercial Press 2005). *Lingnan daxue Sanfan shi tongxuehui jianbao* [Bulletin of Lingnan University Alumni Association in San Fancisco, CA], May–August 2006, Alumni Day Special Edition. For more details on the nostalgic attachment of Lingnan alumni to their long gone alma mater, also see Conclusion.

26. Jean-Paul Wiest, "Religious Studies and Research in Chinese Academia: Prospects, Challenges, and Hindrances," *International Bulletin of Missionary Research* 29, no. 1 (2005): 21–26.

27. Wang Licheng, *Meiguo wenhua shentou yü jindai Zhongguo jiaoyü: Hujiang daxue de lishi* [American cultural penetration and the modern education of China: a history of the University of Shanghai, *sic*] (Shanghai: Fudan daxue chubanshe, 2001); Xie Bizhen, *Fujian xiehe daxue: xiangpiao Weiqicun* [Fukien Christian University] (Shijiazhuang: Hebei jiaoyü chubanshe, 2004); Sun Haiying, *Jinling nüzi*

daxue: Jinling baiwufang [Ginling College in Nanking] (Shijiazhuang: Hebei jiaoyü chubanshe, 2004); Zhang Liping, *Huaxi daxue: Xiangsi Huaxiba* [West China Union University] (Shijiazhuang: Hebei jiaoyü chubanshe, 2004).

28. President's Report by Charles Edmunds, 1919–1924, p. 27. Trustees of Lingnan University, microfilm roll 26.

29. President's Report by Charles Edmunds, 1919–1924, p. 28. Trustees of Lingnan University, microfilm roll 26.

30. Ibid, p. 22. Lingnan originally had a four-year preparatory school (equivalent of a middle school).

31. *Canton Christian College Bulletin: President's Report, 1909–1910*, New York: Trustees of Canton Christian College, 1911, pp. 66–67. Trustees of Lingnan University, microfilm roll 25.

32. Marianne Bastid approaches China's educational relations with other countries from the perspective of "servitude" and "liberation." See Bastid, "Servitude or Liberation? The Introduction of Foreign Educational Practices and Systems to China from 1840 to the Present," in Ruth Hayhoe and Marianne Bastid, eds., *China's Education and the Industrialized World: Studies in Cultural Transfer* (Armonk, New York: M.E. Sharpe, 1987.) Ruth Hayhoe's concluding chapter sums up the different educational influences of Britain, the U.S., Germany, Japan, and the Soviet Union on China. Ruth Hayhoe, "Past and Present in China's Educational Relations with the Industrialized World," in op. cit. pp. 270–89. In a further article, Hayhoe maps the interrelations between China's cultural traditions and modernity along three dimensions—geographical disparities, female participation, and the knowledge issue. Ruth Hayhoe, "Cultural Tradition and Educational Modernization: Lessons from the Republican Era," in Ruth Hayhoe, ed., *Education and Modernization: The Chinese Experience*, Oxford: Pergamon Press, 1992, pp. 47–72.

33. "President's Report, 1911–12," p. 76. Trustees of Lingnan University, microfilm roll 25.

34. As aggressive fundraisers, Lingnan's Chinese presidents bore little resemblance to their Chinese counterparts in other institutions. In his edited volume *Jidujiao daxue huaren xiaozhang yanjiu* [Studies of the Chinese Presidents of Christian Universities] (Fuzhou: fujian jiaoyü chubanshe, 2001), Wu Ziming (Peter Ng) portrays ten Chinese presidents of Christian universities in China (but excluding the Lingnan presidents).

35. Lingnan daxue Xianggang tongxuehui [Lingnan University Hong Kong Alumni Association], ed., *Zhong Rongguang xiansheng zhuan* [Biography of Chung Wing Kwong] (Hong Kong: Lingnan daxue Xianggang tongxuehui, 1996), p. 95.

36. Chung Wing Kwong, "Guoji de Lingnan," [International Lingnan University] reprinted, *Lingnan xiaoyou* [Lingnan alumni], Guangzhou, 1988, vol. 16, pp. 15–16.

37. Qi Liang, "Chongping Chen Xüjing," [Reassess Chen Xüjing] *Zhejiang shehui kexue*, No. 6 (1998): 111–27.

38. In his resume, Ch'en gave his degree from the University of Berlin as a Ph.D. This probably would correspond to a *Promotion*. Lingnan daxue Chen Xüjing cailiao [Files on Ch'en Su-ching], Guangdongsheng dang'an'guan, file # 38-4-5.

39. Lingnan daxue Chen Xüjing cailiao [Files on Ch'en Su-ching], Guangdong-sheng dang'an'guan, file # 38-4-5. Chen Qijin, "Chen Xüjing xiaozhang zhuchi Lingnan daxue," [President Ch'en took the helm of Lingnan University] *Lingnan tongxun* [Lingnan newsletter], No. 151 (September 15, 2001): 15–17.

40. Charles H. Corbett, *Lingnan University*, p. 153.

41. Chen Xüjing (Ch'en Su-ching), *Zhongguo wenhua de chulu* [The future of Chinese culture] (Shanghai: Commercial Press, 1934). Also, see Yang Shen, ed., *Zuochu dongfang* [Going beyond the East: Collected works of Chen Xüjing on culture] (Beijing: Zhongguo guangbo dianshi chubanshe, 1995), p. 139.

42. *Lingnan daxue gongchao yunniang ji jiejue shimo ji* (pamphlet) [A record of the origins and resolution of the labor unrest at Lingnan University], Guangdong-sheng dang'an'guan, file # 38-1-27. Corbett, *Lingnan University*, pp. 100–101.

43. *Record of the Testimonial Dinner to* [sic] *Dr. Charles K. Edmunds*, New York, March 2, 1922, pp. 4–5. Trustees of Lingnan University, microfilm roll 39.

44. Peter Ng, "Lingnan daxue de diyiwu xuesheng—Chen Shaobai" [The first student of Lingnan University: Chen Shaobai], *Zhongguo lishi xuehui jikan*, No. 23 (July 1991): 139–48.

45. Kenneth W. Rea, ed., *Canton in Revolution: The Collected Papers of Earl Swisher, 1925–1928* (Boulder, CO: Westview Press, 1977). Earl Swisher's diary dated March 24, 1927, p. 49.

46. Ibid. Swisher's letter dated March 6, 1927, p. 44–46.

47. Lingnan daxue Xianggang tongxuehui [Lingnan University Hong Kong Alumni Association], ed., *Zhong Rongguang xiansheng zhuan* [Biography of Chung Wing Kwong] (Hong Kong: Lingnan daxue Xianggang tongxuehui, 1996), p. 94.

48. President's Report by Charles Edmunds, 1925, p. 10.

49. Earl Swisher, *Today's World in Focus: China* (Boston, MA: Ginn and Company, 1964).

50. Rea, ed., *Canton in Revolution: The Collected Papers of Earl Swisher, 1925–1928.*

51. Edmund W. Meisenhelder, III, "The Foreign Exchangers at Lingnan," manuscript given to the author by Lee Sui-ming.

52. Correspondence of Edmund W. Meisenhelder, III with Lee Sui Ming, December 16, 1998. I am indebted to Lee Sui Ming for providing a copy of this letter. Meisenhelder, a 1936 exchanger at Lingnan, also wrote a valuable memoir, *The Dragon Smiles*, New York: Pageant Press, 1968. See also Arthur Eaton, "Lingnan: 62 Years Later," *Lingnan daxue Sanfanshi tongxuehui jianbao* [Lingnan University alumni association at San Francisco], October–December 1999, pp. 19–27.

53. Clough's works include: *Cooperation or Conflict in the Taiwan Strait?* Lanham, MD: Rowman & Littlefield Publishers, 1999; *Reaching across the Taiwan Strait: People-to-People Diplomacy*, Boulder, CO: Westview Press, 1993; A. Doak Barnett, Ralph N. Clough, ed., *Modernizing China: Post-Mao Reform and Development* (Boulder, CO: Westview Press, 1986). "Taiwan's Globalization Dilemma," National Committee on American Foreign Policies, Northeast Asia Projects, February 2003, http://www.ncafp.org/projects/NEasia/articles.htm, accessed on December 16, 2005; "Progress and Problems in Taiwan's Cross-Strait Relations," National Committee on American Foreign Policies, Northeast Asia Projects, August 2003, http://www.ncafp.org/projects/NEasia/articles.htm, accessed on December 16, 2005.

54. Hugh Deane, *Good Deeds & Gunboats: Two Centuries of American-Chinese Encounters* (San Francisco, CA: China Books & Periodicals, 1990), Hugh Deane, *The Korean War 1945–1953* (San Francisco, CA: China Books, 1999), Hugh Deane, ed., *Evans F. Carlson on China at War, 1937–1940* (New York: China and U.S. Publication, 1993).

55. Correspondence of Edmund W. Meisenhelder, III with Lee Sui-ming, December 16, 1998.

56. Rea, ed., *Canton in Revolution: The Collected Papers of Earl Swisher, 1925–1928.* Preface.

57. W. Henry Grant, Secretary of the Board of Trustees of Lingnan University, March 2, 1922. *Record of the Testimonial Dinner to [sic] Dr. Charles K. Edmunds*, New York, March 2, 1922, p. 2. Trustees of Lingnan University, microfilm roll 39.

58. Charles K. Edmunds, *Record of the Testimonial Dinner to [sic] Dr. Charles K. Edmunds*, New York, March 2, 1922, p. 14. Trustees of Lingnan University, microfilm roll 39.

59. James Sheehan, "The Varieties of History," Perspective, Vol. 43, No 9, December 2005, p. 2. Also see http://www.historians.org/Perspectives/issues/2005/0512/0512pre1.cfm, accessed on December 11, 2005.

60. Adam McKeown, "Chapter 1: Introduction: The Continuing Reformulation of Chinese Australians," in *After the Rush: Regulations, Participation, and Chinese Communities in Australia 1860–1940*, ed. Sophie Couchman, John Fitzgerald, and Paul Macgregor (Kingsbury, Australia: Otherland Literary Journal 2004).

61. On May 30th, 1925, students, workers, and merchants in Shanghai rallied against the killing of Gu Zhenghong. British forces stationed in the International Settlement fired on the protesters, killing thirteen people and injuring many more. This became known as the May 30th Incident and triggered waves of anti-imperialist protests, strikes, and boycotts in China. See chapter 5 of Ka-che Yip, *Religion, Nationalism and Chinese Students: The Anti-Christian Movement of 1922–1927* (Bellingham, WA: Western Washington University, 1980). Nicholas Rowland Clifford, *Shanghai, 1925: Urban Nationalism and the Defense of Foreign Privilege* (Ann Arbor, MI: Center for Chinese Studies, University of Michigan, 1979). Jessie Gregory Lutz, *Chinese Politics and Christian Missions: The Anti-Christian Movements of 1920–28* (Notre Dame, IN: Cross Cultural Publications, Cross Roads Books 1988).

62. Edward J. M. Rhoads, "Lingnan's Response to the Rise of Chinese Nationalism: The Shakee Incident (1925)," in *American Missionaries in China: Papers from Harvard Seminars*, ed. Kwang-Ching Liu (Cambridge, MA: Harvard University Press, 1970). Also see Chapter 1 of the present study for more information.

63. Letter drafted by R. D. Rees, R. T. Rich, H. B. Graybill and Alex Baxter on June 6, 1925, Guangdongsheng dang'an'guan, file # 38-4-60.

64. Referring to the eighteen Christian colleges in China.

65. Guangdongsheng dang'an'guan, "Situ Wei cailiao" [the Sz-to Wai files], file # 38-4-6.

66. Among the very scanty scholarship on the financing of Christian colleges in China, Liu Jiafeng's study, "Qilu daxue jingfei laiyuan yü xuexiao fazhan: 1904–1952," [Qilu University—income sources and development: 1904–1952] provides a fresh perspective from Shandong Christian University (Qilu daxue). See also

Zhang Kaiyuan and Ma Min, eds., *Jidujiao yü Zhongguo wenhua congkan* [Christianity and Chinese culture series] (Wuhan: Hubei jiaoyü chubanshe, 1999), vol. 3, pp. 81–130. Jonathan J. Bonk examines the perplexing consequences of missionary affluence in a world polarized between the rich few and the poor many. Jonathan J. Bonk, *Missions and Money: Affluence as a Western Missionary Problem* (Maryknoll, NY: Orbis Books, 1990).

67. President's Report, 1919–24, p. 21, Trustees of Lingnan University, microfilm roll 26; *Sili Lingnan daxue yilan*, pp. 229–330; President's Report, 1943–1944, Trustees of Lingnan University, microfilm roll 19; "Academic Year, Semester II, 1945–1946, Lingnan University," Lingnan daxue renshi cailiao [Personnel files of Lingnan University], Guangdongsheng dang'an'guan, file # 38-4-59. The 1927 figure comes from C. K. Edmunds letter to Wm. Summer Appleton in Boston, MA dated June 28, 1927, "Memorandum re. Lingnan University," Office of the Trustees in New York City, Yale Divinity School Library.

68. Xi Lian uses the term "reflex influence" to describe the impact of the China experience on Western missionaries' understanding of their faith. Lian Xi, *The Conversion of Missionaries: Liberalism in American Protestant Missions in China, 1907–1932* (University Park, Pennsylvania: The Pennsylvania State University Press, 1997).

1

✛

The Setting: Honglok, Guangzhou, and Canton Christian College (Lingnan University)

HONGLOK AND CANTON CHRISTIAN COLLEGE: A HERITAGE

At Lingnan in the glow of sunset light
The Pearl casts forth a brilliant sheen;
While to and fro, o'er watery surface, bright,
The sampans move across the scene, [*sic*]
On Honan's shore are trees and factory spires.
Beyond the masts are lights—the city's fires.

A pearly way that casts the sunset's glow
Makes joy, for such as see, o'erflow.
A glorious stream where boatmen earn their rice
Is pearl, indeed, of greatest price.
And so the waterway has been well named
The Pearl—a stream throughout the region famed.[1]

—"The River Pearl at Sunset" by George Weidman Groff
(Gao Lufu, on Lingnan faculty 1907–1941)

In 1929, Kenneth S. Latourette described Lingnan as a landmark in the history of Christian higher education in China. It was also a striking physical landmark:

To the visitor to China in the year 1926 one of the most interesting and thought-provoking features of the landscape was the physical evidence of the activities of Christian missionaries. . . . If he [the visitor] came by way of Suez and Singapore, and if he paused at Hongkong long enough to visit Canton, the tourist saw, as his steamer carried him up one of the two principal channels toward the city, the extensive campus of Lingnan University, or, as it was formerly called, Canton Christian College.[2]

Honglok, the Honam Island, Canton, Hongkong (Hong Kong), the Pearl River, wharfs, junks, sampans, water channels, greenery, rice paddies—all places and features mentioned in the above quotations—were the geographical and cultural markers which connected Canton Christian College with the outside world. In Chinese, the name Lingnan refers to the area "south of the mountain range," a general term for the Guangdong region. It was this environment, infused with a new conception of modern education, that made Lingnan special among Christian universities and colleges in China.

The origins of Lingnan were intimately connected with Andrew P. Happer, who was born 1818 in Washington County, Pennsylvania, and died on October 27, 1894, in his home in Wooster, Ohio. He was a graduate of Jefferson College in 1835 and studied at the Western Theological Seminary from 1840 to 1843. After graduating from the Medical School of the University of Pennsylvania in 1844, Happer set sail to China to preach the Gospel.[3] In 1879, after thirty-five years preaching in the Canton area, but with few converts, Happer made an unsuccessful proposal to the General Council of the Presbyterian Church to establish a Christian college in China.[4] Despite this initial rejection, another approach was made by Benjamin C. Henry (Xiang Bianwen), a Presbyterian missionary stationed in Canton, to the Presbyterian Board of Foreign Missions for the founding of a Christian college in 1885. This plan was likewise not approved.[5] Later in 1885, Happer proposed a modified scheme. Permission was finally granted by the Board of Foreign Missions when Happer proposed that a separate board of trustees be responsible for the finances of the college.[6]

Self-financing made Lingnan special in relation to other denominational colleges and universities in China. At the time there was some uncertainty about the site of the new college—whether it should be in Chefoo (in Shandong province), or in Shanghai, Canton, or somewhere else altogether. A petition (*gonghan*), signed by over four hundred officials, degree-holders and members of the distinguished Hanlin Academy (Hanlin yuan)[7] of Guangdong descent, was presented to the American backers of the proposed college. Representing all sectors of the aristocracy in the entire Guangdong Province (*Guangdong hesheng shenqi*), this document expressed the desire to have Happer's school opened in Canton.[8]

Classes started in 1888 in Shaki (*Shaji*), outside Canton city, in a school simply named the Christian College in China (*Gezhi shuyuan*). The college was incorporated under the auspices of the University of the State of New York in 1893, with a board of trustees managing its finances, thus making it independent of any denominational body.

Happer saw the model for a Christian college in the nonsectarian American University of Beirut, founded in 1866. He contemplated the foundation of a modern Christian college of national scope on a "wider basis," not just a "Training School for preparing mission assistants."[9] Happer found himself at odds with Francis F. Ellinwood, secretary of the Presbyterian Board of Foreign Missions, and the Canton Mission, both on this issue and on the question of the medium of instruction. Contrary to the practice in "ordinary lower or higher mission schools," Happer favored "making the study of English prominent in the curriculum, partly as an attraction to pupils, and partly as a valuable means of enlightening those who may be thus attracted."[10] Twenty years later, Happer's successors used the similar arguments to defend the use of English in higher courses at Lingnan. Citing Chinese demand as the most important reason for the college's use of the English language in its higher courses, Andrew H. Woods, vice-president of Canton Christian College, reported that

[a]t present this College cannot take in all the students who apply. They and their parents tell us that they do not want us to teach them through Chinese. It was once feared that this demand for English was an expression of the desire to use it merely in business. The twelve years experience of the College has demonstrated that the Chinese desire English because it leads them more quickly and more surely to the coveted knowledge than any other medium. For genuine Christian altruism and for effective service the students of Canton Christian College are in a class by themselves.[11]

The controversies and bickering over the language issue and the purpose of the Canton Christian College (C.C.C.) among missionaries and missions in the late nineteenth century are detailed in Charles W. Hayford's article. Hayford's article also reveals the bigger role which Benjamin C. Henry—the "devout college man"—had played in the founding of the C.C.C.[12]

During the Boxer Movement of 1899–1900, the Christian College in China took up temporary quarters in Macao under the presidency of Oscar F. Wisner (Yin Shijia, President 1899–1907). Because of difficulties in buying land and the turmoil created by the Boxer Rebellion, it was not until 1904 that the college got a permanent home in the village of Honglok (*Kangle*) on the north side of Honam ("south bank"), an oval-shaped island some fifteen miles wide in the Pearl River opposite the old city of

Canton. Before the opening of Canton as an accessible treaty port in the mid-nineteenth century, the island of Honam was one of the few places which foreign merchants were permitted to visit on certain days of the lunar calendar. The villas and gardens of well-to-do Canton merchants (the most noted belonged to Howqua, or Houqua) were also located here from the late eighteenth to the mid-nineteenth centuries. In 1793 and 1817, Lord Macartney and Lord Amherst respectively were housed on Honam during stopovers in Canton.[13] The main campus was about four miles from the old city and about ninety miles from Hong Kong, and was connected with Canton by regular bus and launch services. (See map 1.1; map 1.2.)[14]

Today, a wander along the shady avenues of the old Lingnan campus evokes nostalgic thoughts. (See photo 1.1; photo 1.2.) The historic campus serves as a reservoir where past and present meet and where memories and emotions flood back and converge. Commenting on the sweeping renovations that restored luster to the eternal city of Rome, Tony Perrottet describes similar emotional associations:

> In 1930, Sigmund Freud famously compared modern Rome to the human mind, where many levels of memory can coexist in the same physical space.

Map 1.1. Map of Guangdong Province. By Shirley Houston and author.

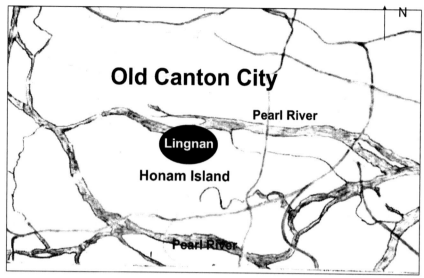

Map 1.2.   Map of Canton (Guangzhou), Pearl River, and Lingnan University. By Shirley Houston and author.

It's a concept those classical sightseers would have understood: the ancient Romans had a refined sense of *genius loci*, or spirit of place, and saw Rome's streets as a great repository of history, where past and present blurred. Today, we can feel a similarly vivid sense of historical continuity, as the city's rejuvenated sites use every conceivable means to bring the past to life.[15]

In the late 1940s, Lingnan was at its zenith and had over 600 acres of land and 98 permanent buildings, plus 172 temporary buildings, several athletic fields, 4 college dormitories, 8 middle school buildings, 7 primary school cottages, and 40 residences. Over half of the campus area was devoted to market gardening, nurseries, fruit and mulberry culture, grain-growing, dairying, stock-raising, and other farming activities. In addition to the agricultural station on campus, Lingnan's College of Agriculture had a substation of about 10,000 mows (mu, 2,000 acres) of hilly land for forestry and fruit-growing, as well as for the study of dry land management and intensive farming.[16]

The distinctive style of Lingnan's campus architecture symbolized the combination of American education and Chinese values.[17] According to Charles K. Edmunds, the buildings at Lingnan were designed to blend Western with Eastern design, "chiefly expressed in the roofs [of those built after 1911] which are of green glazed tile and ornamented and curved according to the best native style."[18] This style of roof was forbid-

Photo 1.1.   Sun Yat-sen Avenue at Sun Yat-sen University (Old Lingnan Campus), Guangzhou, Guangdong. Photograph provided by Li Xia.

Photo 1.2.   *Xingting (Xing Pavilion, Bell Tower), Sun Yat-sen University (Old Lingnan Campus), Guangzhou, Guangdong. Photograph provided by Li Xia.*

den for private dwellings under the Qing empire (1644–1912).[19] All buildings were equipped with modern plumbing, and were sturdily constructed: "All of the permanent buildings are built of red brick with reinforced concrete floors, being thus both fire-proof and white-ant proof."

Most of the old college buildings remain intact on today's Sun Yat-sen University campus. In his foreword to a book on the architecture of the campus by Yü Zhi, an engineering professor at Sun Yat-sen University fascinated by these red buildings, Li Yanbao sheds light on their contemporary impact:

> [The] Honglok red buildings remain a unique landscape of the campus of Sun Yat-sen University. As a key component of the campus culture of Sun Yat-sen University, they became [an] important carrier of cultural heritage for cultivating and educating the students. . . . Each student of Sun Yat-sen University could realize from the red buildings the spirit of Western and Chinese culture. . . . [original English translation][20]

The following is a list of some of the main Lingnan buildings in chronological order of construction.[21] (See Table 1.1). The diverse sources of funding which enabled their construction attest to the dynamics of what

I term the "multiparty alliance"—the eclecticism and adaptation characteristic of the Lingnan enterprise. (See photo 1.3; photo 1.4.)

Table 1.1 clearly indicates the diverse funding that flowed into Lingnan from sources that included Chinese and Westerners, private and public donors, and local Cantonese and overseas Chinese. This is a deviation from what is normally known of the Christian colleges in China.[22] The importance of local sources becomes even clearer in the late-twentieth-century rebirth of the university when the bulk of the funding for over a dozen new buildings constructed after 1988 came from Hong Kong Chinese, loyal Lingnan alumni.[23] In the 1920s Chinese nationalists demanded full control of foreign institutions of higher learning; eighty years later, Lingnan embodies the realization of their aspirations. The significant role played by Chinese in financing and collaborating on an institution of Christian higher education such as Lingnan University staggers the imagination. Today, Lingnan (University) College is a genuine Chinese institution, albeit with American origins and receiving some American aid.

What made Lingnan an institution with a special character among the Christian colleges and universities in China? To answer that question, we must now take a look at the larger geographical area in which Lingnan is situated.

Photo 1.3.   *Swasey Hall (Huaishi Tang) Today, Sun Yat-sen University (Old Lingnan Campus), Guangzhou, Guangdong. Photograph provided by Li Xia.*

Photo 1.4.   Swasey Hall (Huaishi Tang) Yesterday. Postcard by Lingnan (University) College, Sun Yat-sen University (Zhongshan University).

CANTON (GUANGZHOU), HONG KONG, AND THE PEAR RIVER DELTA (*ZHUJIANG SANJIAOZHOU*)

This section examines the region surrounding Lingnan—Canton (Guang-zhou), Hong Kong, and the Pearl River Delta—and suggests three elements that might account for its distinctive character.

First, throughout history Canton has had extensive connections with the outside world. A survey conducted in 1982, just a few years after China's reopening to the world, showed that 1.02 million residents of Guangzhou had either lived overseas or had relatives in Hong Kong, Macao, or other countries. In the same year, over 1.33 million ethnic Chinese residing in more than seventy countries and regions—the so-called overseas Chinese (*haiwai huaren*)—were of Guangzhou ancestry.[24] In addition, one-third of the population of Guangzhou has overseas connections, including links with Hong Kong and Macao.[25] According to the Guangdong provincial archives, in the later nineteenth century and the first half of the twentieth century, more than 90 percent of Lingnan students were from Guangdong Province, including Hong Kong, and over 25 percent from

Table 1.1.   Construction of Major Buildings at Lingnan University

Name	Year of Completion	Function	Significance
Martin Hall (Mading tang)	1906	Main library (from 1948)	Erected in honor of Henry Martin, a donor from Cincinnati, OH. One of the earliest concrete buildings in China
Swasey Hall (Huaishi tang)	1915	Assembly hall (seating 800)	Built with funds from Ambrose Swasey
Grant Hall (Gelan tang)	1915	Administration building, bank and departmental offices of the College of Arts	Built with funds from Mrs. J. S. Kennedy
Infirmary	1918	Dispensary, physicians' offices, operating rooms, wards	Built with funds from Ma Ying-Piu (1861–1944)
Java Hall (Zhaowa tang)	1919	College dorm	Built with funds raised by Chung Wing Kung, and given by Chinese in Java
Chang Hall (Zhang Bishi tang)	1921	Overseas students' dorm and school building	Gift of Chang Pik-shih (founder of Changyu Pioneer Wine Company and initiator of the International Chinese Businessmen's Conference)
Guest House	1922	Reception	Gift of Ma Ying-Piu
Wing Kwong Hall	1924	College dorm	Gift of students
Alumni House	1925	Reception	Gift of Tam Lai-Ting
Atwood Reeling Lab	1925	Built to house silk-reeling machines	Gift of Eugene Atwood, temporary site for Union Theological College (1948)
Lingnan Hospital	1925	For villagers and workmen	Built with funds provided largely by General Lee Fuk-lam (Li Fulin), Sun Yat-sen, and others
Willard Straight Hall	1928	Depts. of Biology, Chemistry, and Physics	Built with funds from Mrs. Willard Straight and the Rockefeller Foundation
Agriculture Hall	1929	Classrooms, labs, exhibition hall, garden, store	Gift of ten Chinese friends
Luk Yau Hall (Lu You tang)	1931	College dorm	Gift of two alumni, brothers Wong Yung Cheung and Wong Yung Hong, together with funds raised by the Alumni Foundation Committee
Engineering Hall	1931	Classrooms and labs	Gift of the Ministry of Railways, Nanjing Government

Women's Dorm (Guanghan gong)	1933	College dorm for women	Built with donations from American friends, particularly from Orange, NJ, raised by the American Trustees of Lingnan University, and from Chinese women raised by Chung Wing Kwong
Four Middle School Dorms	1909–1916		Gift of Chinese friends
Primary School Group	1916–1931	Classrooms and dorms	Gift of Chinese friends
New Middle School Group	1933–1947	Classrooms and dorms	Gift of Chinese friends
Lingnan Chapel	1936	Morning service	Gift of the Lingnan community and friends abroad
Medical Unit	1934–1937	Canton Hospital	Built with funds from American friends and the Nationalist Government

By author.

Hong Kong itself.[26] Many overseas Chinese traditionally sent their children back to their homeland to study, and many whose families came from Guangzhou went on to college studies at Lingnan. In response to this demand, the Lingnan Overseas Chinese School was launched in 1918, accounting for the strong support enjoyed by Lingnan from overseas Chinese since its inception, and explaining why the Overseas Chinese School has remained high on Lingnan's priority list.[27] Today, this important source of income has been extended to Lingnan (University) College at Sun Yat-sen University in Guangzhou, which has no parallels in contemporary China.

Second, a strong tradition of trading and commerce, combined with remittances and investments from overseas Chinese, significantly contributed to the comparative wealth of the Pearl River Delta, thus allowing Lingnan to appeal to the parents of Lingnan students for financial support.[28] The Pearl River Delta comprises the fertile alluvial area at the Pearl River mouth where the river flows into the South China Sea. It covers the Guangzhou, Shenzhen, Zhuhai, Dongguan, Zhongshan, Foshan, Huizhou, Jiangmen, Hong Kong and Macao regions. Economically, the Pearl River Delta is the most dynamic region in contemporary China: With only 0.4 percent of the land area and 3.2 percent of the population of mainland China (2000 census), the Pearl River Delta accounted for 8.7 percent of national GDP, 32.8 percent of total trade, and 29.2 percent of utilized foreign capital in 2001.[29] Between 1912 and 1921, the annual overseas remittances sent to the two cities of Chaozhou and Shantou in the Pearl River

Delta amounted to 21 million Chinese yuan.[30] Thus, unlike other similar institutions, Lingnan was well positioned to benefit from the most commercially powerful sector of Chinese society. I shall discuss this aspect in detail in chapter 3.

Third, Lingnan's proximity to the Portuguese and British colonies of Macao and Hong Kong provided Canton Christian College with communication and transportation networks. Extensive water and rail networks connected Canton, Hong Kong, and Macao. From 1918, steamers operated by the Hongkong, Canton and Macao Steamboat Company and the China Merchants' Steamboat Company plied regularly between Canton, Hong Kong, and Macao. Passenger junks, towed by launches, were run between Canton and important cities and towns in the Pearl River Delta, and on the East, North, and West Rivers. In addition, the 110-mile Kowloon–Canton Railway, opened in 1911, offered daily express services between Canton and Hong Kong.

The two colonies also offered Lingnan ready protection. As we have seen, in 1900 the college took refuge in Macao for four years before finding a permanent home at Honglok. In 1938, after Guangzhou fell to Japan, Lingnan once again went into exile in Hong Kong, borrowing facilities from the University of Hong Kong and other organizations. Its proximity to Hong Kong also enabled Lingnan to transfer scientific and medical equipment from Honglok for classroom use in Hong Kong. Commenting on teaching conditions during this period of exile, Y. K. Chu, dean of Lingnan, noted:

> We set up our own Biology, Physics and Pre-Clinical Medical laboratories in rented quarters and the Chemistry laboratory in a building belonging to Hong Kong University. Our present science equipment is very inferior to what we had in Canton, but it is, in relation to the number of students, much superior to that found in most 'refugee' universities in the interior.[31]

On the other hand, proximity to Hong Kong had its drawbacks for Lingnan as well. Since the university paid its bills in Hong Kong dollars but received a significant proportion of financial aid in U.S. dollars, fluctuating exchange rates wreaked havoc on Lingnan's budgets. On July 1, 1927, a board of directors in China officially assumed responsibility for the governance of Lingnan University including complete financial responsibility for the Chinese faculty and staff. At the same time, the Board of Trustees of Lingnan University became known as the American Foundation, responsible for the hiring and the sponsoring of Western personnel at Lingnan. At the handover of Lingnan to the Chinese in 1927, it was arranged that the salaries of Western staff be paid by the American Foundation (the Board of Trustees of Lingnan University) at a fixed rate of 0.5 U.S. Gold per Hong Kong dollar. In a letter dated April 9, 1935 to James M. Henry, provost of Lingnan, Olin D. Wannamaker, American director of the American Foundation,[32] revealed a financial dilemma for the institution:

> The matter which drew my very special attention when I took this [budget] up again was the item of Exchange rates. The manner in which the University and the faculty respectively are affected by the change in the Exchange rates is a queer thing. When the Hong Kong dollar dropped to 25 cents [US Gold], we sent additional American money to the staff. The guaranteed rate resulted in placing in the hands of each faculty member almost twice as many Hong Kong dollars per month as he was getting when the Hong Kong dollar was worth 50cents gold. At the same time, the American Trustees were assisted to a considerable extent through having to pay only 40cents gold for the Hong Kong dollar instead of 50cents gold. An unmarried man's salary cost to the Trustees during this period was $720.00 U.S. currency instead of $900.00. Now the Hong Kong dollar is almost back to 50cents gold. If the Trustees pay only the $720.00 U.S. currency as the salary of an unmarried man, the teachers will probably suffer severely.[33]

However, overall Lingnan benefited a great deal from its location in Canton, a crucial contact point between China and the outside world, particularly since the beginning of the European age of exploration in the fifteenth century. The significance of Canton has been assessed from a number of different angles. It has been variously viewed as a "staging area," along with other Southeastern Asian cities, for the Protestant mission enterprise in China in the first forty years of the nineteenth century;[34] as the main site of the Sino–British clash during the Opium Wars (1840–1842, 1856–1860);[35] as the center of revolutionary activity in Guangdong from 1895 to 1911;[36] as the site of the fledgling Chinese Communist Party's and the Nationalist Party's unsuccessful attempts to construct a cohesive modern nation-state through mobilizing workers and peasants from 1922 to 1927;[37] and as the only accessible window through which China could be viewed from the Communist takeover of 1949 to 1968, before China's reopening to the West from 1979.[38] Canton also figured prominently in both Western and Chinese art from the 1770s to the 1870s.[39]

Guangzhou (Canton), known as the "city of the rams" (*yangcheng*) and the "city of flowers" (*huacheng*), is the capital city of the Guangdong province and one of the foremost metropolises and international ports of China.[40] Lying at a similar latitude to Mecca, Calcutta, Honolulu, and Havana, the city is located approximately seventy-five miles from the South China Sea, at the northern end of the Pearl River Delta where the West, North, and East Rivers meet. River and sea channels forming an A-shaped gulf forty miles long link Guangzhou to the former British colony of Hong Kong at its right foot, and to the former Portuguese colony of

Macao at its left.[41] The city's other neighbors are the provinces of Hunan, Jiangxi, Fujian, and Hainan, and the Guangxi Zhuang autonomous region.

Guangzhou is situated on the plain of the Pearl River Delta, backed by mountainous land to the north. Located in the subtropical and monsoon zone, the city has a year-round average temperature of 20° to 22° C (68°–70° F), with 79 percent average humidity. Guangzhou's annual precipitation is about 2,200 mm (87 inches). Warmth, humidity, and the fertile delta soil provide ideal conditions for flowering trees, subtropical flowers, and abundant fruits such as banana, citrus, lichee, and pineapple—all features that figure frequently in the songs and reminiscences associated with Lingnan and its alumni.

From early in its history, Guangzhou has been the key center of the *lingnan* ("south of the mountain range") region of South China, as well as the hub of domestic and international trade in the province. Municipal Guangzhou has a population of about 6 million, and covers an area of 7,434 square meters (8,891 square yards). Many Cantonese have emigrated to Southeast Asia, the Americas and Africa, as well as to other parts of the world, and this provides Guangzhou and South China with a significant link to overseas Chinese and the outside world. As we have seen, Lingnan University has capitalized on the Guangzhou heritage, enabling it to form significant ties with both local businessmen and overseas Chinese.

As the starting point of the Silk Road on the coast, Guangzhou had already established a trade relationship (in silk) with Rome in 116 A.D. Other trading partners were India, Ceylon, Syria, Persia, and Arabia. In the eighth century the foreign trade market was regularized with the founding of the *Shibo Si* (Bureau of Sea Trade). Buddhism and Islam were introduced into Guangzhou with the arrival of Indian and Arab merchants.

The coming of the Portuguese to Guangzhou in 1517, followed by the Spaniards in 1575 and English in 1636, ushered in a new era of colonialist penetration of China, in which the Arabs lost their dominant position. In 1685, the Manchu Qing regime lifted its ban on the entry of foreign vessels, thus facilitating foreign trade. From 1715, with the signing of a favorable trade agreement with the Guangdong Customs, to the first Opium War (1839–1842), the British East India Company was the dominant foreign trading power in Guangzhou. In 1720, the *cohong* system was instituted by the Qing government authorizing certain Cantonese merchants, known as the Thirteen Hongs (guilds), to conduct business with the English, Dutch, French, Americans, Swedes, Danes, Spaniards, and other foreigners who maintained their "factories" in designated areas of

Guangzhou. In 1757 all foreign trade in China was restricted to Guangzhou.

Friction occurred when foreign traders found the *cohong* system manipulative and inconvenient, as the Qing authority did not allow foreigners to trade freely or to establish diplomatic relations with China. Unable to sell manufactured goods in the China market, British merchants began smuggling Indian opium into China to make up their trade deficit. In response to the Qing government's crackdown on opium traffic, Britain went to war with China in 1840, and in 1842 forced the defeated Qing regime to sign the Treaty of Nanjing. This treaty opened up five ports, including Guangzhou, to foreign traders, and conceded Hong Kong to Britain.

Guangzhou has played a key role in the Chinese revolutions of the twentieth century. After the demise of the Qing government in 1912, the city became the headquarters of the Nationalist Party (Guomindang, GMD) and the base, shared by both the GMD and the Chinese Communist Party (CCP), of the anti-warlord and anti-imperialist Nationalist Revolution.

Since the opening-up of China in 1979, Guangzhou again emerged as a prominent center of commerce and has been at the forefront both of China's domestic economic reforms and its interactions with the outside world. Guangzhou's urban population in 1995 was over 3.8 million.[42] Along with Shanghai, the city's labor force is one of the most productive in China. Guangzhou's economic, political, and social influence in contemporary China is further reinforced by its proximity to Hong Kong and to the two Special Economic Zones of Shenzhen and Zhuhai.

THE LINGNAN ENTERPRISE

In this section I trace the history of Lingnan University, combining a narrative and a thematic approach. The history of Lingnan falls into three phases: inception (1888–1903), expansion (1903–1937), and war, recovery, and disestablishment (1938–1952). Since the first phase has been covered above, I focus here on the periods of 1903–1937 and 1938–1952.

EXPANSION, 1903–1937

The decades between 1903 and 1937 witnessed phenomenal growth, both in Lingnan's physical size and in the number of enrolled students. Starting from the original 35 acres of grounds, by 1918 the university had a campus of 135 acres. By 1934, this had grown to 560 acres.[43] Student numbers climbed rapidly too, especially between 1927 and 1930 when total collegiate enrollment increased by over 46 percent.

Lingnan was one of the pioneers of coeducation in China. In 1903, girls were first admitted to classes, and subsequently Lingnan was coeducational in all grades.[44] The medical school started in 1906. In the same year, the Guangdong government approved a proposal by Chung Wing Kwong (1866–1942), who later became Lingnan's first Chinese president in 1927, to send qualified Lingnan students overseas to benefit South China.[45] In 1910, four of the five students in the medical school received scholarships to study medicine in America.[46] The first three collegiate male students graduated from the College of Arts and Sciences in 1918, which marked the full development of Canton Christian College as a higher educational institution.

Teaching staff also increased rapidly during this period, with an astounding growth spurt in the years 1927–1930, when faculty numbers doubled. There were only three faculty in 1899: Rev. O. F. Wisner, M. R. Alexander (instructor in electrical engineering), and A. H. Woods, professor of biology.[47] In 1930, among 101 faculty, twenty-one (21 percent) possessed doctorates, and thirty-four (34 percent) had a master's degree.[48] Furthermore, 69 faculty had foreign degrees, mostly from American universities.[49] The proportion of academic staff to collegiate students fluctuated in the 1920s and 1930s. In 1927, the ratio was 5.02:1; in 1930, it was 3.5:1;[50] in 1934, it had climbed to 5.7: 1; and in 1947, it was even higher, 6.8:1[51]—but it was still the lowest among all Christian colleges and universities in China. In comparison, the student–faculty ratio at Shanghai University in 1934 was 18.8:1—higher than the national standard of 10:1 for schools with enrollments of less than 300, and 12:1 for those with more than 300 students.[52]

Unlike most Protestant schools, the college was managed by an interdenominational board of trustees in the United States, despite the fact that in its early years most of its teachers and board members in China were Presbyterians.[53] Lingnan's nonsectarian approach drew students from various backgrounds. A tolerant admissions policy is reflected in the 1906–1907 *Canton Christian College Catalogue*: "No creed, religious or philosophic, which does not interfere with attendance and proper deportment, will exclude an applicant for admission; nor will it prevent his full enjoyment of all the privileges of the institution after he has been received."[54] Besides an eagerness to pursue one's education, evidence of industry and moral character were also required for admission.[55] Students were drawn mainly from well-to-do families in Guangdong, Hong Kong, and the Macao area.

Continuity and coherence was strongly stressed at all levels of study, which included elementary, preparatory, and collegiate grades. English was the medium of instruction for all modern subjects beyond the second year of the secondary school. In the meantime, all students were required to study Mandarin. However, there had been a growing trend of adopting Mandarin in teaching in place of English, a trend supported by the Chinese Nationalist government (1928–1949) in Nanjing. The loosening of the English requirements for admission to Lingnan, together with turning English into a subject of study, was entrenched in 1935 when the government banned the use of English in the teaching of history, geography, and other subjects in Lingnan's middle schools. Such government enforcement was perceived as "jeopardizing Lingnan's reputation for excellence in English."[56]

A total of 140 credits including electives were required for graduation and students were required to amass 18 credit hours per week. The education offered at Lingnan was designed to be "one continuous course which should be followed by the student from beginning to end, if he is to have any adequate preparation for a life work." Not until the end of the second year of college were students deemed to be "properly prepared" to do specialized work.[57] Hence, a general liberal education was considered the foundation for later specialization.[58]

All students were required to live in school (*jisu*) as a part of their liberal arts education. Residential life was aimed at achieving the dual goals of an American liberal arts education—character-building and the pursuit of truth. In 1909, expenses for one year at the preparatory level—including tuition, rent, board and incidentals, laundry, books and school supplies, uniforms, athletic association fees, military and medical fees, guarantee deposit, and registration fees—ranged from HK$204.20 to $240.00. The elementary school costs were identical, except for tuition fees (HK$5) for the three semesters. The college tuition fee was $50 plus lab fees, a drawing class fee of 50 cents, and a deposit of $10; the remaining costs were the same as for the preparatory school.[59]

During the 1920s, the college experienced a proliferation of course-offerings and an increase in course standards. The modern liberal arts education introduced at Lingnan included four components that distinguished it from the old Chinese system—natural sciences, manual training, athletics, and social service. Before its return to Chinese administration in 1927, Lingnan had come of age as a fully fledged liberal arts college, while being on course for becoming a comprehensive university.

The courses offered at Lingnan were partly modeled on those taught in American liberal arts colleges. For example, in the Department of Western Languages, courses on English (freshman English, sophomore English, debate and oratory, phonetics, oral English, advanced composition, fundamental English, and the teaching of English), French (first- and second-year French), and German (first- and second-year German) were offered. Literature-related courses were integral to the degree program and those offered included: Classical Mythology, Survey of English Literature, Russian Literature, 19th-century English Literature, Contemporary English Novel, The Short Story, English Poetry, Contemporary Poetry, Contemporary Drama, Contemporary European Literature, European Drama of the 18th & 19th Centuries, Poems of the Romantic Movement, Victorian Poetry, Literary Criticism, Shakespeare, and introductory studies of Dante and Goethe.

For the history degree, the program, besides a general historiography course and a world history course (An Outline of History and The World at War and Since), offered a variety of courses on Europe (Europe in the Half Century before World War I, Economic History of Modern Europe, History of European Civilization Since the Renaissance), the United States (History of the United States), England (English Constitutional History, Development of Civilization in England in the 19th Century), Greece and Rome (The Civilization of Greece and Rome), and Japan (The Beginnings of Modern Japan, Imperial Japan to 1931, Cultural and National Characteristics of Japan). However, there was a clear emphasis on China, in courses such as Chinese Civilization (for overseas students), Modern China's Foreign Relations, Pre-Manchu Foreign Relations of China, Ancient History of China to 222 B.C., Medieval History of China from 222 B.C. to 906 A.D., History of the Manchu Dynasty, and The Republic of China. In the 1931–1932 *Catalogue*, in addition to the above courses, Latin American History and Turkish Reform History were also offered.[60]

The notion of liberal arts originally covered those "arts" and "sciences" that were considered "worthy of a free man," in opposition to the "servile" or "mechanical" arts. In later use, the concept of liberal arts came to refer to general skills of expression in language, speech, and reasoning as well as broad intellectual refinement.[61] Besides building up the liberal arts programs, the Lingnan leaders, both Chinese and expatriates, also took an interest in technical and professional training by developing a college of agriculture (formed in 1922), a college of sericulture (in 1927), of civil engineering (in 1928), a college of commerce (in 1929), and a medical school (since late nineteenth century). It was Chung Wing Kwong with his deep and enduring personal commitment who inspired both the Chinese and foreign staff at Lingnan, and thus gave a decisive impetus to the founding and development of the above four colleges.[62]

Lingnan lived the first half of its life at a time when the imperial Qing government was fading away and republican China was struggling unsuccessfully to create order and prosperity. In the 1920s, the college had its finger on the pulse of the anti-imperialist movements in Canton, albeit involuntarily. As discussed briefly in the Introduction, the tempo of political involvement increased after the May 30th Incident in Shanghai in 1925. The whole campus was shaken by the Shaki/Shameen shooting of June 23, 1925,[63] when Lingnan lost one teaching faculty member, Au Lai Chow, aged fifty, and one student, Hui Iu-cheung, aged eighteen, who died on the spot. Four students were severely injured and twelve students were slightly wounded in the incident.[64] James M. Henry (1880–1958), son of one of the founders of Canton Christian College, Benjamin Couch Henry, then president of Lingnan (1924–1927; executive secretary 1919–1922; provost 1927–1948, American director 1948–1951), was caught in a difficult situation: He tried to ameliorate the tension caused by anti-foreign agitation, including a workmen's strike on campus, while helping Alex Baxter—an Englishman who was made a scapegoat in connection with the June 23 incident—leave the college as quickly as possible. At the same time, Henry had to handle the repercussions in foreign circles that followed the publication of a resolution by seventeen American staff, without Henry's approval, in Guangzhou and Hong Kong on June 24. The resolution was controversial in allegedly rating Chinese eyewitnesses over English and French informants. In a statement issued on July 27, 1925, Henry, having decided to withdraw the resolution drawn up by the American staffers, expressed his grief over the loss of "family members":

> No outsiders can appreciate the feeling on the campus upon the part of for-eigner and Chinese alike when it became known that a much honored teacher and one of the students had been killed and at least two others wounded. In a very intimate sense it was a family affair.

Henry then gave his reasons for withdrawing the resolution, while emphasizing his sympathy for the Chinese cause and his commitment to mutual understanding:

> No one had had any chance to hear from the Shameen side [i.e., the English and French possessions in Guangzhou], but what was definitely and fore-most in everyone's mind—and this could not have been seriously objected to on June 24—was a protest against what seemed to be unnecessary severity in the Shameen defense and the apparently indiscriminate machine-gun fire. . . . Had the wording of these resolutions been as clear in this as I have satis-fied myself was the intention of those who drew them up I am confident so much misunderstanding would not have arisen, nor so regrettable and, I beg to say, undeserved bitterness evoked against an institution which, despite every assertion to the contrary, has been striving steadily to promote interna-tional goodwill, and as an institution with Chinese, British and American on its staff and on its Board of Trustees, has, we believe, been to no small degree successful in this and we hope will continue to be. . . . It is our belief that the only settlement of China's external difficulties will be one wherein mutual rights are mutually recognized, and where the foreigner is willing to do what has been so well suggested recently by a group in London, put Chinese interests first.

Although Henry's statement pleased neither the Europeans nor the Chinese, the college's fair-minded handling of the crisis was less confrontational and violent than was the case in other schools, based on available sources.[65] At St. John's University, for example, nineteen Chinese teachers and over 500 students withdrew from the university on June 3, 1925, when the president forbade them to fly the Chinese flag at half-mast to commemorate the Chinese killed in the May 30th Incident. And on July 7 about 600 students at the British Anglo-Chinese College in Tientsin staged a walkout.[66]

In 1927, Lingnan passed into Chinese hands, with Chung Wing Kwong as the first Chinese Christian president, serving until 1937.[67] In comparison with the controversial English and Chinese versions of constitutions during the power changeover at Yenching University, the legal documents guiding such a transition at Lingnan were straightforward and unequivocal.[68] The transfer of power was achieved by and large in a spirit of cooperation on both the American and Chinese sides, reflecting the multiparty bond that had formed over the years. Preparing to take up his new post, President-elect Chung reasserted the importance of the college's American connections:

> The new management of the Lingnan University is asking the American Foundation [Lingnan's Board of Trustees, then situated in New York] for the continued support of at least as many foreigners as are at present on the staff. We are asking this not merely for the financial aid which they represent. Even if we had a million dollars at our disposal we should still want foreign professors in this University. We should want them *just because it is a university.* For a middle school we might get along without them but not for a University, where we must draw on the knowledge of the whole world. Such an institution must be international in character. As it grows and departments multiply we shall need more rather than fewer foreigners.
>
> We want Americans especially here, because we have been working together with them for so many years in the building up of the University and because we have closer relations with Americans than with the rest of the world.[69]

On March 16, 1927, shortly after the transfer of the college to the Chinese, Sun Fo, son of Sun Yat-sen, mayor of Guangzhou, later president of Lingnan's board of directors, recognized the "splendid work" that Lingnan "has done and is continuously doing for the advancement of modern education in China." He added: "The maintenance of institutions like the Lingnan University as an institution of higher learning under Christian influences and international auspices would be most helpful to China in her great struggle for national freedom and independence."[70]

Referring to the handover, James M. Henry, former president and then

provost of Lingnan University from August 1927, expressed similar sentiments from the American side in 1932:

> I was President of the University until we turned the presidentship [over] to
> a Chinese scholar, Mr. Chung. . . . Our legal name is "Trustees of Lingnan
> University, incorporated in the State of New York." I am a sort of liaison
> officer between our New York office which owns the property and which
> leases it at one dollar a year to the Chinese and the people in the field. This
> arrangement is working very happily. . . . Our arrangement provides that if
> we feel the agreement is not being kept we resume control in six months'
> notice. . . . The feeling is better now than it ever has been.[71]

However, the handover was not accomplished without difficulty, as the
growing influence of Chinese in university administration led to the pos-
sibility of shelving some veteran American faculty, such as Clinton N.
Laird (tenure at Lingnan 1905–1942), Wilfred E. MacDonald (1911–1943),
and William E. Hoffmann (1924–1951), and replacing them with Chinese
staff.[72]

WAR, RECOVERY, AND
DISESTABLISHMENT, 1938–1952

As we have seen, in December 1938 Lingnan was forced to move to Hong
Kong after the fall of Guangzhou to the Japanese, borrowing space from
the University of Hong Kong, Chung Ching Medical College, and other
institutions. Later the Lingnan College of Agriculture relocated to a new
site in Pingshih (Pingshek, Pingshi) in Northern Guangdong. In December 1941, Japan occupied Hong Kong, thus forcing Lingnan to embark on
a new round of moves, first to Kukong, to Taitsuen (*dacun, Shaoguan, Xian-
renmiao*), and then to Meihsien (Meixian), only stopping in late 1945 with
the end of the war. During those difficult years, Lingnan in exile had to
suspend classes or evacuate its premises as the Japanese occupied Canton
and Hankow, the two largest cities on the Canton–Hankow Railway.

In his English report for 1943–1944, President Y. L. Lee gave some idea
of what it was like to run Lingnan while constantly on the move:

> On account of the uncertainty of the Military situation around Kukong, the
> University had been urged by our friends to move on from our recent evacu-
> ation to Hingning in the eastern Kwantung. I left Kukong on Dec. 10th [1943]
> with a colleague in a private car which was not in good condition. Both the
> brake and the second bearing were out of order but we did not know it then.
> We went on about 120 kl. from Kukong, then the steering broke down while
> coming down from a slope. The old car fell over on the right between two

trees and turned over 270 degrees into a rice field, about ten feet below. I was badly shaken and became unconscious for a few moments. The chauf[f]e[u]r stepped on [me] which woke me up. Later on I was pulled out from the car and was able to pull the damaged car up with the help of the others. . . . Our University has been somewhat like my experience. When there is life, we must proceed. . . . The year 1943–1944 has witnessed two Japanese movements from both ends of the railway [Canton and Hankow] but fortunately happened between the end and beginning of the academic year. We were able to carry on our work most of the year in not much abnormal condition.[73]

Although Lingnan came through these years of chaos and suffering, during the war both the American director, Olin D. Wannamaker (in New York), and the Chinese president, Lee Ying Lam, feared Lingnan might be irretrievably lost.[74] The war exerted extreme pressures on Lee Ying Lam who had to finance Lingnan's toing and froing between various places— Canton, Hong Kong, Kukong (Qüjiang), Taitsuen, Kuiling, Meihsien (Meixian), etc.—in addition to regular staff salary. In Lee's account,

Financially we have been very desperate. Between June first and July 31 [1944] I received either from Mr. Edwards or Rev. Coole $310,000 and drew from Mr. Lockwood $200,000 [*sic*]. I had to borrow from the local banks $200,000 and General Yui Han Mou $200,000 and other sources $300,000 to meet the emergency. With these amounts I have paid all of our staff their salaries of June, July and August and evacuation subsidy. I have sent away our books and equipment from Pingshek and Sinyanmiou.[75]

In 1944, Lee spent three months in Chongqing, then interim capital of the Nationalist government, to secure funds as well as to keep the communication lines open to the outside world. In mid-January 1945, having just settled in Taitsuen for three months, Lingnan had to evacuate into the mountains, upon learning about the renewal of the Japanese military advances. Once again Lee Ying Lam was on the move, sometimes even on foot, to seek out relief.[76]

In the economic stringency of wartime, Chen Lifu, Minister of Education of the Nationalist government in Chongqing, even proposed that Lingnan be nationalized (*Lingnan guoli*), something which would have jeopardized its independence had Lee agreed.[77] However, the war did propel Lingnan to form a broader coalition with government and nongovernment officials as well as with religious and nonreligious leaders. In 1944, through Madame Jiang Jieshi, Lingnan received £5,000 from the British Fund. And, through Horace Seymore, British Ambassador to China, the British United Aid Fund to China bestowed 1 million dollars upon Lingnan.[78]

After the Sino–Japanese War ended, a fully operational Lingnan was reopened at its permanent home of Honglok, and was gearing up for further development. The road to recovery, however, proved to be challenging.[79] Lingnan issued desperate appeals for help, in particular help to remedy the shortage of highly trained personnel. In a personal letter to Henry S. Frank, Lee Ying Lam wrote that "[t]he reasons that the Board of Directors formal request [sic] of your and Brownell' return is much more from the public demand of faculty, students and alumni [sic]. At this stage of University struggle, we need men like yourself and other old-time professors like Brownell, who should stay with us during this critical period [sic]."[80] Loyal American Lingnanians such as Henry S. Frank found themselves caught in conflict between what they considered the call of duty and their hardly settled life back in America.[81] Eventually Frank did come back to Lingnan and assumed the role as Associate Provost after the war.

The war had failed to dampen the resilient spirit of Lingnan; on the contrary, the war and the national emergency it created encouraged the university's senior management to stick to their pursuit of academic excellence. In May 1941, when the university was operating out of Hong Kong, Dean Y. K. Chu (Chu Yau-kwong, Zhu Youguang) offered his views (in English) on Lingnan's wartime role:

> What should universities do to help the nation in its twofold task of armed resistance to aggression and comprehensive national reconstruction? In my opinion, contributions of universities shall be made of a scholarly nature. At the same time participation in wartime reconstructional activities shall result in further development of learning and technology. Members of the University [Lingnan] should do many things expected of them as citizens, but as a university their contributions must be related to knowledge and scholarship.[82]

Chu saw an opportunity for Lingnan to make a difference at national level: "Many universities which have moved into the interior on account of the war are operating under very great handicaps which affect unfavorably on teaching efficiency. If we can train qualified personnel on a high plane, it may constitute a significant national contribution."[83] Chu argued that the quality of teaching and research at Lingnan in exile would be determined by four factors—the quality of the faculty; improvements in resources and equipment such as library collections and labs; the quality of the students; and the quality of academic research.

Lingnan was also assessed favorably in postwar planning, which likewise stressed the need to achieve new levels of academic excellence. In a document titled "The Future of Lingnan," Dr. Andrew Woods, who taught at the college from 1900 to 1907 and again from 1912 to 1917, reflected:

It was impossible fifty years ago for the Trustees of Lingnan to foresee the exact service for China which they should aim to render. . . . Courses of sound quality in the ordinarily approved subjects of our best colleges should receive the chief emphasis. Spoken and written English must not be given as competitors with Chinese language, but as valuable tools for the single purpose of communication in the field of world thought. Biology, physics and chemistry, with thoroughgoing laboratory experience, would be kept on a high plane, not only as preparatory work for later professional courses in Chinese and foreign universities, but as valuable assets in the careers of all thoughtful persons. . . . Lingnan thus far has supplied for imitation in the whole of China lower schools and a college that are worthy of being accepted as models. Its graduates have become marked men and women. . . . If this can be continued into the future, this Canton institution will prove to be a creative influence in determining a high quality for all future education in China.[84]

High academic standards continued to be emphatically stressed in the Lingnan records. Unprecedented numbers of applicants gave Lingnan the opportunity to raise admission standards. In 1946, applications for admission reached a peak of 1,710. "Entrance examinations were held at five centers of [in] different parts of the Province [Guangdong] and Macao so that graduates of all secondary schools in this part of the country might have a chance to try." The success rate for fall 1946 was 28.3 percent (amounting to 472 new students in total), much lower than the 60 percent admission rate achieved in wartime.[85] In fall 1947, there were 1,944 applicants for places at Lingnan but only 14.1 percent (232) were accepted, with a view to raising admission standards and keeping the total enrollment around 1,000.[86]

By the end of the 1940s, the University was in possession of 600 acres of land with 98 permanent brick and concrete buildings, including four academic buildings, four college dormitories, eight middle school buildings, seven primary cottages and forty residences. Also there were 172 buildings and several athletic fields.[87] The total funds of Lingnan University as of March 31, 1946, were US$2,372,847.69 including a current surplus of $180,838.55, plant $1,199,921.36 and endowment $939,917.81.[88]

In August 1948, Ch'en Su-ching (Chen Xüjing) assumed office steering Lingnan towards high academic standards, financial solvency and administrative efficiency. [89] Clouded by the impending change of regime in China, Ch'en, within a short period of time, reorganized the Medical College that, in Henry S. Frank's opinion, "has now a staff which in any period would be recognized as among the strongest in China." Ch'en was also able to recruit into the College of Arts some scholars such as Wang Li (Linguist) and Chen Yinque (Historian), who were renowned as "national treasures" (*guobao*). Lingnan was carrying on in "such a wonder way" that

Ch'en received immediate recognition and praise from a wide range of people for his wise administration.[90]

In 1948, Lingnan consisted of the College of Arts (with seven departments, i.e., the departments of Chinese Literature, Western Literature and Languages, History and Government, Sociology, Economics and Business, Education, Psychology and Philosophy, with a total enrollment of 427), the College of Agriculture (three departments, i.e., Department of Agronomics, of Animal Husbandry, of Horticulture with an enrollment of 98), the College of Science and Engineering (five departments, i.e., Department of Biology, of Chemistry, of Physics, of Mathematics with an enrollment of 360), the College of Medicine (with an enrollment of 171).[91] The same 1948 survey has no figures for the Union Theology College, for which the present author shall venture some accounts in the conclusion of the book. In 1949, the reestablishment of the College of Commerce was being planned, and the university student body was set to be kept at about 1,500.[92]

In the postwar period, the shortage of American teaching staff became acute. In 1947, there were only 13 American teachers out of 154 teaching members (i.e., 141 Chinese, 9.2 percent) as compared with "more than twice that number before the war [the Sino-Japanese War]."[93] In 1934 the proportion of foreigners to Chinese was 33 to 234 (14.1 percent).[94] During Ch'en's presidency, "a further increase in Western staff so as to maintain and extend the international character of the institution" was given priority, although Ch'en was clear about his preference for permanent foreign hires in English and natural sciences. To this end, the Exchange Student program was renewed as well.[95]

The postwar records from Lingnan bear witness to a measured anxiety, arising out of the uncertainties experienced by China engulfed in a civil war between the Communists and the Guomindang Nationalists. In this uncertain political situation, Ch'en Su-ching carried on the work with great calm so as to bolster up campus morale. Further implementation of the college's postwar plans came to an end as a result of the change of political power in China in 1949 when the Communists defeated the Nationalist Party and established the People's Republic of China. With the outbreak of the Korean War in 1950, the entire American contingent on the Lingnan campus were branded as imperialists and forced to leave China.[96] In 1951, the Chinese government decided to merge Lingnan with Sun Yat-sen University (Zhongshan daxue). In 1952, Lingnan University, as an institution, ceased to exist.[97] In 1967, Lingnan College was established in Hong Kong, and gained university status in 1999. In 1988, Lingnan (University) College was reconstituted within the governance of Sun Yat-sen University.[98]

CONCLUSION

This chapter has provided an overview of the history and operation of Lingnan University by placing Lingnan in its geographical, cultural, and economic contexts, both broad and narrow. Perceiving Lingnan as both a local and international institution, firmly rooted in South China yet with inseparable ties with the outside world, I have also taken some initial steps toward mapping out the history of the university around the significant but hitherto underexamined issues of adaptation and integration with reference to the transmission of American higher education to modern China. In chapter 2, I pursue these issues further with a view to understanding cultural encounter in the case of Lingnan University.

APPENDIXES

The proportion of women collegiate students in 1924 was 17 percent (24.5 percent in 1930, 29.3 percent in 1943, 34.2 percent in 1946, 30.1 percent in

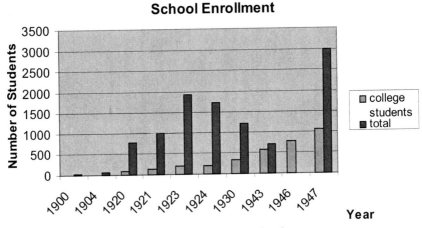

Figure 1.1.   School Enrollment. By Jessica Foster and author.

Year	1900	1904	1920	1921	1923	1924	1927	1930	1943	1946	1947
College students	0	0	85	128	205	194	340	330	565	777	1,058
Total enrollment	17	65	773	1003	1930	1727	1360	1214	714*	?	3,000

Sources: Canton Christian College, 1906–07 *Catalogue*, p. 56; President's Report, 1919–1924, p. 21, Trustees of Lingnan University, microfilm roll 26; *Sili Lingnan daxue yilan*, pp. 229–30; The 1927 figures are taken from C. K. Edmunds' letter to Wm. Summer Appleton in Boston, MA dated June 28, 1927, "Memorandum re. Lingnan University," Office of the Trustees in New York City, Yale Divinity School Library; President's Report, 1943–1944, Trustees of Lingnan University, microfilm roll 19; "Academic Year Semester II, 1945–46, Lingnan University," Renshi cailiao [Personnel files], Guangdongsheng dang'an'guan, file # 38-4-59; Untitled and undated [End of 1947 my inference] document, "Renshi canliao" [Personnel files], Guangdongsheng dang'an'guan, file # 38-4-58.
*This number derives from the statistics regarding the first semester, i.e. fall 1942, of school year 1942-43: Fall 1942 total enrollment was 488 collegiate students, plus 226 middles school students. See *Lingnan daxue xiao-bao* [Lingnan University newspaper], April 1, 1943, citation provided by Lee Sui-ming.

Female Collegiate Students

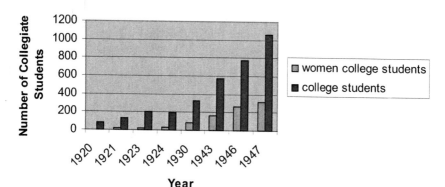

Figure 1.2. Female Collegiate Students. By Jessica Foster and author.

Year	1920	1921	1923	1924	1930	1943	1946	1947
Women	5	18	25	33	81	166	266	319
Collegiate students	85	128	205	194	330	565	777	1,058

1947), well above the national average of 2.5 percent in the same year.[99] (Sources: see figure 1.1 sources.) On June 30, 1927, Lingnan granted bachelor degrees to 26 candidates, 19 men and 7 women. The proportion of women collegiate graduates that year was 26.9 percent. (Source: C. K. Edmunds' letter to Wm. Summer Appleton in Boston, MA dated June 28, 1927, "Memorandum re. Lingnan University," Office of the Trustees in New York City, Yale Divinity School Library.)

NOTES

1. G. Weidman Groff, *Glimpses of China 1939* (Canton, China: Lingnan University, 1938). This is a calendar booklet compiled by Groff and printed and bound in Hong Kong in 1938 for Christmas 1939.

2. Kenneth S. Latourette, *A History of Christian Missions in China* (New York: MacMillan, 1929), p. 1.

3. Happer's biography, Trustees of Lingnan University, microfilm roll 1.

4. Charles Hodge Corbett, *Lingnan University: A Short History Based Primarily on the Records of the University's American Trustees* (New York: the Trustees of Lingnan University, 1963), p. 7. Charles W. Hayford, "Andrew P. Happer and the Founding of Canton Christian College: A Problem in Missionary Strategy," unpublished seminar paper, Harvard University, 1966. For Happer's correspondence from 1845 to 1889, see Yale Divinity School Library, Group 8: China Records Project Miscellaneous Personal Papers Collection, Box 107, Folders Mr. & Mrs. J. S. Kunkle.

5. Jessie Lutz speculates that many mission boards, with no direct experience

in China, were concerned that educational work might displace missionary and pastoral work and were therefore cautious about calls for funding. See Jessie Lutz, *China and the Christian Colleges, 1850–1950* (Ithaca, New York: Cornell University Press, 1971), p. 13. Charles Hodge Corbett, *Lingnan University: A Short History Based Primarily on the Records of the University's American Trustees* (New York: the Trustees of Lingnan University, 1963), p. 10.

6. A slightly different depiction of the founding of the Canton Christian College can be found in Charles W. Hayford's "Andrew P. Happer and the Founding of Canton Christian College: A Problem in Missionary Strategy."

7. Hanlin yuan was an elite academy founded in the eighth century A.D. and disbanded in 1911. Functioning as the emperor's "think tank" and pool of personal secretaries, it conducted court secretarial, archival, and literary work.

8. For the content and signatories of the letter, see Gao Guantian, compiler, *Lingnan daxue jiehui guoren ziban zhi jingguo ji fazhan zhi jihua* [The process of Lingnan's return to the Chinese and its development plan] (Guangzhou: Lingnan daxue, 1928), pp. 2–5.

9. Andrew P. Happer's letter to F. F. Ellinwood, dated February 19, 1894. Trustees of Lingnan University, microfilm roll 1.

10. Andrew P. Happer's letter to Rev. F. F. Ellinwood from Peking, China, dated June 1, 1892. Trustees of Lingnan University, microfilm roll 1. Ironically, Happer's strong stance on teaching English and building the college on a broad basis triggered his request for the return of his US$10,000 subscription bond as he feared that the college's trustees were prejudiced against both the use of English and his support of a broad Christian education. Andrew Happer's letter to Rev. F. F. Ellinwood, Secretary of the Presbyterian Board of Foreign Missions, dated February 19, 1894, Trustees of Lingnan University, microfilm roll 1. Later A. P. Happer (son of Andrew Happer) and the trustees of the college settled their dispute out of court, the trustees accepting a payment of $6,000 in lieu of the defaulted bond. Charles Hodge Corbett, *Lingnan University: A Short History Based Primarily on the Records of the University's American Trustees* (New York, NY: The Trustees of Lingnan University, 1963), pp. 27–28.

11. Andrew H. Woods, M.D., "Why the English Language is Used in the Canton Christian College," Trustees of Lingnan University, microfilm roll 39.

12. Charles W. Hayford, "Andrew P. Happer and the Founding of Canton Christian College: A Problem in Missionary Strategy." See Footnote 4.

13. See chapter 10, "Across the River: Honam and Fati," in Valery M. Garrett, *Heaven Is High, the Emperor Far Away: Merchants and Madarins in Old Canton* (Oxford: Oxford University Press, 2002). Phyllis Forbes Kerr, ed., *Letters from China: The Canton-Boston Correspondence of Robert Bennet Forbes, 1838–1840* (Mystic, CT: Mystic Seaport Museum, Inc., 1996).

14. Untitled document, Guangdongsheng dang'an'guan [Guangdong provincial archives], file # 38-4-58. One Lingnan American exchange student of 1936 recalled in 1999: "In those days, one of our primary connections to then Canton, and the Lingnan campus was by small poled or rowed watercraft, which, together with seagoing junks constituted the primary river traffic. Today, there are still a few junks to be seen and occasional sampans pass along with varied styles of

motorized boats." Arthur Eaton, "Lingnan: 62 Years Later," *Lingnan daxue Sanfanshi tongxuehui jianbao* [Lingnan University alumni association at San Francisco], October–December 1999, pp. 19–27.

15. Tony Perrottet, "The Glory That Is Rome," *Smithsonian*, October 2005. pp. 90–91.

16. Guangdongsheng dang'an'guan, untitled document, file # 38-4-58.

17. For the architectural and spatial hybridity of Christian universities and college campuses in China, see Jeffrey W. Cody, "American Geometries and Christian Campuses in China," paper presented at the conference, "The American Context of China's Christian Colleges," Wesleyan University, September 5–7, 2003. Jeffrey W. Cody, *Building in China: Henry K. Murphy's "Adaptive Architecture", 1914–1935* (Hong Kong: Chinese University Press, 2001). Jeffrey W. Cody, *Exporting American Architecture* (London: Routledge, 2003).

18. Charles K. Edmunds, "Modern Education in China," *The Journal of International Relations*, Vol. 10, No. 2, October 1919, p. 195.

19. Yü Zhi, *Kangle honglou: Zhongguo daxue xiaoyuan de dianfang* [Red buildings on Honglok campus, *sic*.], p. 20.

20. Yü Zhi, *Kangle honglou: Zhongguo daxue xiaoyuan de dianfang* [Red buildings on Honglok campus, *sic*], Foreword by Li Yanbao.

21. My sources for this list are drawn from: Guangdongsheng dang'an'guan [Guangdong provincial archives], untitled document from late 1947 (my inference) and Yü Zhi's *Kangle honglou: Zhongguo daxue xiaoyuan jianzhu dianfan* [Red buildings on Honglok campus, *sic*] (Hong Kong: The Commercial Press, 2004).

22. William P. Fenn, *Ever New Horizons: The Story of the United Board for Christian Higher Education in Asia, 1922–1975,* (New York: The United Board for Christian Higher Education in Asia, 1980), p. 8.

23. See Introduction.

24. Guangzhou Social Sciences Research Institute, compiler, *Handbook of Investment and Tourism in Guangzhou* (Beijing: Beijing Review, 1986), p. 8.

25. Graham E. & Glen D. Peterson Johnson, *Historical Dictionary of Guangzhou (Canton) and Guangdong* (Lanham, MD: The Scarecrow Press, Inc., 1999), p. 66.

26. Guangdongsheng dang'an'guang, untitled document, file # 38-4-58.

27. Guangdongsheng dang'an'guang, untitled document, file # 38-4-58.

28. Y. M. Yeung and David K. Y. Chu, eds., Guangdong: Survey of a Province undergoing Rapid Change, 2nd ed. (Hong Kong: The Chinese University Press, 1998). Guangdongsheng difang shizhi bianji weiyuanhui, ed., *Guangdong shengzhi* [Provincial records of Guangdong] (Guangzhou: Guangdong renmin chubanshe, 1993–present).

29. http://en.wikipedia.orgwiki/Pearl_River-Delta, accessed January 5, 2006.

30. Ding Shenzun, et al., eds., *Guangdong minguoshi* [The history of Guangdong in the Republic of China] (Guangzhou: Guangdong renmin chubanshe, 2004), vol. 1, pp. 186–91. No exchange rates are provided in the source.

31. Y. K. Chu, "The Academic Life of Lingnan," dated May 5, 1941. Trustees of Lingnan University, microfilm roll 26.

32. Corbett, *Lingnan University*, p. 107.

33. Letter to James M. Henry from Olin D. Wannamaker, dated April 9, 1935, Re. Budget, Staff, etc. Trustees of Lingnan University, microfilm roll 12.

34. Murray A. Rubinstein, *The Origins of the Anglo-American Missionary Enterprise in China, 1807–1840* (Lanham, MD: Scarecrow Press, 1996). Wu Yixong, *Zai zongjiao yü shisu zhijian: Jidujiao Xinjiao chuanjiaoshizai huanan yanhai de zaoqi huodong yanjiu* [Between religion and secularism: a study of the earlier activities of Protestant missionaries on the coast of South China] (Guangzhou: Guangdong jiaoyü chubanshe, 2000).

35. Peter Ward Fay, *The Opium War, 1840–1842: Barbarians in the Celestial Empire in the Early Part of the Nineteenth Century and the War by Which They Forced Her Gates Ajar*, 2nd. ed. (Chapel Hill, NC: The University of North Carolina Press, 1997 (1st ed. in 1975)). Maurice Collis, *Foreign Mud: Being an Account of the Opium Imbroglio at Canton in the 1830s and the Anglo-Chinese War That Followed*, Reprint edition. (New York: New Directions Publishing Corporation, 2002, 1st ed. by Faber and Faber in 1946). Jack Beeching, *The Chinese Opium Wars* (San Diego, CA: Harcourt Brace Jovanovich, Publishers, 1975). Arthur Waley, *The Opium War through Chinese Eyes*, (Stanford, CA: Stanford University Press, 1968). Timothy Brook, and Bob Tadashi Wakabayashi, ed., *Opium Regimes: China, Britain, and Japan, 1839–1952* (Berkeley, CA: University of California Press, 2000). Guo Deyan, *Qingdai Guangzhou de Basi shangren* [Parsee Merchants in Canton during the Qing period. *sic*] (Beijing: Zhonghua shujü, 2005). Liu Cunkuan, *Xianggang shi luncun* [Collected works on the history of Hong Kong] (Hong Kong: Qilin shuye youxian gongsi, 1998). For information on the wealth of Chinese and English archives on Guangdong Province held at the Public Record Office in London under file class F.O. 682, see David Pong, *A Critical Guide to the Kwangtung Provincial Archives Deposited at the Public Record Office of London* [Qingdai Guangdongsheng dang'an zhinan, *sic*] (Cambridge, MA: Harvard University, 1975).

36. Edward J. M. Rhoads, *China's Republican Revolution: The Case of Kwangtung, 1895–1913* (Cambridge, MA: Harvard University Press, 1975).

37. Michael Tsin, *Nation, Governance, and Modernity in China: Canton, 1900–1927* (Stanford, CA: Stanford University Press, 1999). Shending Yingfu (Fukamachi Hideo), *Jindai Guangdong de zhengdang shehui guojia: Zhongguo guomindng jiqi dangguo tizhi de xingcheng guocheng* [Political parties, society, and state in modern Guangdong: the Nationalist Party and the formation process of its party–state system] (Beijing: Shehui wenxian chubanshe, 2003).

38. Ezra F. Vogel, *Canton under Communism: Programs and Politics in a Provincial Capital, 1949–1968* (Cambridge, MA: Harvard University Press, 1969).

39. Martyn Gregory, *Canton to the West: Historical Pictures by Chinese and Western Artists 1770–1870* (London: Martyn Gregory Gallery, 2001), Catalogue 77.

40. Dong Wang, Entry for Guangzhou, *Encyclopedia of Western Colonialism since 1450*, ed. by Thomas Benjamin (Detroit, MI: Macmillan Reference, 2006). For further information on the history of Guangzhou, see Graham E. Johnson, *Historical Dictionary of Guangzhou (Canton) and Guangdong* (Lanham, MD: The Scarecrow Press, Inc. 1999). Edward Bing-Shuey Lee, *Modern Canton* (Shanghai: The Mercury Press, 1936). Yong Sang Ng, Canton, *City of the Rams: A General Description and a Brief Historical Survey* (Canton: M.S. Cheung, 1936). Dr. Kerr, *A Guide to the City and Suburbs of Canton*, Reprint ed. (San Francisco: Chinese Materials Center, Inc., 1974, reprint of the 1918 edition by Kelly & Walsh,). Guangzhou shi difangzhi

bianzuan weiyuanhui, ed., *Guangzhou shizhi* [History of Guangzhou] (Guangzhou: Guangzhou chubanshe, 1995–2000), 19 vols.

41. Fay, *The Opium War, 1840–1842: Barbarians in the Celestial Empire in the Early Part of the Nineteenth Century and the War by Which They Forced Her Gates Ajar.* chapter 2.

42. Johnson, *Historical Dictionary of Guangzhou (Canton) and Guangdong*, p. 18.

43. Edmund W. Meisenhelder, III. *The Dragon Smiles* (New York: Pageant Press, Inc., 1968), p. 4. Jian Youwen, "Lingnan, wo Lingnan" [Lingnan, My Lingnan], *Lingnan tongxun* [Lingnan newsletter], vol. 60, p. 9.

44. For more on women's education at Lingnan, see chapter 5.

45. President's Report by Charles Edmunds, 1909–1910, p. 63. Trustees of Lingnan University, microfilm roll 25.

46. "Guide to the Archives of the Trustees of Lingnan University," (Record Group No. 14), compiled by Martha Lund Smalley and Joan R. Duffy, Special Collection, Yale Divinity School Library, 1986, p. 3.

47. See 1899 *Catalogue*.

48. Sili Lingnan daxue (Lingnan Private University), *Sili Lingnan daxue yilan* [Overview of Lingnan University] (Guangzhou: Lingnan University, 1932), pp. 229–35.

49. Collegiate Faculty Directory, Sili Lingnan daxue (Lingnan Private University), *Sili Lingnan daxue yilan* [Overview of Lingnan University] (Guangzhou: Lingnan University, 1932), pp. 11–20.

50. Collegiate Faculty Directory, Sili Lingnan daxue (Lingnan Private University), *Sili Lingnan daxue yilan* [Overview of Lingnan University] (1932), pp. 11–20.

51. Untitled and undated [End of 1947, my inference] document, "Renshi cailiao" [Personnel files], Guangdongsheng dang'an'guang, file # 38-4-58. In 1947, Lingnan had 154 teaching staff with a collegiate enrollment of 1,054.

52. China Christian Educational Association Bulletin, No. 33, 1934. Wang Licheng, *Meiguo wenhua shentou yü jindai Zhongguo jiaoyü* [American cultural penetration and the modern education of China: a history of the University of Shanghai, *sic*] (Shanghai: Fudan daxue chubanshe, 2001), p. 179.

53. Four mission boards cooperated with Canton Christian College by each contributing a representative to its staff: the London Missionary Society (British), the Wesleyan Methodist Missionary Society (British), the American Presbyterian Mission, and the Presbyterian Church of New Zealand. Collegiate missions were the following: the Pennsylvania State College Mission to China, the Teachers College at Columbia University, the Foreign Work of the University of Pittsburgh, Kansas State Agricultural College, University of Kansas, Vassar College, Washington and Lee University, Wellesley College, and Williams College. See President's Report by Charles Edmunds, 1919–1924. Trustees of Lingnan University, microfilm roll 26.

54. *Canton Christian College Catalogue*, 1906–1907, p. 11. Trustees of Lingnan University, microfilm roll 25.

55. *Canton Christian College Catalogue*, 1906–1907, p. 15. Trustees of Lingnan University, microfilm roll 25.

56. Corbett, *Lingnan University*, p. 122.

57. *Canton Christian College Catalogue*, 1906–1907, p. 17. Trustees of Lingnan University, microfilm roll 25.

58. Subjects offered in the college's first two-year course of study included: life of [St] Paul, English, medieval history, solid geometry, trigonometry, general chemistry, chemistry (laboratory), mechanical drawing—first year; teaching of Jesus, English, history of England, analytical geometry, present-day problems in the Orient, physics, physics (laboratory), and translation. See *Canton Christian College Catalogue*, 1906–1907, p. 35, Trustees of Lingnan University, microfilm roll 25.

59. *Canton Christian College* (C.C.C.) 1906–1907 Catalogue, p. 54. Trustees of Lingnan University, microfilm, roll 25.

60. "Courses Offered in the College of Arts and Sciences, 1937–38," in Charles Hodge Corbett, *Lingnan University: A Short History Based Primarily on the Records of the University's American Trustees* (New York, The Trustees of Lingnan University, 1961), pp. 193–97. Sili Lingnan daxue (Lingnan Private University), *Sili Lingnan daxue yilan* [Overview of Lingnan University], pp. 125–28.

61. Oxford English Dictionary, 2nd ed., 1989. Encyclopedia Britannica Online, http://search.eb.com/bol/topic?thes_id=31800&pm=1, accessed on December 11, 2001. Stein Haugom Olsen provided me the sources on the concept of liberal arts.

62. "Zhong Rongguang zhuan," [Biography of Chung Wing Kwong], Guangdongsheng dang'an'guan, file # 38-4-70.

63. Shaki was the name of the road—running parallel to but divided by a canal from the English and French concessions in Shameen (established in July 1859)—where the unarmed marchers were hit by rifle and machine-gun fire. Shanghaishi lishi bowuguan [Shanghai historical museum], et al., ed., *Zhongguo de zujie* [The Foreign concessions in China, sic] (Shanghai: Shanghai guji chubanshe, 2004), pp. 56–59, p. 349. The Anglo-French side disagreed with the Chinese over who fired first on June 23: the Anglo-French blamed the Whampoa cadets among the protesters, while the Chinese blamed the foreign forces. Ding Shenzun, et al., ed., *Guangdong minguoshi* [The history of Guangdong in the Republic of China] (Guangzhou: Guangdong renmin chubanshe, 2004), vol. 1, p. 463. Corbett, *Lingnan University*, pp. 90–94. For details about the June 23, 1925 incident, and particularly Lingnan's involvement, see the untitled document by Gertrude Richarson Brigham, Associate Professor of English, on the Lingnan American faculty. Trustees of Lingnan University, microfilm roll 37.

64. Untitled document on the Canton tragedy, with a foreword by Gertrude Richarson Brigham, Associate Professor of English, July 21, 1925. Trustees of Lingnan University, microfilm roll 37.

65. My findings concur with Edward Rhoads's view on Lingnan and nationalism in 1925. Rhoads attributes Lingnan's riding out the turbulence to James Henry for his management skills as well as his liberal missionary mindset. Edward J. M. Rhoads, "Lingnan's Response to the Rise of Chinese Nationalism: The Shakee Incident (1925)," in *American Missionaries in China: Papers from Harvard Seminars*, ed. Kwang-Ching Liu (Cambridge, MA: Harvard University Press, 1966).

66. Ka-che Yip, *Religion, Nationalism and Chinese Students: The Anti-Christian Movement of 1922–1927* (Bellingham, WA: Western Washington University, 1980),

p. 55. North-China Daily News & Herald, *China's in Chaos: A Brief Outline of the Foreign Concessions with Examples of China's Disruption and Failure to Observe Her Obligations Due to Civil War, Bolshevist Propaganda and Mob Law* (Shanghai: North-China Daily News & Herald, 1927).

67. Gao Guantian, compiler, *Lingnan daxue jiehui guoren ziban zhi jingguo ji fazhan zhi jihua* [The process of Lingnan's return to the Chinese and its development plan] (Guangzhou: Lingnan University, 1928). Lingnan daxue Xianggang tongxuehui [Lingnan University Hong Kong Alumni Association], ed., *Zhong Rongguang xiansheng zhuan* [Biography of Chung Wing Kwong] (Hong Kong: Lingnan daxue Xianggang tongxuehui, 1996), p. 95.

68. "Agreement between the Board of Directors of Lingnan University, located in the District of Honglok, Honam Island, Province of Kwangtung, Republic of China, and the Trustees of Lingnan University, incorporated in the State of New York, U.S.A., hereinafter to be called the American Foundation. For the Purpose of Providing for the Maintenance and Development of Lingnan University as a Private Christian Institution of Higher Learning," "Lingnan Agreement: Section I, Re.: Property Lease," "English Version proposed By-laws of the Board of Directors of Lingnan University," Group 14, Box 1, Yale Divinity School Library.

69. "Memorandum re. Lingnan University," Office of the Trustees, 150 Fifth Avenue, New York City, Yale Divinity School Library.

70. Sun Fo's letter to Charles K. Edmunds, dated March 16, 1927, in "Memorandum re. Lingnan University," Office of the Trustees, New York City, Yale Divinity School Library.

71. Corbett, *Lingnan University*. xvii.

72. Letter from William A. Riley to Olin Wannamaker, dated January 6, 1935. Trustees of Lingnan University, microfilm roll 12.

73. "President's Report to the Members of the Board of Directors of Lingnan University for the Year 1943–44," by Y. L. Lee. Trustees of Lingnan University, microfilm roll 19.

74. Such fears surfaced in letters from Olin D. Wannamaker in October 1944 when Lingnan was cut off from the outside world. Trustees of Lingnan University, microfilm roll 19, Wannamaker's letters to Arthur R. Knipp (dated October 6, 1944), Clinton N. Laird (dated October 4, 1944), and to trustees and faculty members in America, dated October 2, 1944, etc.

75. Lee Ying Lam to Olin Wannamaker, Board of Trustees of Lingnan University in New York City on October 4, 1944. Guangdongsheng dang'an guang, file # 38-4-8 (2).

76. Lee Ying Lam, "Sili Lingnan daxue yü cici Yuebei shibian zhong chuli zhi jingguo" [The process of Lingnan's handling of the recent northern Guangdong Incident], written in June 1945 at Meixian. Guangdongsheng dang'an'guan, "Li Yuanhong yü Lingda laiwang hanjian, 1916–1918," [The correspondence between Li Yuanhong (President of Republic of China, 1916–1917 and 1922–1923) and Lingnan University [This document appears to have been misfiled], file # 38-1-23.

77. Li Xiaobi and Li Xiaoqiong, "'Lingnan niu' yü 'Niulin: huainian fuqin Li Yinglin," ["Lingnan Cow" and "Cow Lin": Remembering our father Lee Ying Lam] *Lingnan xiaoyou* [Lingnan alumni], Guangzhou, 1988, vol. 16, pp. 20–21.

78. Lee Ying Lam's letter from Kukong, Kwangtung to Sir Horace Seymour (Ambassador to China) on November 22, 1944. Guangdongsheng dang'an'guan, file # 38-4-8 (2).

79. Lee Ying Lam's letter to Henry S. Frank, May 30, 1944, Guangdongsheng dang'an'guan [Guangdong provincial archives], file # 38-4-8 (2).

80. Lee Ying Lam's letter to Henry S. Frank, March 31, 1943, "Li Yinglin xin-jian" [Correspondence of Lee Ying Lam], Guangdongsheng dang'an'guan, file # 38-4-8 (1).

81. Henry S. Frank's letter to Olin D. Wannamaker (American Director of the Trustees of Lingnan University), December 10, 1945. Guangdongsheng dang'an'-guan, file # 38-4-8 (2).

82. Y. K. Chu (Yau-kwong Chu), "The Academic Life of Lingnan," dated May 5, 1941. Trustees of Lingnan University, microfilm roll 26.

83. Y. K. Chu (Yau-kwong Chu), "The Academic Life of Lingnan," dated May 5, 1941. Trustees of Lingnan University, microfilm roll 26.

84. Andrew Woods, "The Future of Lingnan," July 17, 1948. Trustees of Lingnan University, microfilm roll 26.

85. Y. K. Chu, "The Academic Life of Lingnan," dated May 5, 1941. Trustees of Lingnan University, microfilm roll 26.

86. Guangdongsheng dang'an'guan [Guangdong provincial archives], untitled document, file # 38-4-58.

87. "Letter from Foreign Claims Settlement Commission of the United States to Trustees of Lingnan University," February 24, 1971. Trustees of Lingnan University Archives, Group 14, Box 37, Folder 439, Yale Divinity School Library.

88. "Trustees of Lingnan University, annual meeting of Trustees, brief report on conditions at the University and prospects," May 21, 1946. Trustees of Lingnan University Archives, Box 25, Folder 372, Yale Divinity School Library.

89. "Confidential report to the Trustees of Lingnan University," submitted by Henry S. Frank, provost of Lingnan, June 1, 1949. Trustees of Lingnan University, microfilm roll 24.

90. Letter from Robert J. McMullen (Executive Secretary of the United Board for Christian Colleges in China) to Ch'en Su-ching on March 10, 1949. Guangdong-sheng dang'an'guan, "Lingnan daxue Chen Xüjing cailiao," [Lingnan University files on Ch'en Su-ching] file # 38-4-5. Chen Qijin, "Chen Xüjing xiaozhang zhuchi Lingnan daxue," [President Ch'en took the helm of Lingnan University] *Lingnan tongxun* [Lingnan newsletter], No. 151 (September 15, 2001): 15–17.

91. The figures are taken from "Report on the First Phase, Lingnan University Planning Survey," (1948). The report was written in May 1948 by Raymond Rich & William Cherin Associates in New York, NY. This report is held at the Yale Divinity School Library, Group 8: China Records Project Miscellaneous Personal Papers Collections, Box 107, Folder Mr. and Mrs. J. S. Kunkle.

92. "Confidential report to the Trustees of Lingnan University," submitted by Henry S. Frank, provost of Lingnan, June 1, 1949. Trustees of Lingnan University, microfilm roll 24.

93. Untitled and undated [End of 1947, my inference] document, "Renshi cai-liao" [Personnel files], Guangdongsheng dang'an'guan, file # 38-4-58.

94. Lingnan daxue jiaozhiyuan yilanbiao [List of staff, Lingnan University, *sic*], 1933–1934, Guangdongsheng dang'an'guan, file # 38-4-224.

95. "Confidential report to the Trustees of Lingnan University," submitted by Henry S. Frank, provost of Lingnan, June 1, 1949. Trustees of Lingnan University, microfilm roll 24.

96. Charles Hodge Corbett, *Lingnan University: A Short History Based Primarily on the Records of the University's American Trustees*, p. 163.

97. For a guide to the Lingnan archives, see Lee Sui-ming, ed., *Lingnan daxue wenxian mulu: Guangzhou Lingnan daxue lishi dang'an ziliao* [Index of the Lingnan University archives] (Hong Kong: Lingnan University, 2000).

98. Despite their generous funding of related programs, the Lingnan Trustees in 1974 decided to discourage any attempts to "restore Lingnan University whether in Hong Kong or elsewhere, as it formerly functioned in Canton." See "Guides to the Archives of the Trustees of Lingnan University" (Record Group No. 14), compiled by Martha Lund Smalley and Joan R. Duffy, Special Collections, Yale Divinity School Library, 1986, p. 5.

99. Zhongguo jiaoyü gaijinghui (Chinese education reform society), ed., *Zhongguo jiaoyü tongji gailan* [Chinese Educational Statistics] (Shanghai: Commercial Press, 1923). Ruth Hayhoe, "Cultural Tradition and Educational Modernization: Lessons from the Republican Era," in Ruth Hayhoe, ed., *Education and Modernization: The Chinese Experience* (New York: Pergamon Press, 1992), p. 56.

2

✛

Cultural Migration: Lingnan as a Foreign and Local Institution

In this chapter I am concerned with discovering the links between Lingnan, as a foreign institution from the start, and the realities of the local society in which it was set. To this end, I utilize the history of Lingnan University to explore the meanings of Lingnan as a foreign and local higher educational institution.

Recent work in anthropology, history, and popular culture has teased out the complexities of interaction and process involved in cultural migration. In *Golden Arches East: McDonald's in East Asia*, edited by James Watson, the authors show localization at work, often in surprising and unexpected ways, as the multinational fast-food chain infiltrates almost every nook and cranny of the planet:

> Key elements of McDonald's industrialized system—queuing, self-provisioning, self-seating—have been accepted by consumers throughout East Asia [including Beijing, Hong Kong, Taipei, Seoul, and Japan]. Other aspects of the industrial model have been rejected, notably those relating to time and space. In many parts of East Asia, consumers have turned their local McDonald's into leisure centers and after-school clubs. The meaning of "fast" has been subverted in these settings.[1]

In a compelling portrait of Godzilla, the king of monsters, William Tsutsui deals with cultural flow in the other direction—from Japan to

America—but arrives at a similar conclusion. Tsutsui shows that, in the process of importing a Japanese film character into America, and eventually becoming an American popular cultural icon, the Godzilla films underwent significant modifications such as dubbing and editing, as well as marketing, for American audiences.[2]

In his *Migration in World History*, Patrick Manning comments on diasporas and cultural migration, especially the transfer of university systems: "Universities, too, are European-based elite institutions that have appeared all over the world. In the nineteenth century, German, British, and French models competed for dominance. The German form, remodeled in the United States, became the most influential, and has brought about the refashioning of the older university systems in South America, the Muslim world, and China."[3] In the lively discussions of Christianity in China, however, the many dimensions of cultural transmission in the history of Christian educational enterprises are still an under-explored topic.[4] Filling the research gap, this chapter attempts to address the following pertinent questions: How did the process of cultural "give and take" involve adjustments over time that helped shape the identity of Lingnan? What were the consequences of being foreign and local for Lingnan? What are the diagnostic markers that characterize a truly localized university?

TAKING AMERICAN LIBERAL ARTS EDUCATION[5] TO SOUTH CHINA: ADAPTATION TO LOCAL CONDITIONS

The issue of the localization of Christianity in China has recently drawn the attention of historians. For example, Eugenio Menegon's study of Spanish Dominican friars in Fuan county in eastern Fujian from the 1630s to 1747 reveals that, while upholding the universality and superiority of Christian tenets in the Chinese environment, the Dominicans reconciled the Catholic concept of vowed virginity with Confucian chastity. This adaptation, in combination with a receptive social environment, resulted in the acceptance by the Chinese of some two hundred Christian virgin converts who would otherwise have been seen as breaking with traditional social expectations and practices privileging marriage and reproduction.[6] Second, through a case study of the "Little Rome"—a Catholic village north of Meizhou City in Guangdoing—Eriberto P. Lozada Jr. has examined the process of localization in a global world. His findings suggest that "transnational Catholicism has become a local religious tradition, a social fact embedded in their everyday lives and in their identity as a rural community in postsocialist southern China. Thus the localization of the Chinese practice of Catholicism has a wider political and social context, which speaks to the more abstract question of what it means to be local in a global world."[7] A close examination of Lingnan's history supports Lozada's wider anthropological conclusion: "[T]ransnational processes do not necessarily challenge state sovereignty, and in many cases buttress state legitimacy and authority."[8]

In this section I also examine the response to American Christian liberal arts education in the late nineteenth and the first half of the twentieth centuries by Lingnan alumni. The pattern of this transnational process was laid down early in the history of Lingnan, a pattern that highlighted a process of adaptation built on a foundation of mutual cooperation.

In the transfer of an American model of higher education to South China, genuine efforts were made to secure mutual appreciation, understanding, and collaboration between Chinese, Americans, and the other expatriates involved. Before his arrival at Canton Christian College in 1904, the physicist Charles K. Edmunds (a graduate of Johns Hopkins University, professor of physics 1903–1908, and president of Lingnan 1908–1924) had been in charge of the Magnetic Survey of China, under the auspices of the Carnegie Institute of Washington.[9] Based on his travels across fifteen Chinese provinces, Edmunds reported that some of the most pressing problems China faced were "of [a] physical nature, such as reforestation, control of rivers and canals to prevent floods, construction of railways, development of mines, and many others of a similar sort."[10]

Besides his deep concerns about China from the perspective of a field worker, Edmunds, who had lived in the country for over twenty years, had an acute appreciation of China's educational needs. Speaking of the gap between the East and the West, Edmunds remarked that the distinction "lies in technique and in knowledge, not in intellectual caliber." Despite the significant cultural differences, "there is no fundamental difference in intellectual character."[11] Edmunds championed the adjustment of education to life-needs in China. In contrast to the Chinese conception of education as an exclusive preparation for a career in officialdom, Edmunds noted that much work needed to be done to instill the "broader idea of education as a training [sic] of each man for all phases of the life he is to live."[12] Secondly, referring to the importation of American pedagogy and curricula into China, he asked that special attention be paid to pupils' backgrounds, ethnically and as individuals, to the status of their communities, and to the need for adjustment in light of the specific problems faced by China.

The offering of highly differentiated courses ranging from elementary to college levels was a distinct feature of Lingnan from the beginning, and Henry B. Graybill (1880–1951),[13] on faculty from 1903 to 1926, offered three points of explanation. The first had to do with the college's publicity efforts in China. In Graybill's view, the differentiation of course levels would make it easier for the college to meet local needs and avoid being perceived as an elite institution. His remarks were tinged with enthusiastic pragmatism: "we must enlarge the school so that the people will see that we are not going to fail them, but can be depended upon. Our medical, agricultural, civil engineering, college and especially educational courses, should more definitely be advertised at once." What the new China needed most, in Graybill's view, was "men of knowledge and character," something that the ostentatious government schools were failing to supply. In reality, "it is the mission school graduates who are doing most of the new work."[14] Secondly, a diversified education would help students develop their own educational and career goals. Graybill's third point reflected the institution's own infrastructural needs: the differentiation of courses promoted "our wish to define more clearly for ourselves and the Trustees our ideas of what the College will mean for the next few years to come, what teachers must be gotten, what equipment, etc."[15]

Educational adaptation was a theory that held good on the other side of the Pacific as well. Charles K. Edmunds argued that Chinese students studying in America should not be subject to the same requirements as American students, "for the reason that the previous history of these Chinese students, both personally and racially, is so entirely different from that of the American student." Edmunds also argued that degree requirements of Chinese students ought to be different from those of American students "as a measure of their preparation for life work" in China. He concluded: "we believe that academic requirements should be adjusted to their real needs without in any wise changing the standard with reference to the American student."[16] With full confidence in the competence of his Canton students, Edmunds urged American institutions to admit them without examination,

> [o]n the basis that any conditions that may need to be imposed in reference to Latin or French or German may be worked off in due course, and that in determining the extent to which such conditions should be imposed, account should be taken of the fact that they are already thoroughly acquainted with two ancient languages, Chinese and Mandarin, and have a much better command of English than the usual college graduate in America has of any language foreign to him.[17]

Conscious efforts were made to enhance mutual understanding and personal development. For example, in his presidential report for 1909–1910, Edmunds proposed that "the Head of the Chinese Department [Chung Wing Kung (Chung Wing Kwong, Zhong Rongguang)] should be given further opportunities for culture and development, especially in the knowledge of American and Western institutions of all sorts."[18]

This pluralist exploration of higher learning helped to move Chinese education beyond its traditional boundaries. Charles Edmunds stated that Canton Christian College aimed "to furnish students [with] a collegiate education of the thoroughness and general excellence of that to be obtained in the colleges and universities of foreign countries."[19] Lingnan's mission statement in its Charter for Trustees, revised in 1930, set out three major goals: "The Board of Trustees is committed to continuing the mission laid out by the founders of the college. We aim at the education of character (*shixing renge zhi jiaoyü*), training academic talent (*yangcheng kexue zhi rencai*), and meeting China's needs (*shihe Zhongguo zhi xüyao*)."[20] The college had won recognition for its success in meeting these goals both nationally and internationally, as evidenced by Chinese President Li Yuanhong's letter to Charles Edmunds praising the role played by Americans in Chinese education: "I am deeply impressed by the great kindness of your fellow compatriots who exhort learning for the public good."[21]

The pursuit of a common cause in both bettering China and rendering service to America (and humanity in general) also accounted for the active role played by Lingnan's Chinese faculty in debating some of the fundamental issues facing Chinese higher education—such as the correlation between modernization and westernization, and the tensions felt between advocates of a broad liberal education and specialized training.

These concerns had a background in debate about the role of education in China. The early twentieth century, along with the Warring States and Weijin periods, has been categorized as the third important phase of cultural pluralism (*duoyuan hua*) in Chinese history. Heated debates about the direction of Chinese educational reforms focused on the relation between tradition and modernity, and between East and West. Guangdong educator Xü Chongqing (1888–1969, president of Sun Yat-sen University 1931–1932 and 1940–1941) proposed that education be seen as a way of increasing social productivity. In his work *Production, Revolution and the New Education*, Xü commented that "the correlation between education and society is equivalent to that between education and production."[22] In contrast to Chinese tradition which separated manual labor from the concept of education, Xü's conception centered on production as the core of the new education (*jinri jiaoyü de jichu shi zai changye*).

Another Guangdong educator, Lin Liru (1889–1977, president of Canton Normal College 1922–1927, president of Beijing Normal University 1950–1952) called for the development of normal schools based on two educational principles, popularization (*minzhong hua*) and modernization (*xiandai hua*).[23] Looking to the future of education in China, educator Chen Qingzhi proposed a three-tier system: basic education, education for production, and scholarship (*xueshu*). Chen's system aimed to orient both primary and secondary education toward practical labor and production for national needs. He argued that specialized technical institutions ought to replace universities and that research institutions be reserved for those very few who were able to engage in scholarly work.[24] In contrast, socialist educator Jiang Qi argued that foreign educational models were unsuited to China. What China needed, in Jiang's view, was specialized programs at primary, secondary, and tertiary levels.[25]

Against the background of this debate on the cultural dimensions of education East and West, Lingnan's president Ch'en Su-ching (Chen Xü-jing, 1903–1967, president 1948–1952) urged—in line with his well-known advocacy of wholesale westernization—that Chinese education, as an integral component of the culture, must be completely modernized (*chedi de xiangdai hua*) in order to avoid the dangers of a regressive return to tradition (*fugu*). Drawing a lesson from the failed efforts of the past, Ch'en called for complete westernization as the sole remedy for Chinese education.: "Since 1872, when the first batch of government-sponsored students were sent to the U.S., all so-called educational modernization movements have been stuck in the quagmire of superficiality (*pixiang qianbo*)." Ch'en poignantly summarized the pitfalls of China's previous experience with sending students overseas:

> Since the Chinese authorities did not want our overseas students abroad to forget their own culture, they built comfortable houses to accommodate them. As a result, except for attending classes and on special occasions, these government-funded Chinese students read Chinese classics, spoke in Chinese, and made Chinese friends—their life in America was much like that in China. . . . As a consequence, the Chinese students missed the opportunity to observe the true spirit of education and life in the West.[26]

Having witnessed the prosperity and advancement of American and European society, Ch'en expressed his confidence in Western capitalist civilization: China "must utilize American learning (*meiguo de xuewen*) to become more like America." At this time, Chinese scholars such as Zou Haibin and Chen Guofu proposed abandoning liberal arts and legal education for the exclusive development of practical, vocational schools. In response, Ch'en pointed out that such proposals were, in essence, a return to the failed "self-strengthening" movement of the Qing era (which focused on importing Western technology while preserving traditional values).[27] At the May 1932 Educational Conference, it was proposed that liberal arts and law majors be suspended or reduced while occupational schools were expanded to meet social and economic needs. In a prompt response, Ch'en observed that "the aim of vocational education lies in practical application (*yingyong*), whereas university education is designed for the pursuit of knowledge (*qiuzhi*). Though the pursuit of knowledge does not in itself necessarily lead to any particular application, the application of knowledge to the world would not be possible if one did not possess knowledge."[28]

Although a cultural radicalist, Ch'en's academic writings were dedicated to the goal of saving China[29] and his work focuses on the fundamental issues in higher education. Joseph Ben-David has argued that "[t]he proper scope of higher education consists of the basic arts and sciences, of professional studies based on basic sciences like medicine, and of professional studies, like law and theology, possessing an elaborate intellectual tradition of their own."[30] Along similar lines, Ch'en advocated the acquisition of knowledge for its own sake, which in his view constituted the fundamental core of higher education.

FORCES SHAPING LINGNAN'S GROWTH

The forces shaping Lingnan's rapid growth into a complex educational enterprise were mainly of Chinese origin. First, inadequate preparation for college education in China made the founding of a middle school necessary. When the Christian College in China first advertised for college students, virtually no students were found qualified for higher education. Not until 1901 did the College enroll its first freshman. Collegiate student numbers grew slowly. By 1906, there were only six enrolled in the college course—a big improvement over the zero enrollments between 1902 and 1906.[31] Soon, there was an increasing need for a primary school to prepare students for the middle school. In 1916 the College of Arts and Sciences was established, organized separately from the lower schools. The first B.A. degrees were awarded in 1918. In Charles Edmunds' words, Lingnan had begun "to realize the hopes and aims of its founders."[32]

Second, the college's rapid development in this period reflected its commitment to meeting the local needs of the Pearl River Delta region. Lacking backing from a specific mission board, nondenominational Lingnan lived on annual private donations. Transforming Lingnan into a comprehensive university comprising several colleges seemed impossible, given the financial constraints. However, long before the Chinese official takeover of the college, Chung Wing Kwong, one of the driving forces of Lingnan, began a program of expansion that he believed was justified by China's situation and needs at the time. The founding of several new colleges, mainly directed at meeting local needs, took place as a result of Chung's stewardship.[33] The formation of the Agricultural College in 1922[34] and of the Department of Sericulture in 1922—it was elevated to a college in 1927—took place in response to the needs of rural Guangdong, as did the founding of the College of Commerce and the College of Engineering. In 1928, the College of Commerce was set up to "meet the demand for business personnel" in international trade in Hong Kong and Guangdong. And in 1929, at the request of the Ministry of Railways, the College of Engineering was established to train civil engineers for the southeastern provinces.[35] Numbers enrolled at the College of Engineering grew steadily from 39 in 1929 to 77 in 1935.[36]

In 1921, Chung Wing Kwong successfully proposed the establishment of the College of Agriculture, managed by the Chinese. Under the auspices of the governor of Guangdong Province, the College of Agriculture received startup funding of 300,000, with an additional 100,000 in Chinese currency. The Guangdong provincial government also assisted in the purchase of land and farms for the college.[37] In 1934, the College of Agriculture had five departments—Agronomy, Sericulture, Animal Husbandry, Horticulture, and Plant Pathology. Besides teaching, the college emphasized the importance of research and its implementation, and practical farming, planting, and dairy production.[38] Over the years, Lingnan's College of Agriculture demonstrated a deep commitment to improving daily life in China. For example, to combat hookworm, a crop infection, in South China, a joint project was carried out by Lingnan, the Hookworm Commission, and the Canton Hospital in 1923.[39] The work included the examination of night soil in the kongs, epidemiologic studies, and fertilization experiments on corn crops. Records also reveal that in 1947 the Agricultural College initiated pioneering phytopathological research aimed at raising crop production.[40] In the words of one Lingnanian:

> All those who are deeply interested in the spiritual well-being of the Chinese people have sooner or later realized the primary need to improve the economic basis of human life in China. Such is the origin of the College of Agriculture of Lingnan University and the Department of Sericulture as one of the divisions of this College. They constitute an effort to lift the whole plane of human life for millions of persons.[41]

Lingnan also helped to modernize Guangzhou and the Pearl River Delta through its deep involvement in local life in a transnational context. Thus, the story of Lingnan's expansion is intimately linked with the history of the city in which it was set, offering a peculiar perspective on the modern development of Canton. In the 1920s, the silk industry in Guangdong and neighboring Guangxi province had a labor force of 2,275,000 people, and 492 square miles of soil devoted to the cultivation of mulberry trees for feeding silkworms.[42] The silk industry occupied a vitally important position in Guangdong's—and China's—international trade. In the first half of the twentieth century, China's two largest exports were soybeans (one third of total Chinese exports) and raw silk (worth approximately £20,290,533 per year).[43] According to a report in May 1933, the Japanese occupation of Manchuria (the three Northeastern provinces of China), the center of soybean production since 1931, had changed this situation, making raw silk the leading Chinese export. The silk industry was considered the "lifeline" (*shengming xian*) of Guangdong's prosperity. However, over a period of nearly two decades, Guangdong's export silk industry had been in slow decline, production falling from 44,326 bales (*bao*) in 1912 to 41,337 bales in 1932.[44]

In response, the Chinese and foreign agricultural scientists at Lingnan offered a road map for raising the efficiency and quality of silk production. One method of increasing silk production was to copy Japan, whose silk exports counted for more than 90 percent of the United States and 80 percent of the world market.

Setting its sights on realizing the full potential of Guangdong's silk industry, with an estimated potential income of $78,480,000 gold, Lingnan worked with American businessmen, its own scientists, and the Guangzhou government to fight a devastating silkworm parasite and to help South China comply with American requirements for reeling for and standard sizes and lengths of skein to reduce the cost of throwing and spinning in the United States.[45]

An important feature of Lingnan as a foreign and local establishment involved support from Guangzhou city, and from Guangdong provincial and national governments, despite the constant changes in the political landscape. Lingnan's modernizing efforts in South China did not necessarily challenge the local authorities. On the contrary, mutual respect and cooperation were exhibited by the different parties involved, such as the Silk Association of America, the Guangdong government, and the Canton (Guangzhou) government, all of whom were involved in Lingnan's glocalization projects. For example, in 1919 the Silk Association of America gave the then Department of Agriculture a building for the production of disease-free silkworm eggs and sericultural experimentation, a dormitory for sericulture students, and other buildings and equipment for scientific experiments. Meanwhile, in the early 1920s, the Guangdong government formed a special Provincial Bureau for the improvement of sericulture at Lingnan, appointing C. W. Howard of the Department of Sericulture at Lingnan as its head. In the fiscal years 1926–1927, 1927–1928, and 1928–1929, the Canton government appropriated around $70,000 gold, $60,000 gold, $130,000 gold respectively to support the College of Agriculture and the Department of Sericulture at Lingnan[46] Local organizations, including the Kwongtung Silk Improvement Association, also became involved.

Chinese faculty played an increasingly predominant role in Lingnan's involvement in improving the quality of silk production. The death of C. E. Howard in a railway accident in America in 1927 meant that in 1928 the entire staff of the Department of Sericulture was Chinese nationals, and the Americans faced the challenge of keeping pace with them.

Chinese sources also document Lingnan's work on silkworm disease and citrus research in South China at both the scientific and practical levels. In 1930, the *Lingnan Science Journal* (*Lingnan kexue zazhi*) published a series of research papers including "Feeding disease-free silkworms in South China" (*Zai nan Zhongguo siyü wubing can'er*) and "Report on the investigation of the parasite attacking silkworms in Guangdong province, 1929–1930" (*Min shiba zhi shijiu nian diaocha Yuesheng can zao binghai baogao*).[47] Meanwhile, Lingnan was able to provide the public with disease-free silkworm eggs raised in its state-of-the-art labs.

The medical work of Canton Christian College is equally a story of transnational collaboration aimed at meeting local needs.[48] The college's long history of medical work began in 1900 when Andrew H. Woods, a graduate of the Medical School of the University of Pennsylvania, was appointed to the staff to attend to the medical needs of college personnel and students. Lingnan enjoyed a close relationship with the Canton Hospital over many years. Known as the first hospital in China, it was founded in 1835 by American medical missionary Peter Parker. After a thirty-year gestation and trial period, the transfer of property from the Canton Hospital to the directors of Lingnan University finally took place on July 23, 1930. Three years later, the Sun Yat Sen Medical College was formed as a result of a merger of Lingnan University, the Canton Hospital, and the Hackett Medical College for Women, founded by Mary Fulton in 1901.

Lingnan's medical work was the fruit of genuinely multiparty efforts. When the transfer of the Canton Hospital to Lingnan was completed, the mayor of Canton, Sun Foh (Sun Fo, Sun Ke), donated nearly twenty acres of land for the construction of Lingnan's Medical School. The final merger of the three affiliated institutions in 1933 was achieved by sickness-stricken Chung Wing Kwong who "became fired with a great ambition to place this old institution [Canton Hospital] on its feet so that it should be second to none in China," as he lay in the old wards of the Canton Hospital. Chung went to Nanjing, then capital of the Guomindang Nationalist government, and succeeded in persuading members of the government's Central Executive Council, including Wang Jingwei and Sun Fo, to immediately appropriate $250,000 in Chinese currency for the erection of new medical buildings and the purchase of equipment.

From the medical work that commenced in the college in 1900 to the merger of 1933, foreign medical staff working at Lingnan, the Canton Hospital, and the Hackett Medical College maintained the close ties between the three institutions. European and American-trained doctors like Andrew H. Woods, William W. Cadbury, H. J. Howard, T. M. Li, and

Frank Oldt split their time between Lingnan's dispensary, the wards and clinics of the Canton Hospital, and the Hackett Medical College. Medical work also brought Lingnan into close contact with its village neighbors. In 1923, General Lei Fuk Lam (Li Fulin), in control of the 5th National Army and Honam Island where Canton Christian College was located, sought ways to provide medical services to the village. Lei contributed $13,000 in Chinese national currency for the construction of a dispensary and a sixteen-bed hospital at Lingnan for the care of local villagers.

Lingnan was also heavily involved in the provision of social services, also with significant local participation. In 1936, Lingnan had a key role in a scheme to create a "model county" near the city of Canton—local and provincial authorities planned to hand over to Lingnan the "task of rehabilitation" for a large district in the area. Envisioning another collaborative social project, the university's leaders hoped "to develop a model district where everything, from better agriculture to better education and a higher moral and spiritual life, shall become an inspiration for all of South China."[49] No further material has been located revealing the outcome of this ambitious project, though.

Another scheme was outlined in a document entitled "Proposed Training Center for Rural Workers," dated October 15, 1930, and prepared by Dr. J. Stewart Kunkle (Gong Yuehan, Lingnan's faculty 1942–1943, 1945–1946).[50] It outlined a proposal by Lingnan's President Chung for a joint training center involving the Agricultural Trade School of Lingnan University and Canton Union Theological College, at Eucalyptus Grove, a property owned by Lingnan near its agricultural holdings. Such a center would allow close contact with nearby villages as an aid to training men for religious and agricultural work in village settings.[51] Although this project was approved by the Lingnan board of directors as early as January 7, 1925, political disturbances in the area in the following years prevented further action on the plan.

Students in the college and its primary, middle, and higher level schools were engaged in community voluntary work of all sorts. In 1916, Chester Fuson reported that students at Canton Christian College were running two village schools (one for poor boys and the other for girls), engaging in open-air preaching on Sunday afternoons, and running a night school where the college's workmen studied Chinese, arithmetic, the Bible, history, geography, English, and singing. In addition, the college's Student Christian Association operated a Farming and Industrial School for poor village children.[52] Lingnan's primary school was first launched as a "Student Christian Association enterprise" in a nearby village and later moved to the college campus in 1914 with the addition of seven buildings, "all being the gift of Chinese friends." After the primary school was transferred to the college authorities, the students started another primary school on the university premises accommodating 300 children of work-men and villagers and offering a night class to 150 adults in reading, writ-ing and other practical subjects. In the fall of 1945 the Lingnan Industrial School was reopened on campus as an orphanage to care for 200 children who had lost their families during the Sino-Japanese war.[53]

THE LINGNAN IDENTITY

What were the consequences of being foreign and local for Lingnan? Four factors in particular helped Lingnan define for itself its identity and succeed in integrating with the local community as well as in its efforts to promote itself in religious, civic, and public life, in both local and global contexts.

The first element is reflected in Lingnan's motto, "Education for Service." This spirit of public service manifested itself in Lingnan's development of a coherent system of education from primary level upwards—a significant achievement as very few Chinese were qualified for college education in the late nineteenth century when the college began its work. Another example is the expansion of what was originally planned as a small liberal arts college into the large comprehensive university needed to serve the needs of the local community in South China. The college's "special place and character" is stressed in the February 1936 issue of *Lingnan*: "Lingnan has a highly important mission. It serves primarily the Cantonese, always the most enterprising and public-spirited of the people. . . . Then, our territory is enormous—one Christian college in a population of 53,000,000. We have always served, not one mission, but all."[54]

Among other branch organizations founded by the college, the South West [sic, Southwest] Social and Economics Institute (sic, Xinan shehui jingji yanjiusuo) gave further evidence of Lingnan's genuine interest in its local setting. Founded in 1932, the institute pursued research on the social and economic conditions of Southwest China.[55] Under the directorship of Wu Yuey Len (Wu Ruilin), professor of sociology, it carried out a series of significant field investigations in the 1930s. From 1932 to 1934, it undertook surveys, led by Wu Y. L. and Ch'en Su-ching, of the population, family structure, occupation, social customs and dialect of the boat people (*danmin*) of Shanam (*Shanan*) Village adjacent to Lingnan and in Ho-kow (*Hekou*), Sam Sui County (*Sanshui xian*), Guangdong. In summer 1932, fieldwork on a Chinese rural community was conducted in Sun Fung Wong Village (*Xin fenghuang cun*) on Honam Island near Canton City by Bernard Hormann. Other field investigations included a survey of the rickshaw coolies in Canton and another of Canton's Muslim community. In 1948 the endorsement of Ch'en Su-ching, the new Lingnan president, boosted the Institute's reputation further. A sociologist by training, Ch'en had argued strongly for field research into Southwestern culture. Ch'en believed that, as a crossroads for many different types of culture, Southwest China was of marked significance in sociology, anthropology, and cultural studies. First there was the influence of the non-Chinese—such as the Arab merchants and the Jesuits—whose initial entry-points were made through Southwestern China. Second, the Southwest was a window onto the pristine Han Chinese culture that was influencing local societies at the dawn of China's recorded history. Third, scores of ethnic groups were concentrated in the Southwest, thus making it ideal for researching ethnic dialects, customs, and social systems. Last but not least, Ch'en noted the important role of overseas Chinese in advancing education and the economy in Guangdong.[56]

This introduces the second factor defining the Lingnan identity—the practice of immigrant Cantonese in sending their children back to their homeland for higher education. As we have seen, in response to this demand the Overseas Chinese School was established in 1918. Third, as noted in several places above, donations from Chinese constituted a significant proportion of Lingnan's income—a remarkable achievement given the limited purchasing power of Chinese currency and the modest standard of living enjoyed by most Chinese. For instance, for the financial year 1917–1918 the college's total income was HK$308,792 (1HK$ =0.8US$), of which 72.2 percent (HK$222,984) came from Chinese sources.[57]

The fourth major factor in making Lingnan a foreign and local institution was its internationalism and regional mix. The heterogeneity of the student body distinguished Lingnan from other Chinese universities. Here sophisticated overseas Chinese students, most of them born in America, mixed with local Cantonese. This group of overseas Chinese students constituted nearly 30 percent of the entire student body (including the sub-collegiate schools) at Lingnan.[58] The student body also included young people from Malaya, Siam, the East Indies, Hong Kong, and the U.S. Edmund Meisenhelder, an exchange student from Harvard University in 1936–1937, observed how differences in fashion enlivened the international mix:

> Almost all the Chinese boys, whether they came from Canton or America, wore Western clothes during the warm months and Chinese gowns in the winter. The girls, except for the Overseas Chinese, attired themselves in the national dress throughout the year. Those from abroad generally wore the type of dresses and skirt and sweater combinations seen on the American campus, though, at times, they imitated the local girls.[59]

The international program at Lingnan was launched in 1933. In his 1968 memoir, Edmund Meisenhelder recorded the numbers of foreign students on the Lingnan campus, out of a total of around 500 collegiate students. In his year 1936–1937 there were 32, of whom 9 were girls, representing 20 American and Canadian universities.[60] The exchange students chosen, according to Meisenhelder, were characteristic "not of the run-of-the-mill American college boy or girl, but of the upper third of a university group in scholastic ability, mental and physical energy, extracurricular activities, and wanderlust."[61]

Meisenhelder also remarked that "it must not be thought that Lingnan was a typical Chinese university."[62] First, it was a college with a very distinctive Christian atmosphere. Second, Lingnan was located in the most progressive part of China, Guangdong province, from which were drawn the great majority of Chinese immigrants overseas. The third point Meisenhelder made about Lingnan was that it attracted a "different kind of students from that in most of the Chinese universities." Lingnan students were "far better acquainted with Western culture," and many of them came from wealthy families. Thus, to students drawn from very diverse backgrounds, the Lingnan ethos represented the dual process of Sinicization and Westernization. Both Easterners and Westerners could find a niche at Lingnan. Meisenhelder wrote:

> We were becoming "Orientalized"—that is, we were beginning to like the East to the extent that the folks at home who don't know it themselves would think crazy. This love of the Orient develops almost insidiously in anyone who has lived there for a year or more. It is what plants in all such persons a great longing to go back some day.[63]

How did Lingnanians perceive their place in China and in Sino-American relations? A 1929 issue of *Lingnan: The News Bulletin of Lingnan University* features "a story of co-operation" by Olin D. Wannamaker, the college's American director, which provides us with a window through which we can glimpse Lingnan's perception of itself at that time.

The article starts: "If there is [a] more striking example anywhere in the world of cooperation in Christian education than Lingnan University, we should like to visit such an institution." To Wannamaker, Lingnan's unparalleled place in American Christian education in China lies in its internationalism and the joint participation of both Chinese and Americans, a cooperation symbolized by the two landmark buildings standing side by side on campus—Martin Hall, the college's first permanent building, a gift of Americans, and Java Hall, a then state-of-the-art structure built with funds from Chinese expatriates in the East Indies. (See photo 2.1.)

Photo 2.1. A View Symbolic of Lingnan University. Special Collections, Digital Projects, Yale Divinity School Library.

Wannamaker also singled out two other qualities—an "inter-racial comradeship" that characterized "cooperation on terms of equality," and the "actual sharing of the burden of finance." Wannamaker remarked that in 1929 "of the fifty-four buildings on the campus, fully one half have been paid for with money contributed by Chinese friends. The total investment in land and buildings is now somewhat more than $1,000,000. Probably two-fifths of that amount is the gift of Chinese. There is no parallel case in China."[64] Wannamaker ascribed such a striking degree of contribution by Chinese to the "character of the Cantonese people—enterprising, successful in business, public-spirited."[65] Seven years later in 1936, the Chinese contribution to Lingnan's budget was three fifths.[66] The rapidly growing influence of the Chinese in the Lingnan enterprise prompted Wannamaker to warn the college's American supporters that, "[i]f the Americans fail to keep pace with the Chinese in their forward moves, the whole nature of the institution will undergo a change." The unbalanced Chinese–American staff ratio (171:29 in 1929) elicited an urgent request from Lingnan to both its American and Chinese supporters for more American personnel.

During the Sino-Japanese War, Christian colleges were considered by China's well-known writer and educator Lin Yütang and Charles K. Edmunds, as filling an "important place" in "China's struggle to maintain her freedom and to build for her future."[67] On March 12, 1941, Edmunds, then president of Pomona College, urged that "Americans can render no finer service to China—or to the strengthening of the friendship between the two nations—than by maintaining these Colleges. They are serving the whole of China today; they are training leaders for tomorrow. They embody our American friendship for China, our encouragement to her in a critical hour, our faith in her future."[68]

EXPERIENCING CHINA AND THE CHINESE REVOLUTION AT FIRST HAND

How did Lingnan's expatriate staff feel personally about their time at Lingnan, about their Chinese experience in general, and particularly the turbulent revolutionary movements of the 1920s? Unlike some foreign sojourners, adventurers, and merchants who arrived in China seeking fortune and fame, some of Lingnan's foreign faculty such as Henry B. Graybill (at Lingnan 1903–1926) and F. Earl Swisher (1925–1928) derived great personal fulfillment from their time in China, believing what they were doing was important and had been undertaken for a common cause.[69]

In 1925, as Graybill was about to leave Lingnan after more than twenty years' service, he looked back at his time at Canton Christian College with warm satisfaction:

> Being in an institution that accepts students away down in the primary grades and brings them on up from school to school till they graduate from the college, we have the rare opportunity of watching boys and girls of many types and from a great variety of homes absorb wonderfully from the rich environment here, rise to higher ideals, fill out, become active in affairs of the day, establish themselves as factors in the life of the New China. What is more interesting than that? What could be more satisfying?
> [. . .] In this kind of work there is the satisfaction of the skilled artisan with fine tools and the inspired artist working in the best mediums, but a better comparison is that of a Burbank who watches his many plants respond in ever new and better ways to the improving conditions he is always providing. It is his work, yet not his but nature's, God's.
> [. . .] No, a school is not to be measured and judged by its acres of grounds and the extent of its layout of buildings, nor by the numbers of students that flock to it from all over the world;—though most of us are subject to waves of pride in these things. It should be judged by the results of its spiritual contacts as seen in the lives of those who have shared its life. I find

it pleasant to observe now the men and women who were boys and girls here some years ago. Ideas that were then only ideas have now become people that do things. It is a satisfying thing to watch such a process.[70]

Graybill was not alone in his deep involvement with Lingnan and South China. Swisher, a young man from Lyons, Kansas, came to China fresh out of college at the age of twenty-three. Swisher taught at Lingnan at a time that saw the violent culmination of the Chinese nationalist revolution. As an honest and keen observer of the most turbulent years in Canton (1925–1928), Swisher came to terms with the chaos he recorded all around him and its effects. Later, he returned to America to take up a career teaching about the Far East. In a letter dated June 28, 1926, he confided to a friend:

> As to myself, I have never regretted so far that I signed up for a three year term. . . . It is intensely interesting, and I am just beginning to feel that I am getting some knowledge of the language, and that I am beginning to be in a small way valuable to the students and the university. There is a great responsibility and a great challenge in teaching here, and one feels much more intimately that what he teaches affects the lives of the students and the future of the country.[71]

Swisher was right. In 1924–1925, 38 foreign faculty signed up for the Cantonese language study program at Lingnan. Among them, Earl Swisher "made notable progress."[72] Again, on March 24, 1927, Swisher wrote that:

> Heaven allowing, I am going to stay here one more year. I like my work a lot and enjoy the toil and trouble, although it is rather wearing and gives me the blues once in a while. I am learning a lot of history both out of the books and from the developments that are going on around. . . . Labor has the ascendancy here and the government is in on [a] position to check it. . . . One has a great many more opportunities here of meeting important people than an ordinary person would have at home. A great many prominent people stop here on their way around the world and they make the campus their home while in Canton. Thus we get quite well acquainted with many of them.[73]

Witnessing the labor movement at first hand Earl Swisher grappled with the meaning of Chinese nationalism. Initially out of curiosity about the radical developments in Canton, in early March 1926 Swisher, together with some Chinese students, approached two foreign labor delegates, Earl Browder from the United States and Tom Mann from Britain, and eventually entered into extensive talks with them. These labor leaders were in Canton to "arouse labor to a realization of its unequal position, to demand shorter hours and more pay, and to have labor organized so

thoroughly that it can demand and not need to conciliate." Swisher re-
counted: "We asked him [Tom Mann] if he believed in working out his
plans thru [*sic*] the government. 'The government. To hell with the government. We don't care. Our only interest is for the laborers. Shorter
hours, shorter hours, shorter hours. More leisure, more leisure, more leisure.'"[74]

In reaction, Swisher commented that:

> It is rather sad, I think, that such men as these can influence so many others.
> They do not realize, of course, that the real problem in China is to build up
> industry and not to cripple it. They are demanding more equal distribution.
> . . . But it is hard to see . . . anything constructive for China in this kind of
> demonstration, because industry is steadily declining and capital is being
> driven away.[75]

By and large, Lingnan stayed calm during the widespread strikes, boycotts, and rallies that engulfed Canton at this time. As a small, liberal and
upscale society, Lingnan provided a window onto the larger environment
in which it was set. The aggressive and violent behavior of the labor activists made them unpopular with the majority of Lingnanians. Hence, Lingnan occasionally bore the brunt of nationalist attacks in the mid and late
1920s. As the authority of both the government and police in Canton was
undermined by the labor movement, Lingnan was forced to deal with
labor unrest on its own turf. As a result of Lingnan's dismissal of three
radical students—Guomindang activists and legal advisers for the labor
union—by a vote of around five hundred to twenty-three, Lingnan was
"subjected to all kinds of abuse in the [radical] newspapers."[76] "[T]he
school [Lingnan] is always referred to as an American imperialistic institution, and the students are the running dogs of the imperialists."[77]

Although the political, cultural, financial, and managerial challenges
confronting the college were substantial and manifold, Lingnan managed
to sustain itself during the political disorder and instability that followed
the inauguration of the Republic of China in 1911. Table 2.1 gives some
indication of the constant administrative chaos experienced by the
Guangdong government from July 1912 to September 1924, involving
twenty-nine different heads of government. The newspaper *Shenbao* also
gives us a full and relatively balanced chronological account of the political situation in Guangdong.[78] Michael Tsin's study of Canton reveals that,
despite trying to consolidate its power base in Guangzhou, "[b]y mid-
1924, however, it seemed that the Guomindang-led government had
made little headway in bringing the different segments of society together
under its direction. In fact, it had achieved exactly the reverse: the alienation of most of the residents of Canton."[79] Tsin attributes the hostility

Table 2.1. Administrative Heads of Guangdong from July 1912 to September 1924

Seat of government	Title	Name	Term
Dudu fu (Governor's office)	Dudu (Governor)	Hu Hanmin	Nov. 1911–Dec. 1912
	Daili dudu (Acting gov.)	Chen Jiongming	Dec. 1911–Jan. 1912
		Chen Jiongming	Jan. 1912–Apr. 1912
	Dudu	Hu Hanmin	Apr. 1912–June 1913
	Dudu & Minzheng Zhang	Chen Jiongming	June 1913–Aug. 1913
		Long Jiguang	Aug. 1913–Aug. 1914
	Dudu		
	Dudu		
Sheng xingzheng gongshu (Provincial Administrative Bureau)	Minzheng zhang (Governor of administrative affairs)	Chen Zhaochang	June 1913–Aug. 1913
		Su Zhenchu	Aug. 1913–Aug. 1913
		Li Kaixian	Sept. 1913–May 1914
		Zhang Woquan	Aug. 1913–Sept. 1913
Xun'an'shigongshu Office of Civil Governor	Xun'an'shi Civil Governor	Li Kaixian	May 1914–Sept. 1914
		Li Guojun	Sept. 1914–July 1915
		Zhang Mingqi	July 1915–June 1916
		Long Jiguang	June 1916–July 1916
Shengzhang gongshu (Governor's office)	Shengzhang (Governor)	Zhu Qinglan	July 1916–Aug. 1917
		Chen Bingkun	Aug. 1917–Sept. 1917
		Li Yaohan	Sept. 1917–Sept. 1918
		Zhai Wang	Sept. 1918–June 1919
		Zhang Jinfang	June 1919–May 1920
		Yang Yongtai	May 1920–Sept. 1920
		Chen Jiongming	Sept. 1920–Apr. 1922
		Wu Tingfang	Apr. 1922–Aug. 1922
		Chen Xiru	Aug. 1922–Jan. 1923
		Hu Hanmin	Jan. 1923–Feb. 1923
		Xü Shaozhen	Feb. 1923–May 1923
		Liao Zhongkai	May 1923–Jan. 1924
		Yang Shukan	Jan. 1924–June 1924
		Hu Hanmin	Sept. 1924–July 1925

Guangdongsheng difang shizhi bianzuan weiyuanhui [Commission on the local history of Guangdong Province], ed., Guangdong shengzhi [History of Guangdong] (Guangzhou: Guangdong renmin chubanshe, 2003), Zhengquan zhi [Chronology of governments], pp. 232–33.

of the locals and the ultimate armed confrontation between the Canton Nationalist government and the Merchant Corps on October 15, 1924, to the Nationalist Party's (Guomingdang) oppressive measures relating to private property.[80] The insurgence of the Merchant Corps—established in 1911 and led by Cantonese merchants Cheng Tiangu, Cen Bozhu and Chen Bolian—was suppressed by Sun Yat-sen's Nationalist forces in the Xiguan District of the City of Canton.[81]

In contrast to the recurrent breakdown of law and order in Canton during the early twentieth century, Lingnan represented a different direction for China. With the exception of the occasional act of hostility from radical elements, the moral and financial support and protection given to Lingnan from both the merchant community and military forces in Guangzhou and the Pearl River Delta attests to the peaceful nature of the transformation undergone by Lingnan. This unwillingness to challenge the local power structure demonstrates that Lingnan—the most modern and efficient educational establishment in the area—was evolutionary rather than revolutionary in nature. Second, this local protection and support stood in stark contrast to the experience of the fledgling Guomindang Canton government at the same period, especially with regard to the merchant class. In many ways, Lingnan managed to stand aloof from the politically and militarily fragmented world of Canton after the collapse of the last Chinese dynasty, the Qing, in 1911.

The notorious kidnap incident of 1924 exemplified the contrast of protection and order enjoyed by Lingnan with the instability and chaos generated by the Nationalist revolution and warlordism in the larger environment. The kidnapping of twenty-nine Lingnan students and seven staff took place on December 6, 1924, when six Chinese bandits boarded Lingnan's launch on its return trip from the city that evening. On learning of the incident, Lingnan's acting president, Alexander Baxter, immediately requested the Civil Governor, Wu Hon Man (Hu Hanmin), and General Lei Fuk Lam (Li Fulin) to rescue the hostages. General Lei swiftly dispatched a large number of soldiers to hunt down the bandits, and was able to have all the kidnapped students and staff safely returned to Lingnan five days later. At the subsequent banquet given in honor of General Lei, the general was courteously apologetic:

> As the situation of Kwangtung is so bad and troubled, we did not take good care of you, and caused you to suffer from the robbers for a few days. I hope you will excuse us for this reason. . . . From now on, I can say that the condition in this college will be perfectly safe. We must bear our duties for the welfare of you all. [Original English translation][82]

CONCLUSION

Taking a historical perspective, this chapter identifies the dynamics and multidimensional interactions that were present simultaneously at Lingnan in the American and Chinese context. I have examined the elements—including changes in curriculum, debates on the direction of higher education in China, multiparty cooperation, and local participation and protection—that shaped the cultural migration process undergone by Canton Christian College in transplanting an educational system based on the American Christian liberal arts model. More discussions about the interplay between American liberal arts education and the Lingnan model can be found in the conclusion of the present study. The significant local contributions to the finances of the college, discussed in detail in chapter 3, further demonstrate that Canton Christian College, as a foreign-initiated institution in South China, had become an integral part of the local establishment. As Olin Wannamaker put it, "in unique measure, Lingnan has found its way to the hearts of the Chinese."[83]

NOTES

1. James L. Watson, ed., *Golden Arches East: McDonald's in East Asia* (Stanford, CA: Stanford University Press, 1997, 2006), p. 37.

2. William Tsutsui, *Godzilla on My Mind: Fifty Years of the King of Monsters* (New York: Palgrave Macmillan, 2004). See particularly Chapter 4, "The Making of an American Icon."

3. Manning also identifies four categories of human migration: home-community migration, colonization, whole-community migration, and cross-community migration. Patrick Manning, *Migration in World History* (London: Routledge, 2005), pp. 7 and 159.

4. For an assessment of the state of research on Christianity in China, see Daniel H. Bays, "Chinese Protestant Christianity Today," *The China Quarterly* 174, no. Special Issue: Religion in China Today (2003): 488–504. Ryan Dunch, "Protestant Christianity in China Today: Fragile, Fragmented, Flourishing," in *China and Christianity: Burdened Past, Hopeful Future*, ed. Stephen Uhalley Jr. and Xiaoxin Wu (Armonk, NY: M.E. Sharpe, 2001). Richard Madsen, "Catholic Revival During the Reform Era," *The China Quarterly* 174, no. special issue (2003): 468–87. Michael D. Suman, *The Church in China: One Lord Two Systems* (Bangalore: SAIACS Press, 2006).

5. For information on the history of American higher education, see Frederick Rudolph, *The American College and University: A History*, 2nd; 1962, 1st ed. (Athens, Georgia: The University of Georgia Press, 1990).

6. Eugenio Menegon, "Child Bodies, Blessed Bodies: The Contest between Christian Virginity and Confucian Chastity," *Nan Nu* 6, no. 2 (2004): 177–240.

7. Eriberto P. Jr. Lozada, *God Aboveground: Catholic Church, Postsocialist State, and Transnational Processes in a Chinese Village* (Stanford, CA: Stanford University Press, 2001). p. 1. For the localization of religions, also see William A. Christian Jr., *Local Religion in Sixteenth-Century Spain*, 1981, 1st ed. (Princeton, NJ: Princeton University, 1989). William A. Christian Jr., *Visionaries: The Spanish Republic and the Reign of Christ* (Berkeley, CA: University of California Press, 1996).

8. Lozada, *God Aboveground: Catholic Church, Postsocialist State, and Transnational Processes in a Chinese Village*, p. 9.

9. E. Wilson Lyon, *The History of Pomona College 1887–1969*, Claremont, CA: Pomona College, 1977.

10. Charles K. Edmunds, "A Missionary Scientist in the Field," *The Chinese Recorder*, February 1914.

11. Charles K. Edmunds, "Modern Education in China," *The Journal of International Relations*, Vol. 10, No. 1, July 1919, p. 52.

12. Ibid, p. 75.

13. Chiu-sam Tsang, *A Tribute to Henry Blair Graybill (1888–1951)* (Hong Kong: Chung Chi College, Chinese University of Hong Kong, 1960). Susan Graybill Carter, ed., *Gladly as This Song* (Huntington, WV: University Editions, Inc., 1991).

14. "President's Report, 1911–12," p. 77. Trustees of Lingnan University, microfilm roll 25.

15. Canton Christian College Bulletin: President's Report, 1909–1910, New York: Trustees Canton Christian College, 1911, p. 32. Trustees of Lingnan University, microfilm roll 25.

16. Ibid, pp. 66–67.

17. Ibid.

18. Ibid, p. 11.

19. "President's Report by Charles Edmunds, 1919–1924," p. 27. Trustees of Lingnan University, microfilm roll 26.

20. Sili Lingnan daxue [Lingnan Private University], *Sili Lingnan daxue yilan* [Overview of Lingnan University], (Guangzhou: Lingnan University, 1932), p. 21.

21. Li Yuanhong to Charles K. Edmunds in 1916. See Lee Sui Ming (Li Ruiming), translated and compiled, *Lingnan daxue* [Lingnan Univesity] (Hong Kong: The Lingnan (University) Development Fund, Ltd., 1997), p. 260.

22. Xü Chongqing, ed. by Xü Xihui, *Xü Chongqing wenji* [Collected works of Xu Chongqing] (Guangzhou: Guangdong jiaoyü chubanshe, 2004), p. 164. Ou Chu, *Minguo shiqi de jiaoyü* [Education in Republican China] (Guangzhou: Guangdong renmin chubanshe, 1996), pp. 59–66.

23. Lin Liru, *Lin Liru wenji* [Collected works of Lin Liru] (Guangzhou: Guangdong jiaoyü chubanshe, 1994), p. 804. Ou Chu, *Minguo shiqi de jiaoyü* [Education in Republican China] (Guangzhou: Guangdong renmin chubanshe, 1996), pp. 67–80.

24. Chen Qingzhi, *Zhongguo jiaoyü shi* [Chinese educational history] (Shanghai: Shangwu yinshuguan, 1936), pp. 794–810.

25. Ruth Hayhoe, ed., *Education and Modernization: The Chinese Experience*, (Oxford: Pergamon Press), pp. 58–59.

26. Ch'en Su-ching (Chen Xüjing), "Jiaoyü de Zhongguo hua he xiandai hua" [Sinification and modernization in education], *Duli pinglun* [Independent commentaries], March 26, 1933, no. 43. Also see Yang Shen, ed., *Zouchu dongfang: Chen Xüjing wenhua luzhu jiyao* [Going beyond the East: Collected works of Chen Xüjing] (Beijing: Zhongguo guangbo dianshi chubanshe, 1995), pp. 204–13.

27. Ibid.

28. Ch'en Su-ching, "Duiyü xiandai daxue jiaoyü fangzhen de shangque" [Discussion of the principles of modern university education], in Chen Xujing, *Daxue jiaoyü lunji* [Selected works on university education] (Guangzhou: Southwest Economic Institute of Lingnan University, 1949).

29. Ch'en Su-ching, *Dongxi wenhua guan* [My view on Eastern and Western cultures], 3 volumes, *Lingnan xuebao* [Lingnan Journal], vol. 5, no. 1–4 (July, Septem-

ber & December 1936). Also see Qiu Zhihua, ed., *Chen Xüjing xueshu lunzhu* [Academic works of Chen Xüjing] (Hangzhou: Zhejiang renmin chubanshe, 1998).

30. Joseph Ben-David, *Centers of Learning: Britain, France, Germany, United States* (New Brunswick, NJ: Transaction Publisher, 1992), p. 27. Joseph Ben-David, *American Higher Education: Directions Old and New* (New York: McGraw-Hill, 1972).

31. *Canton Christian College Catalogue*, 1906–1907, p. 56. Trustees at Lingnan University, microfilm roll 25.

32. *President's Report* by Charles Edmunds, 1919–1924, p. 7. Trustees at Lingnan University, microfilm roll 26.

33. Tsang Chiu-sam (Zeng Zhaosen), "Lingnan daxue yuanxun Zhong Rongguang xiansheng xingzhuan" [Biography of Zhong Rongguang: Lingnan University's pioneer], *Lingnan tongxun* [Lingnan newsletter], March 25, 1972, p. 8.

34. "Proposed Revised By-laws of the Board of Managers of the College of Agriculture of the Canton Christian College as Amended and Adopted November 12, 1922," in English, "Lingda Nongxueyuan huiyi jilu he yuanzhang Li Peiwen cailiao, 1922–49" [Minutes of the College of Agriculture meetings at Lingnan University and Dean Li Peiwan files], Guangdongsheng dang'an'guan, file # 38-4-17.

35. Huang Jüyan, ed., *Jindai Guangdong jiaoyü yü Lingnan daxue* [Modern education in Guangdong and Lingnan University] (Hong Kong: The Commercial Press, 1995), p. 48.

36. "Lingnnan daxue gongxueyuan gaikuang" [General situation of the College of Engineering at Lingnan University], Lingnan daxue gongnong liang xueyuan gaikuang [General situation of the engineering and agricultural colleges at Lingnan University], Guangdongsheng dang'an'guan, 1929–1934, file # 38-1-6.

37. "Lingnnan daxue nongxueyuan chengli jingguo ji gaikuang" [The formation and general situation of the College of Agriculture at Lingnan University], Lingnan daxue gongnong liang xueyuan gaikuang [General situation of the engineering and agricultural colleges at Lingnan University], written in May 1934, Guangdongsheng dang'an'guan, file # 38-1-6.

38. Ibid.

39. "Program approved by Horkworm [*sic*] Investigation Committee and sent to Dr. Grant by Dr. Oldt in May, 1923," "Minutes of Meeting of Hookworm Committee held at Dr. Cadbury's residence, Friday, February 29, 1934," Guangdongsheng dang'an'guan, file # 38-4-17.

40. "An Opportunity for Pioneering Phytopathological Work in South China," by Kung-Hsiang Lin, Associate Professor, Plant Pathology Laboratory, Agricultural College, Lingnan University, Guangdongsheng dang'an'guan, file # 38-4-17.

41. *Lingnan: The News Bulletin of Lingnan University*, vol. 5, no. 4 (November 1928), Canton.

42. Ibid.

43. Liao Chongzhen, "Guangdong cansi fuxing zhi tu" [A road map for the revival of Guangdong's silk industry], dated May 1933, a report for the celebration week held by the Guangdong Construction Bureau (*Jianshe ting*). Guangdongsheng dang'an'guan [Guangdong provincial archives], file # 38-1-11.

44. For detailed breakdowns for the years 1912–1932, see ibid.

45. *Lingnan: The News Bulletin of Lingnan University*, vol. 5, no. 4 (November 1928), Canton, China, Yale Divinity School Library.

46. Ibid, and vol. 6, no. 2 (1929, month unknown).

47. "Sili Lingnan daxue min ershi nian canbing yanjiu gongzuo baogao" [Report on the research into silkworm disease by Lingnan Private University in 1931]. Guangdong'sheng dang'an'guan, file # 38-1-11.

48. This paragraph is based on William W. Cadbury's "History of the Medical Work of Lingnan University," Yale Divinity School Library, Group 8, Box 107, Folder Mr. and Mrs. J. S. Kunkle. Barron H. Lerner, "The University of Pennsylvania in China: Medical Missionary Work, 1905–1914," a senior thesis presented to the Department of History of the University of Pennsylvania, April 16, 1982, Yale Divinity School Library.

49. *Lingnan* (Canton Christian College), vol. 9, no. 1, article by Frederick Osborn, president of the board, and Olin D. Wannamaker, American director, Yale Divinity School Library.

50. Dr. J. Stewart Kunkle was president of the Canton Union Theological College, which officially became part of Lingnan in the early 1940s. Lee Sui-ming, ed., *Lingnan daxue wenxian mulu: Guangzhou Lingnan daxue lishi dang'an ziliao* [Index of the Lingnan University archives] (Hong Kong: Lingnan University, 2000), p. 154.

51. Guangdongsheng dang'an'guan, file # 38-4-70.

52. Chester Fuson, "Brief Report on Social Service in the Canton Christian College," *Chinese Recorder* 47 (March 1916): 209–11.

53. Untitled and undated [late 1947, my inference] document, "Renshi cailiao" [Personnel files], Guangdongsheng dang'an'guan, file # 38-4-58.

54. *Lingnan* (Canton Christian College), vol. 9, no. 1 (February 1936), article by Frederick Osborn, president of the board and Olin D. Wannamaker, American director, Yale Divinity School Library.

55. *Lingnan daxue xinan shehui jingji yanjiusuo gaikuang* [The South West Social and Economics Institute Lingnan University: A Review of Its Activities—*sic*] (Guangzhou: Lingnan daxue, 1949). Also see "The South West Social and Economics Institute, Lingnan University—A Review of Its Activities," Chen Xüjing cailiao [Lingnan University files on Ch'en Su-ching], Guangdongsheng dang'an'guan, file # 38-4-5.

56. Ch'en Su-ching, "Xinan wenhua yanjiu de yiyi" [The significance of doing research on Southwestern culture], in *Lingnan daxue xinan shehui jingji yanjiusuo gaikuang* [The South West Social and Economics Institute Lingnan University: A Review of Its Activities—*sic*] (Guangzhou: Lingnan daxue, 1949).

57. Jian Youwen, "Lingnan, wo Lingnan" [Lingnan, My Lingnan], *Lingnan tongxun* [Lingnan newsletter], vol. 60, p. 17.

58. *Lingnan University Bulletin No. 41*, Catalogue of College of Arts and Sciences, College of Agriculture, School of Silk Industry, and College of Business Administration (Canton: South China Printing Company, 1928), pp. 11–12.

59. Edmund W. Meisenhelder, III. *The Dragon Smiles* (New York: Pageant Press, Inc., 1968), p. 29. Other former exchange students also recorded their impressions of their time at Lingnan; see "25th Anniversary [Year 1935–36, 25 American exchangers] Lingnan University Exchanger News," published by Morse-Norton,

Ltd., in Los Altos, California. Group 1, Box 18, Folder 241, Yale Divinity School Library.

60. Edmund W. Meisenhelder, III. *The Dragon Smiles* (New York: Pageant Press, Inc., 1968), p. 9–10.

61. Ibid, p. 10.

62. Ibid, p. 27.

63. Ibid, p. 123.

64. *Lingnan: The News Bulletin of Lingnan University,* vol. 6, no. 2 (1929, month unknown), Yale Divinity School Library.

65. Ibid.

66. *Lingnan* (Canton Christian College), vol. 9, no. 1 (February 1936), article by Frederick Osborn, president of the board and Olin D. Wannamaker, American director, held at the Yale Divinity School Library.

67. Letter of C. K. Edmunds, Chairman of Southern California Committee of Associated Boards for Christian Colleges in China, dated March 12, 1941. Archives of the United Board for Christian Higher Education in Asia, Box 7, folder 167, held at the Yale Divinity School Library. Associated Boards for Christian Colleges in China include the following colleges: The Colleges—Cheeloo University (Shantung), Fukien Christian University, Ginling College, Hangchow Christian College, Hua Chung College, Hwa Nan College, Lingnan University, University of Nanking, University of Shanghai, Soochow University, West China Union University, Yenching University; Pacific Region—Robert A. Millikan, Chairman; Southern California, Charles K. Edmunds, Chairman.

68. Letter of C. K. Edmunds, Chairman Southern California Committee of Associated Boards for Christian Colleges in China, dated March 12, 1941. Archives of the United Board for Christian Higher Education in Asia, Box 7, Folder 167, held at the Yale Divinity School Library.

69. See Jonathan Spence's portrait of a group of Westerners in China, Jonathan D. Spence, *Western Advisers in China: To Change China*, Reprint of 1969 ed. (New York: Penguin Books, 1980).

70. Henry B. Graybill, "Looking back in [sic.] C.C.C," in *Ling Naam: The News Bulletin of Canton Christian College*, vol. 1, no. 3 (April 1925): 2.

71. Kenneth W. Rea, ed., *Canton in Revolution: The Collected Papers of Earl Swisher, 1925–1928* (Boulder, CO: Westview Press, 1977). Swisher's letter dated June 28, 1926, p. 40.

72. "Report of [sic] Language Study for the year July 1924 to June 1925." Trustees of Lingnan University, microfilm roll 37.

73. Rea, ed., *Canton in Revolution: The Collected Papers of Earl Swisher, 1925–1928*. p. 49.

74. Ibid. Swisher's letter of March 7, 1927, p. 48.

75. Ibid. Swisher's letter of March 6, 1927, pp. 45–46.

76. Ibid. Swisher's letter of April 10, 1926. p. 34.

77. Ibid.

78. Guangdong dang'an'guan *Shenbao* Guangdong ziliao xuanji bianjizu (Compiling team of selected sources relating to Guangdong appearing in *Shenbao*, Guangdong provincial archives), *Shenbao Guangdong ziliao xuanji* (Guangzhou: Guangdong sheng gongxiao xuexiao yinshuachang 1995).

79. Michael Tsin, *Nation, Governance, and Modernity in China: Canton, 1900–1927* (Stanford, CA: Stanford University Press, 1999), p. 98.

80. Martin C. Wilbur, "Problems of Starting a Revolutionary Base: Sun Yat-Sen and Canton, 1923," *Bulletin of the Institute of Modern History, Academia Sinica* 4, no. 2 (1974). Martin C. Wilbur, *Forging the Weapons: Sun Yat-Sen and the Kuomintang in Canton, 1924* (New York: East Asian Institute of Columbia University, 1966), Martin C. Wilbur, *The Nationalist Revolution in China, 1923–1928* (Cambridge: Cambridge University Press, 1983). Chen Yung-fa (Chen Yongfa), *Zhongguo gongchan geming qishi nian* [Seventy years of the Chinese Communist revolutions] (Taipei: Liangjing, 2001).

81. Tsin, *Nation, Governance, and Modernity in China: Canton, 1900–1927.* p. 90.

82. *Ling Naam: The News Bulletin of Canton Christian College*, vol. 1, no. 3 (April 1925).

83. *Lingnan* (Canton Christian College), vol. 9, no. 1 (February 1936), article by Frederick Osborn, president of the board and Olin D. Wannamaker, American director, Yale Divinity School Library.

3

Financing God's Higher Education: Management and Governance

O ne June 11, 1914, in a document titled "C.C.C. [Canton Christian College] Publicity and Cultivation Brief," James M. Henry, secretary and treasurer of the Trustees of Canton Christian College in New York, laid down guidelines for fundraising to be launched simultaneously from the college's Canton campus (Honglok, Kangle) and from New York, where its board of trustees' office was located. His notes for the former campaign read as follows:

A. From Honglok [Canton].

1. News-Letter, quarterly, to practically everybody who has had a real introduction to the C.C.C. Regularity is necessary. Good style equally so. Pictures good if really nice appearance. Otherwise not. Wording important. Letters of special character for special people very important if by any means possible. . . . Letter should not beg. They should be interesting and should always show a hopeful tone. . . . Great attention must be put on the N-L if it is to go to the important people . . .

2. Series of Multigraph Letters, to be sent with date and name filled in to prospective friends and contributors far and wide to introduce them by mail to the enterprise.

3. Present's Annual Report. . . . Not elaborate or long, but clearly presenting line of development ahead and the encouraging progress of past summed up.

4. Personal Cultivation by Staff and Students. Letters, clippings, articles, pictures from all the staff, not much but fairly frequent and interesting. To

personal friends (asking them to win other friends), to friends of College, to churches, Y.M.C.A.'s etc.[1]

Initiatives undertaken by the New York office, in Henry's opinion, should include "Book of Pictures with full titles and Brief Review Booklet[,] up-to-date and complete but brief," series of letters, the treasurer's report for a selected list of contacts, calls on friends of the college both old and prospective, luncheons, and so on. With regard to pictures, Henry emphasized the value of photographs showing boys preaching in villages and "Chinese staff with our product at one end and the oldest style fellows at other, best at one end and worst at other."[2]

Henry's campaign strategies, as outlined in this briefing document, provide us with a glimpse into the independent financing of Canton Christian College, which contributed significantly to the distinctive character enjoyed by Lingnan among the eighteen Christian universities in China. The story of Lingnan's finances underlines the way in which the trans-Pacific circulation of faith and higher learning in the late nineteenth and early twentieth centuries was thoroughly dependent on and deeply involved with hardheaded business management—an aspect of Christian colleges and universities in China rarely found in scholarly discussions of the subject.

A SKETCH OF LINGNAN'S FINANCIAL SITUATION

The financial condition of Lingnan had much to do with its origins. In 1886, after unsuccessfully suggesting that the college be governed by the Presbyterian Board of Foreign Missions, the university's founder, Andrew P. Happer, resolved to establish Canton Christian College under a separate board of trustees based in the U.S. who would have sole responsibility for its finances.[3] The six founding trustees in 1886 consisted of three clergy and three laymen, with Francis F. Ellinwood, secretary of the Board of Foreign Missions, as secretary of the college trustees.[4]

In the first pioneering years, the annual reports submitted by successive treasurers were incomplete and unclear, although they do give us a rough idea of the college's sources of income and of expenditure. In 1897 the treasurer appointed by the trustees began the fiscal year with a cash balance of US$2,485.01, and the estimated available income in invested funds was $3,122 in gold.[5] By 1903, the college was receiving the support of several principal subscribers giving amounts in excess of U.S.$5,000: R. L. Stuart ($25,000), Henry Martin ($25,000), David Torrense ($10,000), Andrew P. Happer ($10,000), John H. Converse ($5,000), and William

Thaw ($5,000). Large contributions to current expenses for the year ending April 15, 1903, came from the University of Pennsylvania Y.M.C.A ($500) and a Miss Willard ($600). In 1900, Lingnan incurred a total of US$5,334.21 in expenses with a deficit of $544.54, to be set against its total income of US$5,334.21 that included interest on corporation bonds of $3,909.50, donations from the United States ($600) and miniscule donations from Chinese sources ($6.26). Disbursement of salaries absorbed $4,089.55.[6]

The tables that follow (3.1 through 3.6) set out the university's financial situation between 1897 and 1945, with some gaps. All figures are denominated in U.S. Gold unless otherwise indicated. Income and expenses incurred in the Guangzhou (Canton) area were denominated variously in Mexican dollars, Hong Kong dollars, and Chinese dollars, and were converted into U.S. currency. The conversion rates in 1924–1925 were 1 Mexican dollar silver = 0.52 US$; 1 Hong Kong dollar = 0.5 US$; and 1 Chinese dollar = 0.38 U.S.$[7]

Taken with other statistics, these tables illustrate the rapid financial and institutional expansion of Lingnan, matching the increase in student enrollments. First, the college's income (current account), charged against its running expenses, shot up from US$3,122 in 1897 to US$99,791.96 in 1916. Second, the proportion of Chinese donations increased dramatically from U.S. Gold $6.26 in 1900 to $528.68 in 1908, and to $14,029.54 (13,939.01 + 90.53) in 1912.[8] Third, in 1916 income from Chinese sources

Table 3.1. Summary of Income and Expenditure of Lingnan, 1897–1908[1]

	1897 (1898)	1900	1904	1906[2]	1908[3]
Income	Interest on invested funds $3,122 gold	$5,334.21 (deficit $544.54)[4]	$8,997.04 (deficit $1,047.63)	$17,094.27 (deficit-contingent reserve $491.73)	$23,159.92 (deficit $916.52)
Expenses	Estimated $2,423.34 gold	$5,334.21	$10,044.67 (of which salaries = $6,070.40)	$17,586	$24,075.72
Endowment funds	$126,885.62	$123,325.24	$107,824.03	$134,488.81	$132,144.32

1. Trustees of Lingnan University, microfilm rolls 26 and 19, and adjusted by author.
2. Financial Statement, Trustees of the Canton Christian College, April 18, 1906. Trustees of Lingnan University, microfilm roll 26.
3. Financial Statement, Trustees of the Canton Christian College, 1908. Trustees of Lingnan University, microfilm roll 26.
4. Salaries absorbed $4,089.55.

          Chapter 3

Table 3.2. Summary of Income and Expenditure of Lingnan, 1912–1929[1]

	1912	1916	1925	1928/1929[2]
Income	$42,370.77 (deficit 1,023.61)	$99,791.96 (surplus $13,186.8)	$162,584.14 (deficit $59,570.08)	Chinese $409,984.30 (=approx.US$155,794.03) (deficit Chinese $12,035.70=US$4,573.57)[3]
Expenses	$43,394.38	$86,605.16	$222,154.22	Chinese $422,020.00 (=US$160,367.6)[4]
Endowment funds	$224,432.10	$409,754.44	N/A[5]	US$2,314,673.57[6]

1. Trustees of Lingnan University, microfilm rolls 26 and 19, and adjusted by author.
2. As a result of the handover of Lingnan University to the Chinese, the figures for 1928/1929 are taken from the summary sheets and trial balance prepared by Lingnan University under Chinese governance and the American Trustees of Lingnan University separately. Trustees of Lingnan University, microfilm roll 26.
3. This figure is taken from the Chinese report. Trustees of Lingnan University, microfilm roll 26. In 1928, as a result of the nationalization of Lingnan, it received Chinese $104,999.93 (US$52,499.96) in grant monies from the Guomindang (Nationalist) government.
4. This figure is taken from the Chinese report. Trustees of Lingnan University, microfilm roll 26.
5. The 1924–1925 Report of Operations contains no reference to monies received from New York. Trustees of Lingnan University, microfilm roll 26.
6. This figure was obtained from Trial Balance as of February 28, 1929, by the Trustees of Lingnan University in New York. Trustees of Lingnan University, microfilm roll 26. A windfall of US$700,000 from the Hall Estate in 1928 and the Lingnan campus property assets of US$1,002,381.04 contributed to the boost in Lingnan's endowment funds. Corbett, *Lingnan University*. pp. 117–18.

Table 3.3. Summary of Receipts 1911–1912[1]

Total Receipts from All Sources, U.S. Gold $65,786.97

American Sources $34,115.55

Gifts to Defray Current Expenses	$22,006.55
Gifts Designated for Buildings or Equipment	8,000.00
Gifts to Scholarship Fund	1,000.00
Interest on Bonds and Deposits and Scholarship Funds	1,694.39
Rent on Land and Buildings, Honglok	937.22
Staff Earnings	477.39

Chinese Sources $31,671.42

Gifts to Defray Current Expenses	90.53
Gifts Designated for Buildings and Equipment	13,939.01
Receipts from Students	17,641.88

1. Trustees of Canton Christian College, Treasurer's Report, 1911–1912. Trustees of Lingnan University, microfilm roll 26, and adjusted by author.

Table 3.4. Summary of Receipts of Lingnan, 1915–1916[1]

Total Receipts from All Sources, U.S. Gold $108,201.83[2]	
Chinese Sources of Income $53,943.81	
Student Fees—Tuition, Board and Incidentals	$44,428.16
Chinese Gifts to Defray Current Expenses	8,219.06
Chinese Gifts to General and Building Funds	1,296.59
American Sources of Income $42,443.51	
American Gifts to Defray Current Expenses	$32,565.75
American Gifts to General and Building Funds	5,292.11
Interest on Invested Funds and Balance	4,585.65

1. Trustees of Canton Christian College, Treasure's Report, 1913–1916. Trustees of Lingnan University, microfilm roll 26, and adjusted by author.
2. American Sources $42,443.51, Chinese Sources $53,943.75, Miscellaneous Receipts $11,814.51.

exceeded that from the American side, and this pattern continued in the years to come. Fourth, the tables also make it clear that for many years Lingnan was under intense pressure to raise money and posted only a few rare surpluses. The lack of support from a particular denominational constituency was keenly felt by both Chinese and American supporters, as revealed in a memo from the Trustees of Lingnan University on July 1, 1927, as Chung Wing Kwong was about to become chairman of the board of directors and president of the university: "Not having church resources to call upon, we have to depend on broad-minded individuals for support."[9]

Fifth, political unrest and war in China and abroad deeply affected Lingnan's finances. Since Lingnan paid its bills in Hong Kong dollars but received a significant proportion of its financial support in U.S. dollars, fluctuating exchange rates played havoc with the university's budgets. The crisis caused by World War I, for instance, drove the value of the U.S. dollar down from HK$2.27 in 1915 to HK$1.95 in 1916, HK$1.58 in 1917, HK$1.28 in 1918, and HK$1.20 in 1919. In 1917, "US$40,000 would be needed in Canton to do what $25,000 had done in 1914."[10] The financial difficulties caused by the devaluation of the U.S. currency were clearly documented in various records which I shall discuss in the second part of this chapter. Labor disturbances in China in 1927 and 1928 and the unfavorable American perceptions of China that resulted "made it exceedingly difficult to raise money for such institutions as Lingnan, and the Board of Trustees had to borrow money up to the limit of its credit."[11] The difficult financial situation was alleviated by the donation of US$120,000 from the Rockefeller Foundation and a gift of $700,000 from the Charles M. Hall estate. The records make it clear that the operation of Lingnan relied heavily on individual subscribers and donations from a few large foundations, rather than denominational boards or other church organizations.

Table 3.5. Receipts and Expenditures of Lingnan in a Prewar Year [Sino-Japanese War of 1937–1945][1]

Receipts

Appropriation of Provincial Government	$78,000
Provided by American Trustees	119,500
Grant from China Foundation	3,900
Personal Gifts in China	73,253
Student Fees	107,235
Student Rentals	22,860
Other Rentals	2,820
Water, Telephone, Electricity, etc.	1,904
Community Bank	1,477
Community General Store	450
University Bookstore	1,485
Agricultural Products	10,800
Total Receipts	**$423,684**

Expenditures (Current)	Subordinate	University	
Educational	*Schools*	*Proper*	*Total*
General and departmental; Administration and promotion	$17,169	$43,738	
Operation and maintenance of plant	5,768	16,818	
Instruction	40,705	117,015	
Library accessions	1,500	10,425	
Addition to educational equipment	1,746	11,893	
Functioning and development of National History Museum and Survey	—	14,756	
Infirmary	4,177	4,489	
Scholarships, prizes, and student labor	871	4,551	
Publications	150	7,290	
Athletics, etc.	420	856	
Incidental and emergency	800	3,585	
	$73,306	**$235,416**	**$308,722**

Community Service

Bank	$1,477		
Bookstore	1,485		
General store	450		
Subtotal	**$3,412**	**Total Operating Expenses**	**$312,134**

Investment in Plant

Land purchase & improvements	$600	$900	
New buildings	72,000	35,000	
Furniture	500	2,500	
Subtotals	**$73,100**	**$38,400**	**$111,500**
Total of operating and plant expenditures			**$423,634**

¹Figures approximate, based upon exchange rate of 30¢ U.S. for $1.00 Canton currency. *A Romantic Achievement of Chinese and American Cooperation: Illustrated Historical Sketch* (New York: Trustees of Lingnan University, 1941). Microfilm rolls 26 and 19, and adjusted by author.

Finally, the financial data underlines the character of Lingnan as a joint Sino-American venture. During the war years, Lingnan continued to receive a great deal of financial support from American private funders including the university's American board of directors (trustees) and the United China Relief. On the other hand, as table 3.5 shows, the Sino-Japanese War further diversified the sources of Lingnan's funding and brought in some government aid, partly due to the efforts of President Y. L. Lee and the urging of American Director Olin Wannamaker to maintain close contacts with Chinese provincial and national governments.[12] During the 1943–1944 fiscal year Lingnan received $159,650 in National Currency ($NC) from the Ministry of Education and NC$ 50,000 from the Ministry of Finance of the Nationalist Government in Chongqing, and NC$102,000 from the Kwantung Provincial Government. The British United Aid Fund to China gave £6,000. Meanwhile, Lingnan students raised about NC$700,000 for new buildings and Chan Hok Tam, a Cantonese merchant, contributed NC$100,000 towards the student fund.[13]

THE LINGNAN COMPLEX

In this section, I examine the fundraising methods of two resourceful Lingnan presidents, Charles Keyser Edmunds (Yan Wenshi, 1876–1949; president 1907–1924) and Chung Wing Kwong (Zhong Rongguang, 1866–1942; president 1927–1937), to illustrate some aspects of what I call "the Lingnan complex." Although the eighteen Christian universities in China all faced the problem of financing their operations, Lingnan differed from these other institutions in a number of ways.[14]

First, the very existence of Christian higher learning in China was contingent on effective fundraising, and the importance of finances and financial pressures cannot be overemphasized. This was particularly so for Canton Christian College, a nondenominational institution which received no regular funding from the missions and was forced to stand

Table 3.6.   The Financial Statement of Lingnan University in the Year August 1, 1943, to July 31, 1944[1]

Part I Receipts	National Currency
I. Ministry of Education	$159,650.00
II. Kwantung Provincial Government Subsidy	102,000.00
III. Ministry of Finance	50,000.00
IV. British United Aid Fund to China	1,027,373.47
V. Student Fees:	
A. University $657,550.00	
B. Middle School $333,125.00	
VI. Contributions from Chinese Friends (including $832,859.00 contributions to the building fund of $698,762.00)	832,859.00
VII. United China Relief, American Foundation and Government Subsidy in Foreign Exchange	3,076,989.75
VIII. Loans and Overdraft	399,856.53
IX. Miscellaneous	266,327.24
X. Balance on Hand	88,833.34
Total	**6,993,664.53**
	(6,994,564.33[2]**)**

Part II Expenditures	National Currency
I. General	$1,614,3xx.4x
A. Sal[ary] All[ocation]: Wages and Food	
B. Office Expenses	
C. Equipment	
D. Special Expenses	
II. College of Arts (Same spending structure as above)	394,195.04
III. College of Science & Engineering (Same spending structure as above)	266,41x.xx
IV. College of Agriculture	1,027,499.75
V. College of Medicine	394,535.85
VI. Middle School	373,332.03
VII. Emergency	2,608,059.65
A. Books and Equipment	107,700.43
B. Transportation	443,680.30
C. Buildings, Repairs and Furniture	2,056,678.92
Total	**$6,678,687.30**
Balance	**$314,977.23**
	$6,993,664.53

[1]Trustees of Lingnan University, microfilm roll 19. Some figures have been inferred due to the illegibility of the original documents, and there are some discrepancies as a result.
[2]The figure $6,994,564.33 in brackets is my own calculation, tallied up from the breakdowns.

on its own feet throughout its existence. Lingnan was founded in 1888 as an interdenominational institution with a loose relationship with various mission and collegiate boards which each supplied representative to Lingnan but had no binding financial obligations. Those boards included the London Missionary Society, the Wesleyan Methodist Missionary Society (British), the American Presbyterian Mission, the Presbyterian Church of New Zealand, the Pennsylvania State College Mission to China, the Teachers College at Columbia University, the Foreign Work of the University of Pittsburgh, Kansas State Agricultural College, the University of Kansas, Vassar College, Washington and Lee University, Wellesley College, and Williams College.[15]

Second, pressing financial needs forced Lingnan's Chinese and American administrators, in the words of international evangelist John R. Mott (1865–1955),[16] "to take a larger combination organized on the best modern business lines, and flooded with the spirit of God."[17] Third, unlike the situation of other Christian colleges such as Shantung Christian University (*Qilu daxue*), in Lingnan's case Chinese financial contributions were significant, a phenomenon linked to Lingnan's situation in the progressive and outward-looking Pearl Delta area.

The pressures associated with fundraising were especially evident during the college's early years. In 1922, in a letter to Herbert Parsons, president of the trustees of Canton Christian College, President Charles Keyser Edmunds (1876–1949) described the unrelenting pace of his publicity work:[18]

I [Edmunds] was kept quite busy getting out two campaign letters to our friends in America (about 26,000 each time)[,] copies of which were sent to you at the time; in taking numerous photographs for later reproduction in campaign literature, the negatives for which I am bringing with me, and in revising the plans for the proposed Science Building and drafting an appeal to the China Medical Board. . . . It has been a strenuous visit [back to Lingnan]. My sole exercise for the fifty-seven days was carrying my camera over the Campus!

Lingnan administrators in Canton made strong efforts to cultivate relations with Chinese students and in particular with those with well-to-do parents. In 1908, Edmunds recorded one of the fundraising activities organized by Lingnan students which took the form of a meeting to raise money for a new dormitory building attended by around 500 top Chinese officials—with the exception of the viceroy who was too ill to come but sent the head of the Foreign Office as his representative. Others present included the American consul and Sir Liang Cheng, the former Chinese Minister to America, whose five nephews were students at the college.

The main address was given by Shen Zengtong (Shum Cheng Tung), president of the Bureau of Education of the Two Provinces (Guangdong and Guangxi). Edmunds recalled:

> The meeting was presided over by the father of one of the boys, a Mr. Lai, one of the wealthiest men in Canton, who has agreed to head a subscription book for the dormitory. Besides the speeches there were several songs, the student double quartette sang "Old Kentucky Home" in English, the girls sang a song in English, and the whole student body sang the College Song written by Mr. Chung in Chinese.[19]

"After the meeting," Edmunds continued, "the guests were 'refreshed' in East Hall and then went over the building, inspecting it, and an exhibition of students' work and the laboratory, all of which seemed of considerable interest and were much praised."[20] In the later afternoon, the crowds left in a flotilla of twelve steam launches, four large house boats, and many smaller boats organized by the students' parents.

In order to collect the HK$30,000 needed for a student dormitory, letters were sent out asking parents if their names could be entered in the subscription book. Of the ninety approached, eighty parents agreed to donate. Lingnan offered "to name a room, or floor, or the building after the donor who would give the corresponding cash, or after whom[ever] he would designate."[21] Edmunds also offered that, for every $1,000 donated, "we would give the privilege of naming a student for ten years for free tuition, subject to his meeting the regular scholastic and conduct requirements."[22] Edmunds also recorded an incident that illustrated the efficacy of this appeal for funds: "Yesterday I was in one of the fine Chinaware shops and was surprised to find one of the leading men of our fourth year class in there calling on the proprietor to inscribe his amount in the subscription book for the dormitory."[23]

As mentioned above, the devaluation of the U.S. currency in 1917 and again in 1918 threatened Lingnan's financial viability. This situation was addressed by Edmunds in a letter to W. Henry Grant dated April 8, 1918: "[W]e have suffered heavily from the War in that the alteration in exchange alone has added $14,000 Gold to our expenses without any increase in the work itself at all and moreover that we had received, up to the end of January but one-fifth of the usual annual amount of gifts from America."[24] Lingnan had to raise US$37,000 to finish the 1917–1918 fiscal year in the black.[25] This "extreme financial stringency" forced Lingnan to raise tuition fees and to campaign for additional funds among students, their parents and friends, as well as expatriates in Shameen, Canton, Americans in Honglok, and Chinese emigrants living in Singapore, Malaysia, Java, and Indonesia.[26] Both Charles Edmunds and Chung Wing

Kwong spent months of the autumn and winter of 1917 and early 1918 in Southeast Asia on the fundraising trail.

Determined to keep Lingnan solvent, Chung set his sights on overseas Chinese in Southeast Asia and the Americas. He proposed starting an immigrant school on the grounds that "many Chinese immigrants in the strait settlement and the islands on [sic] South China Sea were wealthy and anxious to send their boys back to China for advanced study after a few years studying there Chinese or English or Dutch." Chung believed that through the proposed immigrant school, Lingnan could "keep into [sic] touch with the big merchants of Hong Kong . . . and the wealthy Chinese in the English and Dutch colony . . ."[27]

As a result of the 1917–1918 fundraising campaigns, expatriate Chinese in Southeast Asia contributed HK$20,000 toward the completion of Lingnan's fourth dormitory, HK$15,000 for general use, HK$10,000 toward the erection of the Central Building at the Elementary School, and HK$70,000 toward Lingnan's first dormitory for collegiate students (Java Hall). Chung's knack for raising funds had long been recognized by his colleagues. According to Henry Graybill, Chung "deserves to be far more of a hero than we represent or even consider him."[28] Graybill noted that Chung's success was "due not only to the excellent promise and solidity of our efforts for China, but largely because we have gone at it in the right way; we are not asking for houses for foreign missionaries to live in, or making requests for donations through the Consul, but it is the *man Chung* [Graybill's emphasis] (there is a bigger part of the secret than he [Chung] will admit it [sic]) housing hardworking, patriotic, Chinese boys."[29] Chung had been recognized as one of the central figures in the development of Canton Christian College.

Chung Wing Kwong did not rest complacent with this success. To finance the expansion of the College of Agriculture, Chung, along with Chen Jiwu of Canton Christian College, undertook a further fundraising trip to North and South America. Chung outlined an ambitious itinerary in a letter from Cuba dated May 27, 1925: "[S]ince last August, I set out from Cuba and came down south along the Pacific. This past January, I went up north along the Atlantic from Brazil to the British Indies to appeal for funds. Now I have done this part of America. Staying in Cuba's capital at the moment, I am planning to go on to Central America, Mexico and North America to accomplish the rest of the task."[30] The American campaigns were very successful, bringing in a fortune of US$340,000 for the college.[31] In 1929, Olin D. Wannamaker wrote that Lingnan's achievements had been

> due very largely to the personality of one man—President W. K. Chung, and his capacity for inspiring loyal, active cooperation on the part of the faculty,

students, and outside friends. From the date of the first effort to raise funds among the Chinese in 1908 until the present time, President Chung has moved among his fellow countrymen in almost all parts of the world and has personally secured hundreds of thousands of dollars from them for Lingnan. Out of his effort and that of a loyal faculty and student body, the alumni of Lingnan have developed a spirit similar to that of the finest loyalty of American alumni to their own universities.[32]

The final component of "the Lingnan complex" involved a financial separation between the college's Chinese and American staff. After Lingnan was handed over to the Chinese administration in 1927, the American board of directors (the Trustees of Lingnan University operating from New York) saw its role as "providing the best American faculty" they could secure and finance.[33] Although this arrangement, which required a high degree of cooperation, appeared agreeable to both sides, the relationship between the American and Chinese boards was always a matter of concern. In a letter dated October 15, 1945, Olin Wannamaker stressed the need for a properly integrated institution:

> Our mutual concern must embrace the whole faculty of the university. Hence our present desire for information regarding the existing status of the Chinese faculty and regarding plans for strengthening it. . . . [T]he Trustees are by no means self-satisfied as regards their achievement in supplying an American faculty. Perhaps, it might be well for the Chinese and American Boards to stimulate one another in this important matter of developing an adequate University faculty.[34]

MONEY: A PRIVILEGE OR A DISADVANTAGE?

In the development of the university, the Lingnan complex offered advantages as well as drawbacks. First, it represented Christian optimism. Referring to the extreme financial stringency experienced in 1918, Charles Edmunds wrote: "[T]his is *the most trying* year we have ever experienced and yet in many other respects it is *the most glorious* [Edmunds' emphasis], and you will see from Mr. Baxter's report that in respect to character formation it has been a most fruitful year."[35] Edmunds was referring to "the fact that 110 students had publicly stated their purpose to become Christians, during meetings conducted by G. Sherwood Eddy."[36] Second, the Lingnan complex represented an acceptance of fundraising as part of the college operations and the adoption of modern business methods to acquire funds, paralleling developments that emerged in American Protestant foreign missions in the late nineteenth and early twentieth centuries, but with greater freedom.[37] In 1920, James M. Henry, executive secretary of the Canton Christian College, saw a unique opportunity for the college:

> For some time I have been wondering whether it would be worth while to try and get help from the University of Wisc. in the way of financial support. As you know, F. O. Leiser, formerly in the Y.M.C.A. here in Canton, is in Wisconsin in the University Y.M.C.A. . . . It seems to me that C.C.C. [Canton Christian College] has a unique position in this respect for our organization is such that a university or college association of course can make its contribution to us directly and not necessarily through any complicated ecclesiastical machinery. Any such contribution to Peking or Nanking would naturally have to go through one or another reuniting board. In our case there is nothing of that sort and I imagine we are practically the only Christian College in China of which that is true.[38]

On the other hand, the issue of money often placed Lingnan in conflict with mission organizations, and sometimes caused it considerable embarrassment. As we have seen, no denominational mission board had any obligation to contribute to the running of the college. Consequently Lingnan's relations with these boards were ambiguous and could be strained when questions of money arose. In a letter to Charles Edmunds, James Henry complained of the drawbacks of dealing with the mission boards:

> The more I think about the participation of various missions in our work the more I am impressed with the fact that even the best of them seek to get off with just as small a contribution as possible. When one reflects upon what percentage of our total liabilities the whole maintenance of one staff member is, and then reflects that each mission making such a contribution is entitled to claim a full share credit in the work, the proportion seems a little distorted. . . . When it comes to actually voting anything which would mean in any sense a money contribution from their immediate budget to C.C.C. there is nothing doing. As witness: the fuss was made about the tuition of one student entering the pretheological course. This student is entirely subsidized by the Presbyterian Mission and they insisted on getting a full scholarship for him as well, practically meaning that C.C.C. donates that scholarship to the American Presbyterian Mission . . .[39]

The history of the college offers no better example of the dilemmas and complications associated with securing and distributing funds than Lingnan's long-time but strained relationship with the Harvard-Yenching Institute.

The story begins with Charles M. Hall, the wealthy inventor of a new aluminum extracting method. At his death in December 1914, Hall left part of his estate to support education overseas, especially in Japan, continental Asia, Turkey, and the Balkan States. For over a year before his death, Lingnan's trustees had worked to nurture a relationship with Hall, culminating in the promise of US$1,000,000 from the Hall trustees in 1925. In December 1928, $700,000 was given outright to the trustees of Lingnan University, and the outstanding $300,000 was entrusted to the newly formed Harvard-Yenching Institute as a restricted fund for Lingnan's use contingent upon its performance in the area of Chinese studies.

Difficulties arose when in July 1927 the Lingnan trustees transferred full responsibility for governing the university to the Chinese board of directors, leaving the American board with responsibility for the American faculty only. While Lingnan's American board was legally entitled to administer the full amount of the Hall Estate funds ($700,000 plus $300,000), it was required by the Harvard-Yenching Institute to transfer the interest to the Chinese board of directors who administered the Chinese program in Canton. However, since the Hall Estate funds constituted the major portion of the American board's assets, it was unwilling to transfer the interest on the $300,000 administered by the Harvard-Yenching Institute to Lingnan's Chinese studies program, in which the Americans had no direct interest.[40]

For many years, the American trustees of Lingnan University were relentlessly criticized by the Harvard-Yenching Institute which insisted on Lingnan's full compliance with the terms of the Hall fund.[41] In his annual assessment in 1937, Serge Elisseeff, director of the Institute, gave Lingnan a grade of "CC," while ranking Yenching University, one of the six recipients of the Hall fund, as "AAA."[42] Elisseeff complained that the Lingnan library was "still weak in Chinese books, as well as in Western books on sinology; the most important works are lacking and the people in charge of the library are not even familiar with the newest publications."[43] Elisseeff further expressed his astonishment that the Institute's contribution to Lingnan "is mostly spent for the traveling expenses of the foreign members of the staff."[44]

CONCLUSION

This chapter has explored the trans-Pacific financing of Canton Christian College (Lingnan University), a critically important but hitherto neglected topic by students and scholars of Chinese Christian universities and colleges. It is now possible to draw some conclusions in this area:

First, both the methods of American private higher education and Southern Chinese entrepreneurial vigor left their imprint on the financial management and governance of Canton Christian College. A sizeable proportion of the college's expenses was covered by tuition fees, a situation which paralleled its American counterparts.[45] As Earl Swisher expressed it in 1925: "The running expenses come from fees, which are quite large, charged to students. The rate next year is to be five dollars (Hong Kong currency) per credit hour per semester. These fees cover perhaps one-half to two-thirds of the running expenses."[46] In 1948, Lingnan's President Lee Ying Lam laid stress on "too great a financial dependence upon student fees" as a "defect" that need to be corrected.[47]

The success or failure of private American liberal arts colleges largely hinged upon the capacities of the individual serving as president—i.e., his ability to muster local, denominational, national, and foreign financial and moral support for his institution.[48] In the same way, the survival and growth of Canton Christian College largely depended on the abilities of its presidents, notably Charles K. Edmunds, Chung Wing Kwong and Lee Ying Lam, as effective fundraisers and national and international publicists. Lingnan's hard-nosed marketing tactics showed anything but the Chinese "intellectual aristocratic"[49] (*shidafu*) spirit, which was ashamed of dealing with money and hard labor.[50] Furthermore, the controversial Hall grant mirrored the changing scale of college finances in the first quarter of the twentieth century on both sides of the Pacific, while higher education experienced a growth spurt resulting in mounting financial pressures and competition. John S. Brubacher, et al., note that, up to the period of the American Civil War, a gift to a college of $5,000 was deemed extremely generous. However, "[i]n the twentieth century large-scale giving took a different turn. Not millions but now hundreds of millions of dollars were poured into philanthropic foundations by men like Carnegie, Rockefeller, and Ford . . ." The fortunes of Lingnan were thus an index of the finances of American colleges over this period.

Second, the financing of Canton Christian College reveals a shift of power to local Chinese in the management of the university, a process taking place even before the official handover in 1927. This power shift was unequivocally spelled out in the "Report on the First Phase: Lingnan University Planning Survey," dated May 17, 1948: "The American Board of Trustees today plays a somewhat different role from that of the early 1900s. It is no longer the dominant driving force of the University, nor does it exercise administrative control."[51] The private donations from Canton merchants to Lingnan were considerable and consistent, and have already been noted in several places of the present study. The following anecdote exemplifies the process by which Lingnan gradually came under Chinese financial direction. On October 31, 1945, a ceremony was held at Lingnan, witnessed by the mayor of Canton, Chen Ce, to mark the acceptance of a gift from Tam Lai-Ting (Tang Liting), a Cantonese businessman and a longstanding member of the Lingnan board of trustees. In the aftermath of the Sino-Japanese War, Tam donated all of his properties to the college including a dozen shops, several residences, one large wharf, nine steamers, a number of vacant lots, seventy mows of rice fields, and forty-eight mows of land in the Canton area.[52]

This shift in control formed a stark contrast to most Christian universities in China, although the present author should like to acknowledge that her judgment of other China Christian colleges hereby has been conditioned in reliance on other scholars' research. One conspicuous example is Yenching University. Despite his fundraising acumen and Yenching's national and international reputation, the efforts of Yenching's president, John Leighton Stuart, "to create a Chinese financial base met with constant frustration."[53] The weak position of Yenching's Chinese chancellor, Wu Leichuan, underlined the gap between the desired sinicization of Yenching and the thin Chinese financial base held by Yenching. To some extent, Lingnan's financial situation ("the Lingnan complex") helps explain the nature of the multiparty coalition at work at the college. At the same time, it also defines the process of indigenization and localization which made Lingnan truly Chinese—not just an aspiration expressed in empty rhetoric.[54]

NOTES

1. James M. Henry, secretary and treasurer of the Trustees of Lingnan University in New York, "C.C.C. Publicity and Cultivation Brief." Records of the Trustees of Lingnan University, Harvard-Yenching Library, Box 202 (1914).

2. Ibid.

3. In reply to the board of trustees of the Canton Christian College (C.C.C.), the Canton Mission stated "it [the C.C.C.] had better be under a separate board of trustees," refusing to include the institution in its mission work. "Answers of the Canton Mission to the Questions Asked in the Letter from the Board of Trustees of the Canton Christian College of Nov. 19th 1889," Trustees of Lingnan University, microfilm roll 1.

4. Before his death in October 1894, for fear of the Board of Trustees of the C.C.C. being prejudiced against the teaching of English in the College, Andrew Happer demanded that the Board of Trustees return of his bond for US$10,000 subscription. The grounds for such an action, according to Happer, were that the C.C.C. was drifting away from his vision to establish the C.C.C. "on a wider basis" which would be of great benefit to the Presbyterian Board of Foreign Mission as well as to other Missions. Andrew Happer's letter to Rev. F. F. Ellinwood, Secretary of the Presbyterian Board of Missions, February 19, 1894. Trustees of Lingnan University, microfilm roll 1. Later A. P. Happer (son of Andrew Happer) and the Trustees of the C.C.C. settled their dispute out of court, the Trustees accepting a payment of $6,000 in lieu of the above-mentioned bond. Charles Hodge Corbett, *Lingnan University* (New York, NY: The Trustees of Lingnan University: *A Short History Based on the Records of the University's American Trustees*, 1963), pp. 27–28. Also see chapter 1, endnote 10.

5. Annual Report of the Treasurer, 1897, and Trial Balance. Trustees of Lingnan University, microfilm roll 26.

6. Financial Statement for Year Ending April 30, 1900, and Trial Balance, Christian College in China May 16, 1900. Trustees of Lingnan University, microfilm roll 26.

7. Report of Operations 1924–1925, Canton Christian College. Trustees of Lingnan University, microfilm roll 26. Corbett, *Lingnan University*, p. 116.

8. Trustees of Lingnan University, microfilm roll 26.

9. "History and Present Status of Lingnan University," p. 6. Trustees of Lingnan University, microfilm roll 26.

10. Corbett, *Lingnan University*, p. 68.

11. Ibid, p. 117.

12. W. E. Hoffmann's letter to Olin Wannamaker dated October 2, 1945. Trustees of Lingnan University, microfilm roll 19.

13. "President's Report to the Members of the Board of Directors of Lingnan University for the Year 1943–44," by Y. L. Lee. Trustees of Lingnan University, microfilm roll 19.

14. For the significance of Canton Christian College in the interaction between American Christian higher learning and Chinese education, see Dong Wang, "Circulating American Higher Education: The Case of Lingnan University (1888–1951)," *Journal of American-East Asian Relations* 9, no. 3–4 (delayed 2000, appeared in 2006): 147–67. Dong Wang, "From Lingnan to Pomona: Charles K. Edmunds and His Chinese-American Career," in *China's Christian Colleges: Transpacific Connections, 1900–1950*, edited by Daniel H. Bays and Ellen Widmer, forthcoming.

15. President's Report by Charles K. Edmunds, 1919–1924. Trustees of Lingnan University, microfilm roll 26.

16. John R. Mott was student secretary of the International Committee of the Young Men's Christian Association from 1888 to 1915. He was one of the organizers of the World Missionary Conference held in Edinburgh in 1910, chairman of the Student Volunteer Movement for Foreign Missions (1915–1918) and the International Missionary Council (1921–1942), and president of the World's Alliance of YMCA (1926–1937). As a result of his work in international church and missionary movements, Mott won the 1946 Nobel Prize for Peace. http://www.britannica.com/eb/article?eu=5539, accessed on June 21, 2004.

17. John R. Mott, "The Vision of the Haystack Realized," in *The One Hundredth Anniversary of the Haystack Prayer Meeting* (Boston, 1907), p. 197. Also see Valentin H. Rabe, *The Home Base of American China Missions* (Cambridge, MA: Harvard University Press, 1978), p. 23.

18. As I have noted elsewhere, Charles K. Edmunds later became President of Pomona College in Claremont, California (1928–1941). Charles K. Edmunds's letter to Herbert Parsons, president of the Trustees of C.C.C., dated November 18, 1922. Records of the Trustees of Lingnan University, Harvard-Yenching Library, Box 38 (1922). Also see Trustees of Lingnan University, microfilm roll 7.

19. "Extract from Dr. Edmunds' letter to Dr. Jackson," Honglok, July 9, 1908. Records of the Trustees of Lingnan University, Harvard-Yenching Library, Box 15.

20. Ibid.

21. Ibid.

22. Ibid.

23. Ibid.

24. Charles Edmunds' letter to Clinton N. Laird, April 3, 1918. Trustees of Lingnan University, microfilm roll 6.

25. Ibid.

26. Charles Edmunds' letter to W. Henry Grant, secretary-treasurer of the Trustees of Canton Christian College, March 12, 1918. Trustees of Lingnan University, microfilm roll 6.

27. Chung Wing Kwong's letter to W. Henry Grant, September 21, 1917. Charles Edmunds' letter to W. Henry Grant, January 27, 1918. Trustees of Lingnan University, microfilm roll 6.

28. Letter from Henry Graybill to Henry Grant, November 20, 1908, Honglok. Records of the Trustees of Lingnan University, Harvard-Yenching Library, Box 15.

29. Ibid.

30. Lingnan daxue Xianggang tongxue hui (Lingnan University Hong Kong Alumni Association), ed., *Zhong Rongguang xiansheng zhuan* [Biography of Zhong Rongguang] (Hong Kong: Lingnan daxue Xianggang tongxuehui, 1996), pp. 76–77.

31. Ibid, p. 79.

32. *Lingnan: The News Bulletin of Lingnan University*, vol. 6, no. 2, 1929, Canton, China, held at Yale Divinity School Library.

33. Anonymous letter to James M. Henry dated October 15, 1945, addressed from Washington, D.C. The author is unknown, but is certain to be one of the Lingnan American trustees. Trustees of Lingnan University, microfilm roll 19. Also see "Xiaodonghui di shibaci huiyi jilu" [Minutes of the 18th meeting of the Board of Trustees], March 29, 1930, in Macao, Guangdongsheng dang'an'guan [Guangdong provincial archives], File # 38-1-18.

34. Anonymous letter to James M. Henry dated October 15, 1945, addressed from Washington, D.C. Trustees of Lingnan University, microfilm roll 19.

35. Charles Edmunds' letter to W. Henry Grant, dated April 8, 1918. Trustees of Lingnan University, microfilm roll 6.

36. Corbett, *Lingnan University*, p. 70.

37. Rabe, *The Home Base of American China Missions*.

38. James M. Henry, executive secretary of Canton Christian College, "Letter to Edmunds Concerning Funding," dated November 19, 1920. Records of the Trustees of Lingnan University, Harvard-Yenching University, Box 36. Also see Trustees of Lingnan University, microfilm roll 6.

39. James M. Henry, executive secretary of Canton Christian College, "Letter to Edmunds Concerning the Presbyterian Mission," dated November 19, 1920. Records of the Trustees of Lingnan University, Harvard-Yenching University, Box 36. Also see Trustees of Lingnan University, microfilm roll 6.

40. In his letter to Serge Elisseeff, Olin D. Wannamaker, American director of Lingnan University, explained that "this entire income was involved in the support of the American faculty and certain other items in the total University budget for which the American Trustees have responsibility. On the other hands, the

whole field of Chinese Studies was altogether outside the sphere of responsibility of the American Trustees. The Chinese Board of Directors was responsible for that division of the University, as well as for the total budget except for the specific assistance promised by the American Trustees." Records of the Trustees of Lingnan University, Harvard-Yenching Library, Box 217.

41. Tao Feiya and Wu Ziming (Peter Ng), *Jidujiao daoxue yü guoxue yanjiu* [Christian universities and China studies] (Fuzhou: Fujian jiaoyü chubanshe, 1998). Chapter 6 discusses the Chinese studies programs in the six Christian universities in China affiliated to the Harvard-Yenching Institute (pp. 189–223).

42. "Memorandum of Conferences with Professor Elisseeff, Tientsin, July 21st and 22nd, 1937," by Edward H. Hume. Records of the Trustees of Lingnan University, Harvard-Yenching Library, Box 217.

43. "Observations by Professor Elisseeff on the Work of the Six Affiliated Universities Based on His Visits to China During 1936–37." Records of Trustees of Lingnan University, Box 217.

44. Ibid.

45. John S. Brubacher, and Willis Rudy, *Higher Education in Transition: A History of American Colleges and Universities*, 4th ed. (New Brunswick, NJ: Transaction Publishers, 1997), pp. 36–37.

46. Kenneth W. Rea, ed., *Canton in Revolution: The Collected Papers of Earl Swisher, 1925–1928* (Boulder, CO: Westview Press, 1977). For Swisher's letter of June 28, 1926, see pp. 39–40.

47. "Confidential report to the Trustees of Lingnan University," submitted by Henry S. Frank, provost of Lingnan, June 1, 1949. Trustees of Lingnan University, microfilm roll 24.

48. Brubacher, *Higher Education in Transition: A History of American Colleges and Universities*.

49. John Israel, *Lianda: A Chinese University in War and Revolution* (Stanford, CA: Stanford University Press, 1998), p. 134.

50. Yukichi Fukuzawa, Japan's "father of the enlightenment," lightheartedly recorded the strong influence of this Confucian tradition on the Japanese samurai elite class before the Meiji Restoration in 1868. See Yukichi Fukuzawa, *The Autobiography of Yukichi Fukuzawa* (New York: Columbia University Press, 1980).

51. "Report on the First Phase, Lingnan University Planning Survey," p. 34, prepared by Raymond Rich & William Cherin Associates, in May 1948. Yale Divinity School Library, Group 8: China Records and Project Miscellaneous Personal Papers Collections, Box 107, Folder Mr. and Mrs. J. S. Kunkle.

52. Guangdongsheng dang'an'guan [Guangdong provincial archives], untitled document, file # 38-4-58. Guangdongsheng dang'an'guan, "Sili Lingnan daxue Tang Liting jijinhui baoguan weiyuanhui banli jiguo ji xiaochan xianzhuang" [A report of the Committee of Lingnan University charged with oversight of the Tan Liting funds and the status of associated properties], file # 38-1-68. Guangdongsheng dang'an'guang, file # 38-1-23. Y. L. Lee, "Tan Liting xiangsheng xianchan xingxue ji" [An account of Mr. Tan Liting's donating his property to education], in *Guangdong jiaoyü* [Education in Guangdong], date unknown: 40. Guangdongsheng dang'an'guan, untitled document, file # 38-4-58.

53. Philip West, *Yenching University and Sino-Western Relations, 1916–1952* (Cambridge, MA: Harvard University Press, 1976), pp. 109–16. Zhu Xinran, "Yanjing daxue xiaozhang Wu Leichuan" [Wu Leichuan, Chancellor of Yenching University], Chapter 9, in Wu Ziming, ed., *Jidujiao Daxue Huaren Xiaozhang Yanjiu* [Studies on the Chinese Presidents of Christian Universities] (Fuzhou: Fujian jiaoyü chubanshe, 2001).

54. For studies of the indigenization and contextualization of Christianity in China, see Daniel H. Bays, ed., *Christianity in China: From the Eighteenth Century to the Present* (Stanford, CA: Stanford University Press, 1996). Kim-Kwong Chan, *Towards a Contextual Ecclesiology: The Catholic Church in the People's Republic of China (1979–1983): Its Life and Theological Implications* (Hong Kong: Phototech System Ltd, 1987). Kim-kwong Chan, "Religion in China in the Twenty-First Century: Some Scenarios," *Religion, State & Society* 33, no. 2 (2005): 87–119.

4

✝

The Advance to Higher Learning: Women's Education, Power, and Modernization

One of the significant contributions made by Christian colleges in China, as in other parts of the world, was their empowerment of women. Studies of women in American missions and mission schools in China normally focus on American missionaries' critique of the Chinese gender system, the contrast between the status of American and Chinese women, attitudes toward traditional China and the "modern" West, and women's work and social reform in the construction of identity, nation, and modernity.[1]

As the first Christian college to admit girls to the secondary grades (in 1903) and the first to open its collegiate courses to women students (from 1908),[2] Lingnan University took the lead in launching coeducation and higher learning for women in China. By examining the issues surrounding women's advancement to higher learning at the pioneering Canton Christian College, this chapter shifts the focus from an imagined, rhetorical construct of womanhood, modernity, and nation to the creation and management of educational projects for women at the practical level. Lingnan women worked side by side with men as practical and hard-nosed activists in championing the cause of women, but without drastically altering traditional gender boundaries. Taking ownership of their own projects sharpened their sense of mission to improve the lot of women, men, and society in general, as well as benefiting future generations. I also argue that education for women at Lingnan University was a joint Sino-

American project, spanning the Pacific, in which men and women, Chinese and Americans, had a shared stake in leading "the uneducated masses of their own people to a better life."[3]

GIRLS' SCHOOL, WOMEN'S DEPARTMENT, AND WOMEN'S COLLEGE

In this section, I examine the processes that led to the establishment of the Girls' School, the Women's Department, and the Women's College—what I categorize as the women's movement—at Canton Christian College. The chief goal of women's education at the college had been to develop college grade work, a goal corresponding with that of the college.[4] Through its educational ideals, practices, and organization, the college gave a new meaning to the concept of advanced education for women.

Canton Christian College's interests in coeducation and educational projects for women had begun with its founder, Andrew P. Happer. In 1877, Happer coauthored a paper entitled "Women's Work for Woman" with T. P. Crawford, an American missionary stationed in Dengzhou (today's Yantai), Shandong, for the first missionary conference in China held in Shanghai, May 10–24.[5] The "women's work" listed by Happer included both day and boarding schools for girls. During the first ten years of the twentieth century, in the process of its rapid development from a sort of "Teachers' College"—chiefly preparing teachers for elementary and preparatory schools—to a fully equipped college of arts and sciences, with affiliated schools of medicine and agriculture, Canton Christian College took the lead in promoting coeducation and higher education for women. This was done in response to strong local demand for making modern education available to at least some of the 200 million women of South China.[6]

In a move initiated by faculty Chung Wing Kwong, at a time when Canton Christian College had relocated to Macao, the college opened a school for girls in February 1903. Twelve pupils aged 10–12 attended the school, and initially were all taught in one class.[7] According to alumna Fung Hin Liu (Liao Fengxian), after the college found a permanent home at Honglok, Canton, some well-to-do Chinese petitioned the college to allow their daughters, who had passed the entrance examinations for the Middle School, to sit in the same classroom with the boys. Local Chinese pleaded that "[t]he salvation of the Chinese women, depends upon the educated Chinese women leaders. The only place in South China where we can have our daughters prepared for this leadership is in C.C.C. Unless they are admitted here, the work for Chinese women in this South will be delayed indefinitely."[8] In January 1908, 300 candidates, including four girls, took the college entrance examinations (at high school level). Among the forty successful candidates, all four girls became resident students, joining three others in the Middle School, all of whom lived with the Chungs in a bungalow on campus. These seven girls were the only female college students in South China to sit in the same classroom with boys.

What became of these fifteen privileged girls—the initial twelve studying at the girls' school in Macau and three others attending the college in 1908?[9] The majority went on to study in the United States, England, and Scotland while advocating the advancement of women across the Pacific and Atlantic. After graduating from the Middle School, Fung Hin Liu came to America in 1909, studying first at Wooster University in Wooster, Ohio. In 1914 Liu received a B.A. from Wellesley College and spent a year at the Teachers' College at Columbia University where she received her B.S. in 1916 before returning to Canton Christian College in the same year. Liu was the first dean of women at Canton Christian College.[10] Sui Au graduated from Hackett Medical College in Canton. Under the auspices of the Guangdong provincial government, Yau-tsit (Agnes) Law (Luo Youjie), attended Mount Holyoke College and received a B.A. in 1915 and a B.S. at the Teachers' College at Columbia in 1916. Fung Yan Liu (Liao Fengen) received a B.A. from Smith College in 1915 and a B.S. from the Teachers' College at Columbia in 1916. Lu Mei Lau studied for a time in London, where her father was Chinese Minister to Britain. The two Tang sisters were also distinguished alumnae; Yuet-Mui Tang (Mrs. Y. Y. Chan) studied in Edinburgh, Scotland, and Yuet-Ha (Anna) Tang pursued a B.A. at Oberlin College in Oberlin, Ohio.[11]

The educational opportunities for girls at Canton Christian College developed rapidly. The Girls' School was originally designed for the elementary grades and the Women's Department was set up for women to take collegiate courses. Later, the Girls' School was divided into two classes to prepare girls for college: the First Year, or Middle School class, and the 7th Year—the Grammar School class, equivalent to high school in the United States. Manifold projects in the field of women's education were developed almost simultaneously at Canton Christian College. The establishment of a women's department for collegiate studies, for instance, had been the subject of discussion until 1914 when the college's trustees, faculty, and female students initiated a fundraising campaign that led to the opening of the Women's Department in 1916. A girls' high school to prepare girls for college was also planned to open in 1916 in hopes of raising the academic standards of secondary schools in Canton and the wider Guangdong provincial area. In 1916–1917, there were thirty girl students at the college under the governance of the dean of women.[12] Women students above the 5th grade were housed in a dormitory of their own.

The college deliberately limited the size of the Girls' School until it was sufficiently well-funded to develop collegiate work for girls. The college was equally cautious in developing the Women's College. As the minutes kept by the college council committee on the Women's Department reveal, "[w]henever the number of women students warrant[s] it, the College will consider the advisability of establishing a separate college for women."[13] In the same spirit, council committee member Henry B. Graybill concluded that "until the [women's] department works itself out more fully there had better be a very simple organization, but one made effective by the fact that the President acts as the head of the girls school from the start and assigned work to others as he finds best from time to time. . . . [T]he rate of growth [of the Women's Department] should not be too great." In addition, the financial acuteness shown in the college's management of women's education formed a stark contrast with the practices followed by others, as noted by Gael Graham:

> Missionaries and their Christian Chinese colleagues continued to establish schools without heeding financial considerations in the twentieth century. Chinese and American Methodists in Jinjiang in 1917, for example, opened a school with no appropriation for it. "We have faith to believe that the money will come from somewhere," they asserted confidently.[14]

In 1921, Canton Christian College took pride in graduating Miss Leung Tsau Ming (Liang Jiuming, later Mrs. S. H. Wang), who was the first Chinese woman to receive the Bachelor of Arts degree in China. She graduated from a coeducational institution at the age of 20.[15] Leung won the Barbour Scholarship for Oriental Women and received an MA degree from the University of Michigan in 1922. Although female enrollments at Canton Christian College were long kept low because of the lack of proper accommodation, the percentage of women among collegiate students remained high from the beginning, comparing favorably with its counterparts on the other side of the Pacific (see the conclusion to this chapter). Between 1921 and 1929, 141 men and 40 women (constituting 22 percent of the student body) graduated from the college. In 1934, Lingnan University graduated 51 men and 13 women (22.3 percent), and in 1935, 31 men and 15 women (32.6 percent).[16] In 1946, among 95 senior students, there were 34 females, 35.8 percent of the total collegiate seniors.[17] From the first collegiate class of 3, who graduated in 1918, to 1941, 600 students received a Bachelor's degree from Lingnan University, of whom 150 were women, constituting 25 percent of the entire graduate body.[18]

THE MEANING OF EDUCATION FOR WOMEN
AT CANTON CHRISTIAN COLLEGE

In this section, I address the following questions among others. What did modern education for women mean to Lingnanians? What was the role of Christianity in educating women at Canton Christian College? What was the purpose of education for girls, given the college's acceptance of conventional gender roles?

In the opinion of W. Henry Grant, then secretary of the board of trustees, projects for women helped mold the college into a well-rounded institution of Christian higher learning. In a letter headed "Women's Department and Girls' Schools of C.C.C." written in 1912 to Henry B. Graybill, Grant stated:

> Please remember this one point: *the financing of the girls' schools of the Canton Christian College is not going to take from but add to the financing of the whole.* [Emphasis original] It will immensely add to the interest in the whole. It will give us a more rounded organization, especially in Teachers College work and the necessary schools for observation and practice.[19]

In the letter, Grant highlighted the leading role of women students and faculty in advancing women's projects at Lingnan: "If we find the woman or women there is no doubt in my mind that the rest will follow."[20]

In his 1913 paper, "Developing a Woman's College," Henry Graybill explained that the establishment of a women's college with attached lower schools at Canton Christian College "would accomplish three things: feed the higher school, give the college students opportunities for practice teaching in the lower schools, and spur the establishment of other schools throughout Guangdong province."[21]

Women students and faculty at Lingnan had found resources in Christianity that gave meaning and purpose to both their personal lives and their work for women's education. In her study of Chinese women and Christianity from 1860 to 1927, Kwok Pui-lan argues that transferring Christian concepts to the Chinese context involved a process of "feminization of Christian symbolism," especially in the nineteenth century. According to Kwok, the emphasis in the Chinese context on "the compassion of God, the use of more inclusive metaphors for the divine, the stress on Jesus' relation with women, and the downplaying of the sinfulness of Eve drew appeals to Chinese women and even men."[22] In the process of building up women's programs at Canton Christian College, young women empowered themselves through work and faith.

While pursuing a B.A. degree at Wellesley College in Wellesley, Massachusetts,[23] a former student, Miss Fung Hin Liu, took on the task of publicizing women's projects at her old college. In 1913, Liu wrote to a friend describing how she felt about women's causes back home in Canton and the relationship of women's education to faith:

> College [Wellesley College] began a week ago. I am enjoying it thoroughly. This year I must spend a great deal of time with the girls. I feel I have a

mission to give to them. The west has given much to the east and the east has something to give to the west. It is such an inspiration to feel that I am needed here in the college [Wellesley] as much as I am needed at home [Canton Christian College]. The Christian Association has asked me to lead a mission study class on China. I am praying that I may do a great deal for Him through this opportunity. Won't you be with me in prayers too? As I grow in faith and in love, I realize more and more the power of prayer. There are many things that I can't understand, but I have the trust that God Almighty is in all and through all and guiding all. The great opportunity at home for leading our women to Christ thrills me, but the great responsibility frightens me. May God give us the sound judgment, the earnest effort and the great faith in him to carry this work through this great crisis.[24]

Two years later in 1915, Liu wrote to Henry Grant that "[w]ords cannot express my appreciation of your guidance of me and kindnesses to me during these past three years. It was quite hard for me to leave you and may other true friends in America. After you all left me and I was alone on the train, I began to realize how much I did miss you and how much I will miss. I thank God for giving me so many loyal friends and I pray that He will guide me in all my ways so that I may not disappoint then in their high expectation of me."[25]

Educational work for women ignited mutual enthusiasm among Americans and Chinese alike. Julia Post Mitchell, associate professor of English at Canton Christian College, wrote that "I want a good school for girls here, with a high academic standard, but a flexible curriculum that will bend to fit their needs."[26] There was a visible personal commitment to women's education at the college. In a letter dated March 30, 1914, Mitchell told Henry Grant that:

I want them [students at the girls' primary school] to put [to use] my quarters in Martin Hall as a sort of clubroom until they have other accommodations. I have had a ping-pong table made and the beanbag game still holds its attractions. "Tiddledy Winks" are on their way out and I hope to find suggestions from Miss Jessie Baneroft's book, "Games for the Playground, Home, School and Gymnasium." . . . I have told you a good deal about the girls, not because I am more interested in them than in anything else, but because I *am* interested in them and in the possibilities for them, and because I thought it likely that you heard less of them than of some of the other college matters [emphasis original].[27]

A letter written by Helen Cassidy, a visiting American teacher who taught at the Girls' School from 1916 to 1917, reveals the same enjoyment of her work and affection for the students:

You are right in saying that this year is affording me wonderful opportunities. The whole experience is richer and more enjoyable in every way than I had dreamed it could be. . . . I have found the work and the life here very interesting and congenial. . . . The girls we have are most attractive—most of them come from wealthy homes and have had careful up bringing [sic]. They were the most demure set I ever saw at the first of the year. I despaired of them ever waking up to real fun—they would stick in the classrooms studying all day unless we dragged them out. I found, though, that the fun was there and now that they feel at home here and have become acquainted, they do have the best times![28]

This kind of eagerness was, to no less degree, displayed on the Chinese side as well, as revealed in Fung Hin Liu's letter to Henry Grant in 1913, sent while she was studying at Wellesley College:

I feel so happy that I shall be having a share in the founding of the woman's department of the Canton Christian College. Though at times I had been undecided about my future work,—[sic] that is the place where I should do my work, yet the desire to work in the College has always been dominant. I know that the College will grow higher and higher in the esteem of the Chinese people, and its influence for Christianity will be greater. . . . It became clear to me that I must go home and start this women's department. It is not a question whether I will be best fitted for it or not, but it just seems as if it is "my job." It "falls upon me" to do it, as you said in your letter.[29]

Although Canton Christian College maintained high standards of college work for women, the kind of female education promoted particularly by women at or associated with the college was intended to equip women for the domestic sphere, rather than challenging men's role in public and at home. This emphasis on familial and social harmony is also noted in Weili Ye's study of Chinese students in America in the first third of the twentieth century.[30]

Julia Mitchell held that better educated women made better homemakers, who would be fitted to assist men in performing their public roles:

I am reveling in my teaching. The boys are keen and eager, and work well and do their own thinking; but men's education always runs ahead of women's, and I don't want the Chinese girls to have to wait till Sophie Smith is reincarnated before they can be trained to make homes that will enable the men from here and elsewhere to shape this republic. How much can they do if they all have untrained wives hanging to their necks?[31]

Stimulated by the prospect of the Women's Department becoming a reality, Fung Hin Liu stated without ambivalence in a letter of 1913 to Henry Grant:

I think the chief place for women is the home. During this transitional period of the Chinese Society [*sic*], I think nothing is more important than to give the women of China the idea of the sacredness of the home, to help them understand that marriage is not just a means to secure happiness, but is a responsibility, a responsibility of producing the future generation, to train and educate the artisans of the future, and to promote love and all that is sacred to the human race. Another place for women is the school. Not every woman can teach, but only she who has love for children can teach. There is hardly any position or work women cannot occupy, but they all need to have preparation. The preparation consists in the acquiring of a great love for humanity and a keen sense of judgment concerning the good and the bad for the country and the world, and the power to carry the right judgment into action.[32]

Liu's actions proved her as good as her word. In June 1918 she left Canton Christian College for Mukden and married C. F. Wang, a mining engineer trained in the United States and brother of the distinguished diplomat C. T. Wang (Wang Zhengting). As a cultured Christian Chinese woman, Liu was devoted to her family to the extent that she declined an offer to be principal of a large school for girls in Mukden.[33]

Despite the emphasis on women's domestic and auxiliary role, the college was determined that women should be educated to the same standard as men. In Henry B. Graybill's words, "fees and standards should in general be the same as in the boys' schools. As in the boys' school the grades taught should be always the highest ones practicable in the existing conditions."[34]

The modern education offered to women at Canton Christian College was built on the foundation laid by various Christian missions active in Southeast Asia and South China.[35] Mission schools for both boys and girls founded in Malacca, Singapore, and Siam, and the native schools for girls that had existed in Canton before the advent of Western influence, contributed to the development of education for girls in progressive South China. According to Mary Raleigh Anderson, by 1832 there were at least 157 Chinese girls enrolled in ten overseas schools under the auspices of various Christian bodies in the Southeast Asian region. By 1840 there were about 380 students in 19 schools for Chinese girls. Anderson noted that:

Although this list is probably incomplete, it is clear that the over-seas [*sic*] schools were of great importance to Kwangtung [Guangdong] as most of the Chinese who went abroad were from this province. Since there was constant intercourse between the emigrants and the people of South China, it is probable that the mission schools of the Straits Settlements had much to do with the liberal attitude of the Cantonese toward the education of girls. Indeed, the first work of the Morrison Education Society was a survey of the educational status of the over-seas Chinese.[36]

Education for girls had been firmly pursued by the Presbyterian Church in South China, which funded and established the first girls' boarding school, the True Light Seminary, in 1872 under the leadership of Harriet Noyes. By 1918 the school had matriculated 3,851 students.[37]

CAMPAIGNING FOR WOMEN'S EDUCATION

Lingnan's female students and faculty worked enthusiastically to raise funds for women's education for its own sake, as partners with their male classmates and colleagues rather than subordinates or inferiors. The unusual opportunities and responsibilities with which they were presented enhanced their management skills, helping explain why women played such a decisive role in promoting women's causes both inside and outside Canton Christian College.

While still coping with "culture shock" upon her return from America in 1916, Fung Hin Liu talked freely to Henry Grant, secretary of the college's board of trustees, of some of the obstacles to female education in the region:

> I found quite a good many of the teachers here felt that the college had unwisely taken up this added burden [girls' education] upon her heavily loaded shoulders. The ladies from the True Light Seminary as well as some of the Chinese and American staff of the College feel that we unnecessarily are building up a rival to the True Light Seminary. It is another example showing how we of South China cannot unite in our Christian activities.[38]

Liu's observations played a part in later efforts to improve coordination between Canton Christian College and the True Light Seminary of the American Presbyterian Mission. In 1918, to avoid conflict, an agreement was reached between the seminary and the C.C.C., whereby the college withdrew temporarily from secondary education for girls.[39] Later, further negotiations took place between the True Light Middle School and the college aimed at preventing overlaps in their activities.[40] In fact, Yam-Tong Hoh, a graduate of Lingnan University and the Teacher's College at Columbia University, was the first Chinese principal of True Light Middle School in the 1930s.[41]

Liu also pointed out the problems involved in charging equal tuition fees for boys and girls:

There is no money for us to use for the girls [*sic*] work at all, so the Council feels we must be extremely careful and make the work as much self support-ing as possible, consequently the Council decided the girls [*sic*] tuition to be as high as that of the boys—$100 H.K. This high tuition is beyond the reach of the middle class families. If you realize how much less willing Chinese parents are to send their girls to school than boys you will readily see how this amount of high tuition is almost prohibitive.[42]

A year later, to his vexation, Henry Graybill had to report the surpris-ingly small number of applicants for admission to the Girls' School. Gray-bill's diagnosis of the factors involved in this failure to secure a good enrollment in the school's first year echoed Liu's earlier concerns.[43] Despite her misgivings over the financial aspects, Liu expressed her high hopes to Henry Grant for an effective fundraising campaign in Canton:

From what I have just written you can imagine how I felt when I first came home [Canton]. But now things are beginning to look very much brighter as far as the girls' work is concerned. . . . I am glad you and the Trustees are eager to raise funds for the girls' work. As soon as conditions are more set-tled in the south we will plan to run a campaign here. . . . The small begin-nings of this work is [*sic*] not discouraging me . . . but this work is solely needed. So we must fight for it and die for it if necessary.

In the same letter, Liu set out the college's recruitment needs for girls' education. She added a long list of suitable American female teachers whom she had befriended in her American years, and commented on the qualifications of each in detail. Promoting female education not only gave women a higher profile at the college, but also put Chinese and American female staff on a more-or-less equal footing financially. In the proposed budget for the Girls' School for 1917–1918, Liu was allotted the same sal-ary, HK$960 (US$500) annually, as the American Margaret H. Riggs, who served on faculty from 1916–1921.[44]

Like many other Lingnan projects, the campaign for female education was trans-Pacific and included both Americans and Chinese, women and men, faculty and students. During her years in America, Fung Hin Liu had championed the cause of a women's department and a women's col-lege for Canton Christian College. An address on family life and women's education given by Liu in Hartford, Connecticut, in September 1915 was considered "enlightening, intimate and interesting."[45] Her U.S. schedule for December 1915 gives some indication of the extent of her promotional work for women's education at Canton Christian College. (See table 4.1 and table 4.2 in the Appendix.)

In New York City, the first meeting of the women's section of the cen-tral committee of the Canton Christian College General Association was held on April 22, 1915, in the office of the Trustees at 156 Fifth Avenue, followed by another meeting on December 2, 1915. The Summit Association was formed in the United States on April 5, 1915, to promote the Girls' School and Women's Department. Later, the women's section meetings were held regularly in the United States on the fourth of October, January, and April. They normally opened with prayers and a portion of Scripture. Topics presented at gatherings included the home life of the average Chinese girl; impressions of years spent at Canton Christian College; the need for a Christian education for Chinese girls; the need for a library for the Girls' School; the purchase and donations of books on physical education; and suggestions from Chinese students on recreational activities for girls.

A support network was established in both America and China which included wives of Lingnan trustees, members of the women's section, former members of Lingnan staff in America, and women members of various college support groups including the University of Pittsburgh, Penn State College, Westover School, Smith College, Wellesley College, the New York Women's American Oriental Club, and the New York Women's University Club. At the college, a Women Students' Christian Association was established which was open to all girls, both Christians and non-Christians, enrolled in the Girls' School or in the College Department. However, only Christian members had the right to vote and to hold office.[46] These activities and organizations undoubtedly linked male and female activists for women's education across the Pacific.

Fundraising was a major activity in the promotion of female education at the college. In the fiscal year 1915–1916, the total contribution to the girls' work was US$2,614.58, received from both individuals and organizations. Vassar College was the biggest donor that year, contributing $1,000, which resulted in a flurry of testimonial letters written by C.C.C. girls.[47]

To support women's projects at the college, Fung Hin Liu "wrote a great many letters to her Wellesley classmates asking them to give even if only a small amount to help the Girls' School." Through Liu, the Governor of Guangdong Province promised to give $4,000 in 1918, adding that "this would be given whether he remains in Canton or not."[48]

In order to raise the US$75,000 needed to build the first women's dormitory, with rooms for eighty girls, women students at the college organized a dedicated campaign. The Alumni Association of the Women Students of Canton Christian College was formed on November 26, 1923, with the immediate purpose, in the words of temporary secretary Wong Tsui Fung, of "organiz[ing] a financial campaign for the building of a girls' dormitory."[49] On June 25, 1924, another organization, the C.C.C. Women Student Friendship Association, was formed, which was also dedicated to raising funds for the women's dormitory, envisioned as a "showcase" for the advanced and healthy lifestyle enjoyed at the college.[50] Senior faculty Chung Wing Kwong was determined to make the dormitory "a home rather than a sleeping barracks, . . . [H]is particular idea being that while money from America would be welcome it would be a more glorious thing for the cause if the Chinese themselves would see it through."[51] Avoiding the expected fundraising tactic of bemoaning the menial status of women in China, a campaign flyer instead characterized China's womanhood as "her greatest undeveloped natural resource."[52] On a fundraising postcard, educated young Chinese Christian women were depicted as the greatest "index of hope for a New China."[53] (See photo 4.1; photo 4.2; photo 4.3.)

Under the guidance of Dr. John Griggs, on Lingnan's faculty from 1919 to 1927, and Chung Wing Kwong in particular, the girls were encouraged to campaign "for a high figure" of US$75,000, and to "work away quietly until they get a few good subscriptions and then start a more general campaign." Through students' family connections, Canton Christian College received help from wealthy Chinese in meeting this target. Lam Woo, father of college student Miss Lam, who had already given $10,000 to a girls' school in Hong Kong and was one of a group of four who had

Photo 4.1.   Women's Campaign for the First Women's Dormitory, 1924–1925. Trustees of Lingnan University archives, Special Collections, Yale Divinity School Library.

Photo 4.2.   *Women's Campaign for a New Dormitory and Girls' Volleyball Team, 1930. Lingnan (Canton Christian College), vol. VI, no. 4, November 1930.*

pledged $10,000 for the college's agricultural building, set aside $100,000 for women's dormitory. Another girl, Miss Liao, whose father was the Civil Governor of Guangdong, contacted a number of provincial officials for assistance with the campaign.[54]

To the great disappointment of Chinese and foreign supporters alike, the momentum of the campaign tapered off as a result of the precarious political and military situation in Canton in the 1920s.[55] However, as the

Post Card

Domestic and
Hongkong 1c
Japan and
Korea 1½c
Foreign 4c

THIS SIDE FOR MESSAGE   THIS SIDE FOR ADDRESS

There is no greater index
of hope for a New China
than the educated Chris-
tian Chinese young woman.

Pub. for College Book Store, Canton Christian
College, Canton, China.

Photo 4.3.   *Women and Campaign. Trustees of Lingnan University, microfilm roll 37.*

situation in Canton showed signs of settling down, the college's campaign for women's education started to pick up in early 1927. There was a general consensus that the Women's Department should continue to grow. The new plan for women's education proposed in 1927 by Yau-tsit (Agnes) Law (Luo Youjie), dean of women, included a dormitory for 80–100 women budgeted at HK$100,000; a college hall, gymnasium, swimming pool, and social center (HK$100,000); and a music hall (HK$10,000).[56]

In 1930, Lucy Liu, the new dean of women at Lingnan University, wrote to James Henry, provost of Lingnan, urging an appeal for a girls' dormitory and better recreational resources for women students:

> How urgently we need the girls' dormitory. At present we are using two houses. One is the old hospital, and the other a building put up for temporary use. From the experience I had last year, the house is very unhealthy for any one to live in. . . . In spite of the unsanitary condition of the present building, we have used all available space there. Even the entrance hall has been used as a bedroom. . . . The next question is that of physical education for the girl students. We are trying our best to find a part-time physical director for the girls this year, but so far have not been successful. What I hope you will note in your next drive is to secure a gymnasium with a swimming pool for the girls.[57]

Along with the letter, Liu enclosed a picture with the caption: "We are forced to house girls in this temporary building, endangering their health."[58] The first women's dormitory at Lingnan University was erected in 1933 with funds donated by both Americans and Chinese—particularly from a supporters' group in Orange, New Jersey, and from Chinese friends of the college, attesting to wide cooperation in a common endeavor across racial and geographical boundaries.

CONCLUSION

By the late nineteenth century, women had become a topic in both scholarly research and public discourse in China, a transformation in attitudes brought about by China's growing interaction with the outside world. The development of education for women at Lingnan came about as a combination of increasing public discussion in the news media and American–Southern Chinese pragmatism. In newspapers such as *Wanguo gongbao* (Global Magazine), started in 1868 by Young John Allen (1836–1907), an American missionary from the Methodist Episcopal Church, extensive coverage of women's rights and education for women (*nüxue*) in countries such as Japan, the United States, Germany, India, Switzerland, Russia, Persia, Turkey, England, Mexico, France, Sweden, and New Zealand prepared the theoretical ground for the liberal conception and discourse of women's education in China.[59] The issue of *Wanguo gongbao* for May 1906 (the 32nd year of Emperor Guangxü's reign) featured an article on Mount Holyoke College, the first American institution of higher learning for women that opened in 1837 in South Hadley, Massachusetts.[60]

The plans for women's education outlined above, and the attempts to implement them, coincided with the process of building Canton Christian College into a fully fledged collegiate institution. The project of educating women at the collegiate level was carried out in a spirit of cooperation and practicality by the college. According to the minutes of the council committee on the Women's Department, "[t]he courses of the College of Arts and Sciences (including the Sub-Freshman year) are, in so far as they are suitable for women to take, open to women students. Whenever the number of women students warrants it, the College will consider the advisability of establishing a separate college for women."[61] After careful consideration of the financial implications, as well as any potential conflict with the True Light Middle School, in 1918 the college had set aside its original scheme for a separate girls' school and women's college. Although not all the college's efforts came to fruition, Lingnan University was ultimately successful in its push for higher education for women, as the high rate of female student enrollment in the twentieth century demonstrated.

Across the Pacific, the same evolutionary ferment of coeducational and women's colleges was experienced from the first half of the nineteenth century. In 1833, the admission of women to its full college course at Oberlin College in Ohio marked the beginning of the American experiment with collegiate coeducation.[62] Edward Power states that by 1900 women "made up about a quarter of all students attending regular college" in America,[63] a ratio to which Canton Christian College also aspired from its launching of women's education in 1903. Interestingly, in the United States by the beginning of the twentieth century, "the question of coeducation was often referred to as 'a dead issue,'" as "[t]he American people have settled the matter."[64] Set against the various phases of development in the advancement of education for women in the United States, the women's projects at Lingnan University and other Chinese higher educational institutions were an important aspect of the westward advance of American liberal arts education across the Pacific. At Canton Christian College, women's education was touted as an evolutionary, not revolutionary process—a victory not just for women, but for humanity in general.

As we have seen, the position of women at Canton Christian College was greatly strengthened by the return of former graduates as members of the faculty. In the end, what advantages did modern education hold for Chinese women? Liu Fung Hin, a female leader and former student of the college who returned to her alma mater after graduating from Wellesley College and the Teachers' College at Columbia University, enumerated her ideals for modern women and women's education in her commencement oration, delivered in English:

> The task that the modern woman has before her is not the copying of the West here and the East there, but rather of creating a new thing through a deeper appreciation of what is best in both. . . . In this particular moment when the cry for emancipation is raging high, have we ever stopped to consider that our epic women have not only contributed to the achievement of the past but have a distinct contribution for our modern world? . . . The woman of China in her eagerness to follow her western sisters must not forget the legacy that has been handed down to her. Her duty is to make music and harmony out of the world of strife. . . . It is the task of the modern woman to extend this influence throughout society and to fill the whole world with the melody of calm and peace.[65]

APPENDIXES

Table 4.1. Schedule Miss F. H. Liu [*sic*][1]

1915	
Dec. 3, Friday eve. 8:30	Leave N.Y. on Lackswanna a Nickel Plate, # 9
	Arrive Cleveland 11:15, Sat. A.M.
Dec. 4 Saturday	Cleveland
Dec. 6, Monday	Leave Cleveland on Nickel Plate, #15, 7:23 for Chicago
Dec. 7, Tuesday	Arrive Chicago 7:44 A.M.
Dec. 8, Wednesday	Leave Chicago in time to arrive Kansas City 8:45 A.M.
Dec. 9, Thursday	Leave Chicago 8:05 P.M., Santa Fe, #3
Dec. 9–10, Thu. Fri.	Kansas City, K., meeting the Wellesley Club and a few individuals in a parlor meeting
Dec. 11, Sat.	Morning at Lawrence,—Mrs. Stubbs, Parlor meeting
Dec. 11, 12, 13, Sat–Mon	Topeka. Baptist Church Sunday, 12th, and a few friends the 13th
Dec. 13–15, Mon–Wed	Manhattan. Address chapel 14th and a meeting of the Domestic Science Dept. of about 1000 girls

Dec. 15, Wed. night	Emporia, Kas
Dec. 16, Thurs.	Emporia Normal College
Dec. 16–17, Thurs–Fri.	Hutchinson, Kas
Dec. 18, Saturday	Colorado Springs, Col. (subject to change)
Dec. 20, Monday	Leave Colorado Springs

LEAVE
12/23: Wed: 7:00 am: Colorado Springs: Arrive: 7:12/22: 10:00 am: Denver, Col.
12/22: Wed: 12:25 pm: Denver, Colo. : UP: 119:12/23: 6:01 pm: Parma, Idaho
12/27: Mon: 6:01 pm Parma, Idaho : OSL: 16:12/28: 8:10 pm: Seattle, Wash.
1/9: Sun: 10:45 am: Seattle, Wash. : OWR&M: 13:1/11: 7:30 am: San Francisco
1/11: Tue: 6:00 pm: San Francisco : SP: 26:1/12: 8:45 am: Los Angeles
1/28: Fri: 8:00 pm: Los Angeles, Cal. : Sp: 76: 1/29: 9:45 am: San Francisco
2/5: Sat: sail from San Francisco on T. K.K. s/s "Shinyo Maru"

[1] Trustees of Lingnan University, microfilm roll 37.

Table 4.2.   Council Minutes, December 23, 1916[1]

Girls' School Assignments

The assignment of work in the Girls' School was presented by the President and is appended below.

Teachers	Hours per class	Total hours per week
Miss Helen Cassidy		
1st Year English	5	
1st Year Arithmetic	5	
Pry. Class English	5	
Music	2	17
Fung Hin Liu		
1st Year English	5	
Prep. Class English	5	
Prep. Class Arithmetic	5	
Prep. Class Sunday School	2	17 (classroom work)
Mr. L. C. Au		
Chinese Classic	2	
Mr. T. W. Ch'an		
Chinese Composition	3	
Mr. C. W. Ch'an		
Chinese History	3	

Mr. Sz-to Wai		
Drawing	2	
Mrs. Brownell		
Bible (1st Year)	2	
Mrs. Laird		
Household Science	3	
Mrs. Y.C. Kwan		
Physiology	3	
Mrs. E. H. Groff		
Physical Training	5	
Mrs. Pomeroy		
Piano[2]	.5	23.5

The following assignments were also reported by the President.

Miss Cassidy (new assignments)	
1st Yr. (Middle School) English	4
Education in the College[3]	1

[1] Trustees of Lingnan University, microfilm roll 37.
[2] Mrs. Pomeroy gives half hour piano lessons to three girls.
[3] In place of work given up in the Girls' School.

NOTES

1. Gael Graham, *Gender, Culture, and Christianity: American Protestant Mission Schools in China, 1880–1930* (New York: Peter Lang, 1995). p. 20, p. 98. Jane Hunter, *The Gospel of Gentility: American Women Missionaries in Turn-of-the-Century* (New Haven, CT: Yale University Press, 1984). Heidi A. Ross, "'Cradle of Female Talent': The McTyeire Home and School for Girls, 1892–1937," in Daniel H. Bays, ed., *Christianity in China: From the Eighteenth Century to the Present* (Stanford, CA: Stanford University Press, 1996). Judith Liu, and Donald P. Kelly, "'An Oasis in a Heathen Land': St. Hilda's School for Girls, Wuchang, 1928–1936," in *Christianity in China: From the Eighteenth Century to the Present*, ed. Daniel H. Bays (Stanford, CA: Stanford University Press, 1996). Gail Hershatter, "State of the Field: Women in China's Long Twentieth Century," *The Journal of Asian Studies* 63, no 4 (November 2004): 991–1065. For an overview of women and Christianity in China, see Pui-lan Kwok, *Chinese Women and Christianity, 1860–1927* (Atlanta, GA: Scholars Press, 1992). Pui-lan Kwok, "Chinese Women and Protestant Christianity at the Turn of the Twentieth Century," in *Christianity in China: From the Eighteenth Century to the Present*, ed. Daniel H. Bays (Stanford, CA: Stanford University Press, 1996). Ethel L. Wallace, *Hwa Nan College: The Woman's College of South China* (New York: United Board for Christian Colleges in China, 1956). Women were left off in the pictorial volume on the history of foreign educated Chinese students compiled by Xiang-gang lishi bowuguan [Hong Kong Museum of History], *Xuehai wuya: Jindai Zhong-*

guo liuxuesheng zhan [Boundless learning: Foreign-educated students of modern China. *sic*] (Hong Kong: Government Logistics Department, 2003).

2. "Women's Departments, Canton Christian College," Trustees of Lingnan University, microfilm roll 37.

3. *A Romantic Achievement of Chinese and American Cooperation, Illustrated Historical Sketch* (New York: Trustees of Lingnan University, 1941).

4. Letter from Henry Graybill (secretary of the council committee on the Women's Department at C.C.C.) to Rev. J. W. Creighton, secretary of the American Presbyterian Mission in Canton, dated April 12, 1917. Trustees of Lingnan University, microfilm roll 37.

5. *Records of the General Conference of the Protestant Missionaries of China*, held at Shanghai, May 10–24, 1877 (Shanghai: Presbyterian Mission Press, 1878).

6. This figure is inferred from Fung Hin Liu, "Samples of English Work by Chinese Girls", date unknown. Trustees of Lingnan University, microfilm roll 37.

7. Henry Grant, Secretary of the Trustees, "Is It Worth While to Educate Chinese Girls?" in *Ling Naam: The News Bulletin of Canton Christian College*, New York, vol. 1, no. 1 (August 1924). I have used Grant's figure for the initial number of girl students, rather that given by Fung Hin Liu who recorded eleven pupils enrolled in the girls' school in 1903. Letter of Fung Hin Liu dated September 20, 1915, to Helen V. Frey. Trustees of Lingnan University, microfilm roll 37.

8. Letter of Fung Hin Liu dated September 20, 1915, to Helen V. Frey. Trustees of Lingnan University, microfilm roll 37.

9. Again, Grant's account of the year 1906 as the start of enrolling fifteen girls in the C.C.C. disagrees with Liu and others' recollection in which it was 1908. See the previous note.

10. Henry Grant, Secretary of the Trustees, "Is It Worth While to Educate Chinese Girls?" in *Ling Naam: The News Bulletin of Canton Christian College*, New York, vol. 1, no. 1 (August 1924). Letter dated April 24, 1916, from Fung Hin Liu in Canton, China, to Henry Grant in New York. Trustees of Lingnan University, microfilm roll 37.

11. Henry Grant, Secretary of the Trustees, "Is It Worth While to Educate Chinese Girls?" in *Ling Naam: The News Bulletin of Canton Christian College*, New York, vol. 1, no. 1 (August 1924).

12. Henry Grant, Secretary of the Trustees, "Is It Worth While to Educate Chinese Girls?" in *Ling Naam: The News Bulletin of Canton Christian College*, New York, vol. 1, no. 1 (August 1924).

13. Council Minutes, August 30, 1917. Trustees of Lingnan University, microfilm roll 37.

14. Graham, *Gender, Culture, and Christianity: American Protestant Mission Schools in China, 1880–1930*. Chapter 1, footnote 80, p. 34. *Women's Missionary Friend* 49 (May 1917): 173.

15. "Report of the Dean of Women," Trustees of Lingnan University, microfilm roll 37.

16. Mary Raleigh Anderson, *A Cycle in the Celestial Kingdom, or Protestant Mission Schools for Girls in South China (1827 to the Japanese Invasion)* (Mobile, AL: Heiter-Starke Printing Co., 1943), p. 213. For more information on the proportion of female to male collegiate students at Lingnan, see chapter 1, Figure 1.2.

17. "Academic Year, Semester II, 1945–1946, Lingnna University," Lingnan daxue renshi cailiao [Personnel files of Lingnan University], Guangdongsheng dang'anguan, file # 38-4-59.

18. *A Romantic Achievement of Chinese and American Cooperation, Illustrated Historical Sketch* (New York: Trustees of Lingnan University, 1941).

19. Letter of Henry Grant to H. B. Graybill, dated July 10, 1912. "Education for Women, Correspondence, Oct. 4, 1909 to April 4, 1927," Trustees of Lingnan University, microfilm roll 37.

20. Ibid.

21. Henry Graybill, "Developing a Woman's College," p. 31, 1913, Canton Christian College pamphlet, RG 31, Box 273, folder 1944, Yale Divinity School Library. Graham, *Gender, Culture, and Christianity: American Protestant Mission Schools in China, 1880–1930*, p. 40.

22. Kwok, *Chinese Women and Christianity, 1860–1927.* Chapter II, "Feminization of Christian Symbolism," and conclusion.

23. For the story of some female Chinese students in America, see Weili Ye, *Seeking Modernity in China's Name: Chinese Students in the United States, 1900–1927* (Stanford, CA: Stanford University Press, 2001).

24. Letter from Fung Hin Liu to Mrs. Doremus, dated September 27, 1913, and sent from Wilder Hall, Wellesley, Mass.

25. Letter from Fung Hin Liu to Henry Grant, dated December 4, 1915 from Y.W.C.A., Cleveland, Ohio. Trustees of Lingnan University, microfilm roll 37.

26. Letter from Miss Julia Mitchell, Canton, sent February 1914. Trustees of Lingnan University, microfilm roll 7. Mitchell was on Lingnan faculty from 1913–1917, 1942–1943, and 1945–1946. She graduated with a B.A. from Smith College in 1901, gained her Ph.D. at Columbia in 1915, and was a former instructor at Vassar College and the Teachers' College at Columbia.

27. Letter from Julia Mitchell to Henry Grant, dated March 30, 1914. Trustees of Lingnan University, microfilm roll 37.

28. Letter from Helen Cassidy to Margaret Barnee, dated February 3, 1917. Trustees of Lingnan University, microfilm roll 37.

29. Letter from Miss Fung Hin Liu to Henry Grant, dated April 17, 1913. Trustees of Lingnan University, microfilm roll 37.

30. Ye, *Seeking Modernity in China's Name: Chinese Students in the United States, 1900–1927*, pp. 129–36.

31. Letter from Miss Julia Mitchell, Canton, February 1914. Trustees of Lingnan University, microfilm roll 7.

32. Letter from Fung Hin Liu, Wellesley College, to Henry Grant, dated April 17, 1913. Trustees of Lingnan University, microfilm roll 37.

33. "Informal Notes Regarding Lingnan Women Students," Trustees of Lingnan University, microfilm roll 37.

34. Letter from Henry B. Graybill to A. H. Woods, acting president of Canton Christian College, dated March 7, 1916.

35. Anderson, *A Cycle in the Celestial Kingdom, or Protestant Mission Schools for Girls in South China (1827 to the Japanese Invasion).* Chapter 12.

36. Ibid., p. 57.

37. Ibid, pp. 98–99. Harriet Newell Noyes, *A Light in the Land of Sinim* (New York: Revell, 1919).

38. Letter from Fung Hin Liu, Canton, to Henry Grant in New York, dated April 24, 1916. Trustees of Lingnan University, microfilm 37.

39. W. Henry Grant, Secretary of the Trustees, "Is It Worth While to Educate Chinese Girls?" in *Ling Naam: The News Bulletin of Canton Christian College*, New York, Vol. 1, no. 1 (August 1924).

40. Letter from J. W. Creighton to Charles K. Edmunds, dated April 7, 1917. Trustees of Lingnan University, microfilm roll 37. K. Duncan's letter to J.W. Creighton, principal of the True Light Middle School, in Paak Hok Tung, Canton, dated July 7, 1924. Letter from Alexander Baxter, acting president of the C.C.C., to J. W. Creighton, dated July 10, 1924. Letter from Alexander Baxter to James M. Henry, president of the board of trustees of the C.C.C., dated July 10, 1924. Trustees of Lingnan University, microfilm roll 37.

41. Anderson, *A Cycle in the Celestial Kingdom, or Protestant Mission Schools for Girls in South China (1827 to the Japanese Invasion)*, p. 104.

42. Letter from Fung Hin Liu, Canton, to Henry Grant in New York, dated April 24, 1916. Trustees of Lingnan University, microfilm roll 37.

43. Letter of Henry Graybill to W. Henry Grant, dated March 8, 1917. Trustees of Lingnan University, microfilm roll 37.

44. Riggs received a transportation subsidy of US$150 for the trans-Pacific journey. "Proposed Budget—Girls' School, 1917–18," Trustees of Lingnan University, microfilm roll 37.

45. Newspaper clipping from a Hartford, Connecticut newspaper in September 1915. Trustees of Lingnan University, microfilm roll 37.

46. "Constitution of the Women's Students' Christian Association." Trustees of Lingnan University, microfilm roll 37.

47. "Contributions to the Girls' Work, 1915–1916." Trustees of Lingnan University, microfilm roll 37.

48. Letter from Owen E. Pomeroy, Bursar, in Canton to C. K. Edmunds in New York, dated July 3, 1917. Trustees of Lingnan University, microfilm roll 37.

49. Letter from Wong Tsui Fung to Alexander Baxter, dated November 26, 1923. Trustees of Lingnan University, microfilm roll 37.

50. Letter from Liu Fung Kei to Katherine C. Griggs, dated June 25, 1925. "The Constitution of the Canton Christian College Women Student Friendship Association." Trustees of Lingnan University, microfilm roll 37.

51. Letter from John C. Griggs to Henry Grant, dated December 3, 1923. Trustees of Lingnan University, microfilm roll 37.

52. 1924–1925 Lingnan campaign photo caption, held at the Yale Divinity School Library. See Photo 4.1 Women's Campaign for the First Women's Dormitory.

53. Publication for College Book Store, Canton Christian College, Canton, China. See Photo 4.3 Women and Campaign.

54. Letter headed "Campaign for Women's Dormitory," from Alexander Baxter to Charles K. Edmunds, dated December 10, 1923.

55. Letter from Julia Fisher to Henry Grant, May 1924. Trustees of Lingnan University, microfilm roll 37.

56. Letter from Yau Tsit Law to Board of Directors, Lingnan University, dated January 25, 1927. Trustees of Lingnan University, microfilm roll 37.

57. *Lingnan: Canton Christian College*, vol. VI, no. 4 (November 1930): 3, held at Yale University Day Missions Library.

58. Ibid.

59. Li Youning and Zhang Yüfa, *Jindai Zhongguo nüquan yundong shiliao, 1842–1911* (Taibei: Zhuanji wenxueshe, 1975), vol. 1.

60. Ibid, pp. 282–83. The *Wanguo gongbao* article mistakes 1814 as the year of the founding of Holyoke College.

61. "From Council Minutes, August 30, 1917: Policy with reference to the Girls' School and Women's Department." Trustees of Lingnan University, microfilm roll 37.

62. Barbara Miller Solomon, *In the Company of Educated Women: A History of Women and Higher Education in America* (New Haven, Ct: Yale University Press, 1985).

63. Edward J. Power, *A Legacy of Learning: A History of Western Education* (Albany, NY: State University of New York Press, 1991), p. 274.

64. Thomas Woody, *A History of Women's Education in the United States*, Second Octagon printing. 1929 copyright by Science Press ed., 2 vols. (New York: Octagon Books, a Division of Farrar, Straus and Giroux, 1974), pp. 252–53.

65. Liu Fung Ling, "The Epic Woman of China," *Ling Naam: The News Bulletin of Canton Christian College*, vol. 1, no. 1 (August 1924).

5

From Lingnan to Pomona: Charles K. Edmunds and his Chinese–American Career

I n 1928, at the beginning of his presidency of Pomona College in Claremont, California, Charles Keyser Edmunds drew out a number of com-
parisons between the two institutions which dominated his career as an
educator:

> As I glance northward out of my window, the San Bernardino Mountains
> present themselves, and in my mind's eye there arises a vision of that other
> institution of learning which also stands "South of the Mountains" even as
> its name implies. Both Pomona and Lingnan owe much to the inspiration of
> mountains that dominate their north horizon. . . . Both also owe much to the
> lofty ideals of Christian thought and life in which they were conceived and
> through which they have been developed.[1]

Edmunds' observations not only underline the geographical parallels
between Lingnan and Pomona on opposite sides of the Pacific, but also
hint at the reciprocal influences operating between China and America
in the area of higher learning in the late nineteenth and early twentieth
centuries. The Christian colleges in China are widely regarded as one of
the most significant examples of cultural interaction in the global development of institutions of higher education.[2] Nevertheless, to date studies
of this subject leave a number of important questions unanswered. How
different were China's Christian colleges from their counterparts across
the Pacific? What was the educational significance of the U.S.–China link?
What happened to Americans in the process of transplanting American
higher learning into Chinese soil and after their return to their native

land? How did their years in China shape their further experience of American institutions of higher learning?[3]

This chapter focuses on the figure of Charles K. Edmunds (1876–1949), an international educator and college administrator, and the connection between his Chinese and American experiences formed within the perspective of the liberal arts ideals to which he subscribed. (See photo 5.1; photo 5.2.) Edmunds' Lingnan and Pomona stories illustrate a two-way interaction, in areas such as college governance and curriculum, linking both sides of the Pacific. On the one hand, Lingnan University was part of the westward exportation of higher education from America, which in its turn had been inspired by European models. On the other, the influence of the Lingnan experience on Charles K. Edmunds is a striking example of the "reflex influence" of China on America.[4]

Photo 5.1.   Charles K. Edmunds at Lingnan. Special Collections,
Digital Projects, Yale Divinity School Library.

Photo 5.2, Charles K. Edmunds at Pomona. E. Wilson Lyon, History of Pomona College, 1887–1969 *(Claremont, Calif.: Pomona College, 1977), p. 231.*

What did the link with China mean to Edmunds after he returned to his home country? First, as a person who traveled 65,300 miles and left his footprints in every province of China, Edmunds could hardly do other than bring the "Orient" to Pomona.[5] Second, Edmunds' China experience strengthened and broadened his faith in Christian liberal arts ideals, making him ideally suited for a professional career as an educational administrator back home. Third, the Lingnan experience was one important—and very positive—factor influencing the way in which Edmunds managed Pomona for the thirteen years of his tenure there.

THE CHINA LINK: EDMUNDS AT CANTON CHRISTIAN COLLEGE (1903–1924)

In 1876, the year of Edmunds' birth, Daniel C. Gilman became the president of the newly founded Baltimore institution that was to become the

Johns Hopkins University. This was a significant year in the history of American higher education, as the Johns Hopkins University under the leadership of Gilman became the first American university to adopt the new German model of a research university.[6] Edmunds, born in Baltimore, received both his undergraduate and graduate training at this new type of institution, something that was to mark him for life. As Edmunds put it in 1926, "It was a pioneer movement in education that gave birth . . . to the Johns Hopkins University. . . . Advanced study beyond that of the college years, organized and continuous research, and the systematic publication of scientific work made up a field of endeavor in which America was sadly deficient."[7]

After receiving his Ph.D. in physics and electrical engineering at Johns Hopkins in 1903, Edmunds went to China, taking up a teaching post at Canton Christian College and with a commission from the Carnegie Institution to make a magnetic survey of the whole of China. For seventeen years (1907–1924), Edmunds served as president of Canton Christian College.[8] Edmunds had a well-developed social conscience and attributed his desire to go to the Far East to the violence of the Boxer Movement in 1900. He was then a graduate student on assignment from the U.S. Government Geodetic Survey to southeastern Kansas to establish a magnetic observatory. He recalled:

> If you know southeast Kansas, you would realize how the news from Peking kept me alive. I made up my mind then that I would be very willing, if the opportunity arose, to devote a considerable part of my life to help prevent that kind of thing from happening again by building up an understanding between the people of China and America at least.[9]

As we have seen, Canton Christian College was founded by Andrew Happer in 1888, with the approval of the Presbyterian Board of Foreign Missions. It was operated first as an independent college, and subsequently (from 1926) as a university, by the Trustees of Lingnan University, who were incorporated in New York in 1893. In 1927, the management of the institution was taken over by a board of directors in China, acting in association with the American board, an arrangement which lasted until 1952 when Lingnan University was merged with Sun Yat-sen (Zhongshan) University.[10] When Edmunds departed in 1924, the trustees of Canton Christian College had an investment of some US$1,600,000 in the land, buildings, and improvements on the campus, plus around $1,000,000 in funds.[11]

Milestones during the Edmunds years included the procurement of Lingnan's permanent home at Honglok on Honam Island in 1904; an expansion in the size of the campus from 35 acres to 135 acres in 1918; the admission of the first six girls in 1906 and the attainment of a high percentage of women entrants (17 percent of collegiate students in 1924, well above the national average of 2.5 percent in the same year); the opening of an affiliated medical school in 1910; graduation of the first collegiate students in 1918; the formation of the College of Arts and Sciences in 1916 and of the Agricultural College in 1921; and peak enrollments of 1,930 students (including 203 college students) in 1923 and 1,727 students (including 194 college students) in 1924.[12] This development of the college under Edmunds combined higher learning with a concentration on local needs in a diversified teaching and research environment. It represented the "South China way" to which Edmunds was committed.

Imbued with the Johns Hopkins spirit, which manifested itself in profound advances in graduate studies as a variety of higher educational institutions made their appearance in America, Edmunds was determined to create a thoroughly modern institution in South China. Working in concert with the visionary William Henry Grant, executive secretary of the board of trustees, Edmunds was open to the prospect of making Canton Christian College into either a college or a Christian university. In 1913, both men were agreed on the model of a professional or technical school composed of a regular arts and science course, a teachers' college or normal school modeled on the Teachers' College at Columbia University, a medical school, a school of agriculture, a school of commerce and international relations, a school of theology, and a school of industries.[13]

Known as "the Southern Yenching" in China, the college's success under Edmunds' presidency depended heavily on the abilities of Edmunds himself. He was the driving force, capably exercising academic, administrative, and executive control of the college along with the board of trustees ten thousand miles away in New York.

With regard to the role of religion in a Christian college, Edmunds and Grant adopted a comprehensive and liberal view. They preferred to "lay the emphasis on its educational side, and the competent teacher as the all important factor." To Edmunds, acceptance of Christianity as an expression of the "new life" found on the Lingnan campus came naturally and was the *sine qua non* for the educational side.[14] In 1907, Henry Grant remarked in a letter that "it is far more homelike out here in China than you would suppose. . . . The Sunday School is the best opportunity during the week to teach the Bible and make personal application of the truth."[15] Daily Bible classes were a part of the required curriculum.[16] Twenty-two years later, the Christian content had been diluted but had by no means become irrelevant. On the Lingnan campus, three Sunday services were held along with a children's service and a Sunday school. Morning and evening prayers for students were held daily from Monday to Friday, with the average attendance about forty.[17] Despite the influence of secularization trickling through into higher learning throughout the world, Christian life and a Christian atmosphere were—in the words of Charles Thomas Walkley, rector of Grace Episcopal Church in Orange, New Jersey—"evident everywhere" at Lingnan.[18]

Lingnan's nondenominational status was one of the college's greatest assets, as it attracted resources from a variety of church groups including the Catholics. On the other hand, being nondenominational meant that the independent board of trustees assumed full responsibility for the finances of the college. At the same time, it put Lingnan in an ambivalent position in relation to denominational groups and the United Board for Christian Higher Education in Asia.[19]

Driven by a strong sense of mission—by standing head and shoulders above all other educational institutions in South China, it was believed that Lingnan would influence the entire nation—the college's early administrators felt the burden of manifold opportunities. They looked up to German educators as role models and saw themselves as doing in China what the Germans had done for American higher education:

> If some German had come to America and conducted a small school in Jersey City within all the higher studies in the German language, and in the course of ten years the leading American teacher in this school should be selected as superintendent of all the school work for the New England and Middle States, with power to reorganize their whole school system on the new lines which he had worked out in his course in the Jersey City school, it would fairly represent the opportunity and influence of the Canton Christian College.[20]

To Edmunds, understanding China and the Chinese was essential to his job. In a letter declining an offer from the trustees to appoint him president of Canton Christian College in 1906, he laid out several reasons for his decision, focusing particularly on the language problem:

> A man is needed who knows the Cantonese language or Mandarin thoroughly in order to have the confidence of the *Chinese* staff. The development of relations with the gentry and officials, a matter which in my judgment is exceedingly important . . . the development of the Chinese department of study and its oversight, and the development of close contact with the students, the people and the needs of the time, all require a thorough knowledge of the vernacular and a deep understanding of the people which it is hopeless for me to expect to attain within any reasonable time.[21]

Edmunds continued, in a candid vein: "I do not think the Trustees realize our condition in this regard. Imagine being in charge of a school in a country the native newspapers of which you are unable to read and have *no member* (American) on your staff who can."[22] Years later, Edmunds described his efforts to master Chinese, an ideographic language, and to get himself about even more than most of his colleagues. "If you see a man a mile off, waving both arms and both legs at the same time, it's Edmunds talking Chinese!"[23]

In the Edmunds years, the college nurtured amicable relations with its local constituents, who often proved to be a source of patronage and protection. In 1923, as a result of his interest in the college infirmary, General Lei Fuk Lam, the head of the 5th Nationalist Army in control of Honam Island, donated $13,000 in Chinese currency (approximately US$1,667 in today's values) for the erection of a dispensary and a sixteen-bed hospital for the neighboring village.[24] As noted in chapter 2, when, in 1924, twenty-nine students and six staff members were kidnapped by bandits, Lingnan turned to General Lei and Civil Governor Wu Hon Man who successfully rescued all twenty-nine. Later, the victims called on General Lei and presented him with a large silver medallion and a gift of twenty-two roast pigs for his soldiers.[25] Also, the chief of police in Canton presented the college with 30,000 bricks on which it had to pay carriage only.[26]

Edmunds presided over a rapid growth in both curriculum and faculty numbers. His first presidential report shows only the first two years of college courses were available in 1907 (see tables 5.1 and 5.2).[27]

There were only six collegiate students in 1906–1907 (all of whom were freshmen), whereas in 1924, Edmunds' last year as president, the figure stood at 194.[28] According to the president's report, in 1906–1907 there were thirteen Chinese and ten expatriates serving as faculty, instructors, and assistants;[29] in 1916–1917, there were sixty-eight members of staff

Table 5.1. **Course Offerings of Canton Christian College, 1907**

Subjects (Freshmen)	Hours/week		Subjects (Sophomore)	Hours/week	
	1st sem.	2nd sem.		1st sem.	2nd sem.
Life of Paul		2	Teachings of Jesus	2	2
English	5	4	English	3	3
Medieval History	3	3	History of England	3	3
Solid Geometry	4		Analytical Geometry	4	4
Trigonometry		4	Present Day Problems in the Orient	4	4
General Chemistry	4	4	Physics	4	4
Chemistry (Lab)	6	6	Physics (Lab)	6	6
Mechanical Drawing	2		Translation	3	3
	24	23		29	29

Table 5.2. Canton Christian College Faculty, 1909[1]

Name	Degree	Position and Dept.	Start year
Charles K. Edmunds	Ph.D., Johns Hopkins	President, Physics	1903
Clinton N. Laird	M.A., Univ. of Penn.	Treasurer, Registrar, Chemistry	1905
Henry B. Graybill	M.A., Columbia	English	1903
Chester G. Fuson	B.A., Emporia	Geography and Drawing	1905
C. A. Bergstresser	M.A., Lafayette	Mathematics	1906
G. Weidman Groff	B.S., Penn State	Commandant	1907
Josiah C. McCracken	M.D., Univ. of Penn	College Physician	1907
Henry C. Brownell	B.A., Univ. of Vermont	Secretary	1908
F. Wilbur Mottley	B.A., Univ. of Minn.	English	1908
R. S. Kinney	M.A., Boston Univ.	English & History	1909
W. K.Chung	Jü Ren (Chinese M.A.)	Head of Chinese Dept.	1900

[1] Table 5.1 and 5.2, Canton Christian College Catalogue, 1906–1907, pp. 4–5. Trustees of Lingnan University, microfilm roll 25. The 1906–1907 catalogue was apparently written in 1908 since the new and prospective appointments for 1908 and 1909 were included.

(twenty-four expatriates, forty-four Chinese). By 1924 the number of expatriates on the academic staff had risen to fifty-one.[30]

By the end of Edmunds' tenure, Canton Christian College had developed into a fully fledged liberal arts college moving in the direction of becoming a university. Its development was stimulated by, and ran in many ways parallel to, the model of the American liberal arts college. It upheld a carefully articulated Christian view of life with practicality and resilience.[31]

The programs offered at the college were China-focused, designed to respond to the needs of South China, and this was always a key feature in Lingnan's development. Recognizing that China's economy rested on agriculture, Edmunds supported projects involving research into irrigation, flood control, subtropical horticulture, and sericulture, the last two pioneered by the college.

One of the most striking developments during 1919–1924 was in agricultural research, an interest begun in 1907 by G. Weidman Groff who devoted thirty-four years to South China and the college.[32] The agricultural problems of South China interested both Chinese and international organizations. The district magistrate of Shun Tak (the heart of the silk region in South China) was so impressed with the college's work that he sent it fourteen promising young men for a six-month extension course, and even paid the cost of their tuition in a lump sum.[33] K. C. Griggs, executive secretary to Edmunds, reported in a letter to her boss that that there was extensive local interest in the college's potential contribution to the silk industry: [34]

We are continually hearing things which indicate that the present government as well as the silk merchants in Canton are waking up to the importance of improving the condition of the silk industry in this province. The Foreign Silk Association of Canton have now undertaken to get all the foreign silk merchants as well as the Chinese silk merchants to agree to collect 15 cents on each bale of silk sold and turn [it] over to the College for the silk work. They are evidently concerned to have a share in the work done here which they now realize will grow into a big thing.

Persuaded by Chung Wing Kwong, the college's senior vice-president, Guangdong Civil Governor Liu eventually admitted that China was the only country which did not insist on the elimination of disease in the rearing of silkworms. He turned over $5,000 [HK currency] to the college for a silk survey of the province.[35]

One mark of a university founded on the new German model was the strength of its research and publication output. Edmunds deemed publications "a fair index of the institution's vitality." According to Edmunds, the college's publications had helped considerably "to increase interest in China and her problems both throughout China and in America."[36] They had also helped strengthen ties with the United States: "The College has thus contributed not only to the progress of modern education in China, aside from its own work of instruction, but also to the development of mutual appreciation, understanding and confidence between Chinese and Americans."[37] By 1924, periodicals published by the college included *The Canton Christian College Magazine*, *The Ling Nan Agricultural Review* (a technical and scientific journal covering research in agriculture and related sciences, published twice a year in English), *Economic Studies* (in Chinese, published by the Economics Association), *the Daily Meteorological Record*, and *Agricultural Monthly* (in Chinese).[38] The *Lingnan Science Journal*, founded in 1931, had an internationally recognized standing among scientific circles in China and abroad. The journal was in such high demand that complete sets were acquired in 43 countries and 1,000 scientific periodicals were sent to Lingnan in exchange from 450 institutions in 75 countries.[39]

The preparation of suitable textbooks was also considered urgent. Edmunds supported the publication of textbooks in mathematics and English, by C. A. Bergstresser and Henry Graybill respectively, both members of the faculty, by the College Bookshop and the Commercial Press of Shanghai respectively.[40] By 1941, teaching and research were both considered "essential regular work of the University." Standards for ranking faculty members had been revised by the board of directors, "placing an equal emphasis on teaching ability and research publications as well as on degrees and experience."

Edmunds' approach in adapting the American system of higher learning to the college was characterized by pragmatism and flexibility. He recognized that "it will not do at all to force an American curriculum on the Chinese students of the present generation, if ever." Indeed, Edmunds' concentration on the objectives of higher learning was matched by his ability to work in the Chinese system. The Edmunds administration also made great efforts to secure teaching staff of high quality. Constant consideration was given to the improvement of the Chinese Department, which in Edmunds' eyes needed "native scholars properly qualified to teach Chinese history, literature and composition according to more efficient methods than those formerly in vogue, who at the same time understand something of the discipline and management of a modern school." At the American end, he arranged for American academic staff to take special leave from the college to learn the Chinese language.

EDMUNDS AT POMONA (1928–1941)

In 1927, following a brief assignment as provost at the Johns Hopkins University, Edmunds was called to the presidency of Pomona College, a nondenominational liberal arts college established by a group of Congregationalists from New England in 1887 in Claremont, California, thirty-five miles east of Los Angeles.[41] As the founding member of a cluster of seven independent but affiliated colleges—Claremont Graduate School, Scripps College, Claremont McKenna College, Harvey Mudd College, Pizter College, and Claremont University Center—Pomona was entering a new phase of development when Edmunds took the helm in 1928.

The Claremont Group Plan was an innovative undertaking in American higher education conceived by Edmunds' predecessor, James A. Blaisdell. Under pressure to expand Pomona, Blaisdell hoped that "instead of one great, undifferentiated university, we might have a group of institutions divided into small colleges—somewhat on the Oxford type—around a library and other utilities which they would use in common. In this way I should hope to preserve the inestimable personal values of the small college while securing the facilities of the great university."[42] With regard to the granting of degrees, it was decided that while each of the undergraduate colleges should grant its own bachelor's degrees, the M.A. and Ph.D. degrees would be conferred by the Claremont Graduate School. This practice departed from Blaisdell's original conception in 1924 that had designated Claremont University Center as the central, inclusive "university" for the whole group.

Edmunds' presidency at Pomona was marked by four major features: building expansion, an increase in endowments, the promotion of the

"Orient," and the college's consolidation as a liberal arts college with an enrollment set at around 750, divided equally between men and women. In contrast to Lingnan, Pomona strove to retain its size and enhance its identity as a small liberal arts college.[43]

Edmunds took office at a time when American academe was going through extensive changes. One such change was the tendency to appoint laymen instead of ordained ministers as university or college heads. While in 1860, 90 percent of American college presidents had received training for the Christian ministry, in 1933 no more than 12 percent had a theological background.[44] As the first nonordained president of Pomona College, Edmunds' appointment was symptomatic of this change in American academia. Introducing himself to Pomona, Edmunds declared that "though I have been a missionary, I am not a minister."[45] Having spent the major part of his professional career in China, Edmunds' appointment as president of Pomona was clear evidence of the recognition of his qualifications for leadership in higher education as well as of his influential contacts. With his twenty-one years of service in Canton, Edmunds was obviously a good choice for Pomona in an era when raising funds and reconciling the different demands of students, faculty, alumni, and off-campus constituents were considered priorities.[46]

Edmunds impressed people with his capacity for raising money using novel methods. At Canton Christian College, in 1922, Edmunds had nominated James Henry to the trustees for appointment as second vice-president, to assist both himself and Chung Wing Kwong (then vice-president) in the "whole work of cultivation," which involved promoting Chinese interest in the college, representing the institution publicly, and developing its relations with the Canton community, both Chinese and expatriate, as well as producing and distributing campaign literature.[47] The trustees had praised him as someone who "could think up more plans in one month than could be carried out in three," employing "methods as novel as they were successful."[48] In response to one of Edmunds' letters demonstrating his clear grasp of the financial situation at the college, Warren P. Laird, the college's treasurer and registrar, commented: "I feel that we have an asset of extraordinary value in Dr. Edmunds, for he is a figure of exceptional size in the educational work going on in China."[49]

Edmunds brought the same energy and inventiveness to his work at Pomona. In 1929, he appointed Margaret Maple as Pomona's first full-time alumni secretary to administer the new Pomona College Alumni Fund.[50] He also led Pomona successfully through the Depression. In 1931, in a beautifully designed pamphlet entitled *An Invitation*, Edmunds frankly set forth Pomona's capital needs—amounting to additional income of $125,000 annually—to invite "thoughtful citizens" to consider giving.[51] And although he was forced to introduce drastic fiscal cuts, including a 10 percent salary reduction for all members of staff for five years from 1932, he increased the academic reputation of the institution. When Edmunds retired in 1941, he left Pomona in an enviable financial situation with total institutional assets of $7,664,963.91, including $3,863,241.66 in endowment funds. This compared very favorably with endowments of $2,840,495.23 and total assets of $6,500,000 in 1931.[52] The staff/student ratio had been maintained at less than 1:10.

Edmunds was also well received by the students, to whom he was affectionately known as "Prexy." An editorial in Pomona's student newspaper, *The Student Life*, enthused: "We like President Edmunds because instead of standing on his own level and preaching down to us, he stepped to our level and talked to us. No matter how much President Blaisdell wanted to be with the students his many duties kept him from it. We hope that the administration will leave Prexy Edmunds enough time to continue the membership in the Student Body to which he was so enthusiastically received."[53]

As a result of his experience with residential college life in China, Edmunds gave high priority to improving physical facilities such as dormitories and dining halls for the student body and college-owned, well-situated residences for the president, the dean, and selected members of the faculty. Edmunds had learned in Canton that the physical plant was important for educational work.[54] He was determined to make Pomona a fully residential college. When Edmunds took office, there were only two dormitories at Pomona, Smiley Hall for men and Harwood Court for women, with only a single dining hall in a wing of Claremont Inn.[55] During Edmunds' first three years as president, Frary Hall (comprising men's dormitories and dining hall), sections 1, 2, and 3 of the Eli P. Clark Dormitories, and the Harwood Dining Hall and kitchen for women students were all completed, in addition to a swimming pool. Other projects completed in the Edmunds years were the Student Union, the Olney Dining Hall, and the Florence Carrier Blaisdell Hall.[56]

Under Edmunds, the structure and governance of Pomona were streamlined and centralized along the lines of his reforms at Canton Christian College. For example, by eliminating the position of dean of the faculty, Edmunds took charge of faculty appointments and promotions and cultivated staff relations on a person level.[57] He was an active figure both on and off campus. Despite being the first nonordained president of Pomona, Edmunds many times filled the pulpit in Pomona's chapel and outside venues. His chapel talks had titles like "The Search for Value,"[58] "Out of the Midst of the Fire—Ye Heard A Voice,"[59] and "Thinking with the Heart."[60]

Charles K. Edmunds was not only a frequent contributor to journals and newspapers on the subject of China, but also spoke about China on many occasions in the United States and actively promoted Sino-American relations through the college. Having spent twenty-one years on the other side of the Pacific, Edmunds brought the Far East to Pomona and Pomona to the world: "I have crossed [the Pacific Ocean] so often that I am convinced now that it was not established to separate but to connect."[61] In his introductory greetings to students, Edmunds told them that "you are in these college years more systematically in touch with the worlds of thought and aesthetics than you will be in years after years."[62]

Committed as he was to an international perspective, Edmunds launched Pomona's first student exchange program in 1929. On the first study expedition led by Sik Leong Tsui, a student from Canton, ten Pomona graduates and upperclassmen spent one year abroad, mainly in China.[63] Asked about the purpose of study abroad, Sik stated it was to "replace ignorant, narrow provincialism with that more accurate knowledge and broadminded understanding of other countries, typical of the international-minded man and of cosmopolitan friendship."[64] During the academic year of 1934–1935, Fulton Freeman was selected as the first Pomona exchange student to Lingnan University, marking the start of Lingnan's student exchange program.[65]

Students and staff at Pomona were also regularly exposed to things Eastern. On January 18, 1938, *Lady Precious Stream*, an ancient Chinese comedy, was performed at Pomona College in English translation. The play, said to be the "first Chinese play to reach American theaters in English," combined comedy and satire with a magnificent visual spectacle; it played three years in London, one season in New York, a further season on an Eastern tour, and two weeks in Los Angeles. According to a report in Pomona College's *The Student Life*, the translator, top Chinese playwright H. I. Hsiung, had made some changes to suit American audiences; he "corrects Occidental impression that Oriental plays are too long, [and] assures that his work with but few changes is only as long as most American plays."[66]

In addition to setting up the exchange program and a Department of Oriental Affairs (see below), Edmunds reinforced Pomona's capacity for international education by inviting visitors and scholars to the college who had a connection with China. In 1919, the college achieved its largest enrollment to date of 650 students, with thirteen scholars from five foreign countries including six from China and two from France.[67] Under his presidency, China was brought firmly into Pomona's campus life. On May 28, 1930, Edmunds conferred the degree of Doctor of Letters on China's foremost Beijing opera singer, the artiste Mei Lanfang.[68] Julean Arnold, a personal friend of Edmunds and U.S. commercial attaché to China for nearly twenty years, gave talks at Pomona.[69]

Edmunds' commitment to China and his promotional work at the college secured Pomona a grant from the Rockefeller Foundation in 1936. This made a reality of the Department of Oriental Affairs which was said to be the first Asian studies program at a liberal arts college anywhere in the nation.[70] The recruitment of Charles Burton Fahs, who had a Ph.D. in oriental studies from Northwestern University, brought China and Japan firmly into Pomona's curriculum. By 1948, Pomona had Chen Shou-yi, F. Raymond Iredell, Chu You-Kuang, Allan B. Cole, and Kenneth E. Foster on its academic staff, teaching twenty-eight courses on Asian subjects.[71] Few universities and colleges in the United States could offer the range of courses available at Pomona after 1936.[72] The arrival in 1941 of Chen Shou-yi, a scholar with a B.A. from Lingnan University and a Ph.D. from the University of Chicago, greatly strengthened Asian studies at Pomona. Chen's many speaking engagements with alumni, civic organizations, churches, clubs, and in town halls made him "one of the best ambassadors for the college."[73] Pomona's research holdings on the Pacific area, started in 1935, amounted to over 55,000 volumes and was said to be one of the best collections on the West Coast by the end of Edmunds' tenure.[74]

Edmunds' own writings on China varied in their subjects from weights and measures and irrigation systems to politics, foreign affairs, and education.[75] Focusing on more spiritual matters, Chen Shou-yi and other members of the academic staff at Pomona promoted an aesthetic appreciation of Eastern civilization.[76]

What kind of image of the Far East was projected by Edmunds and his fellow Asianists at Pomona? Assuming the burden of interpreting China to the world, Edmunds presented China with objectivity, understanding, and from an international point of view. This offset the usual "black and ugly" picture—floods, famine, earthquakes, bandits, Communist insurgents, Japanese military invasion, disintegration and chaos—presented in the American press.[77]

As "a resident in the field" in South China, Edmunds frequently sent reports back home to correct misinformation. In response to the many alarming American reports about violence against foreigners in China, Edmunds protested: "Many of the reports that we have seen are either entirely erroneous, or contain so much that is incorrect in premise that they are misleading in the impression they make upon those who have not observed for themselves."[78] The anti-foreign disturbances referred to by the press, Edmunds continued, were almost entirely of local origin and so were of "rather small value in forming any generalized statement as to the attitude of the people as a whole toward foreigners."[79] In Edmunds' analysis, the roots of this violence were to be found in growing nationalist sentiment as well as an increasing feeling of national humiliation in China. And Edmunds personally testified to many instances of courtesy and kindness to foreigners by natives: "we can go all over Honam and very seldom hear the cries of 'foreign devil' as compared with formerly, but salutations such as 'Teacher,' 'Great Merchant' meet our ears from the lips of genial farm hands on the wayside."[80]

CONCLUSION

Edmunds' links with China help us address a couple of important questions relating to Christian colleges in China and U.S.-China relations. First, how did China's Christian colleges differ from the American model? Edmunds' China experience illustrates, if not fully, the differences between the American model of a Christian liberal arts education and its Chinese counterpart. For instance, the question of the medium of instruction and the status of Chinese studies had been debated from the outset, and remained contentious issues among all Chinese Christian colleges. Edward Yihua Xü's study of St. John's University in Shanghai reveals both the difficulties and ironies inherent in a liberal arts education conducted in English in a Chinese setting. Xü states that St. John's had adopted English as the medium of instruction because English was seen as most suitable for enhancing the analytical skills of students and broadening their "moral horizon."[81] However, as Chinese nationalism grew in strength in the first quarter of the twentieth century, teaching in English was denounced as drawing Chinese students away from their cultural roots.

From its inception, Canton Christian College insisted on the acquisition of English as a prerequisite for class work in order to train students to become "citizens of the world," as the college's founder, Andrew Happer, had envisioned.[82] As we have seen, before his death in October 1894, fearing that the board of trustees was prejudiced against the teaching of English at the college, Happer demanded that the board return his subscription bond of US$10,000.[83] The student body strongly supported instruction in English, and even voted that from 9:15 AM to 2:30 PM every day nothing but English must be spoken.[84]

Edmunds' keen interest in understanding China, and his efforts to become a competent speaker of the language, did not prevent him from noting what he considered to be the shortcomings of Chinese culture. As a physicist, Edmunds had trouble with the lack of accuracy among Chinese with regard to numbers:

> There is no more vexing factor in the life of a foreigner in China than the lack of accuracy among the Chinese in most matters involving numerical relations. . . . The whole Chinese system of thinking is based on a different line of assumptions from those to which we are accustomed, and they can ill

comprehend the mania which seems to possess the Occidental to ascertain everything with unerring accuracy. The Chinese does not know how many families there are in his village, and he does not wish to know and cannot understand why any human being should want to know. It is "a few hundreds," or "not a few," but a definite number it never was and never will be. . . . Curious enough, concomitant with the early development of their system of weights and measures—a decimal system for the most part—the Chinese have become fixed in the habit of reckoning by tens, and frequently refuse to make a statement of number nearer to the truth than a multiple of ten. [85]

This example helps explain the tensions provoked by the college's use of English as the medium of instruction, during the Edmunds years and later, while stressing the importance of understanding Chinese language and culture.

The second question to be dealt with here is—how were expatriate Americans molded by their experience in China and how did it affect them on their return to America? Edmunds' career started in China and ended in America. His work in China gave him invaluable experience with fundraising and financial management, providing him with the opportunity to develop an ability that has been considered critical for presidents of American universities and colleges.

Unlike other Chinese Christian colleges, Lingnan, as a nondenominational institution with no regular funding from the missions, was under constant financial pressure. Edmunds spent several months in 1917 and early 1918 in Southeast Asia, working hard to keep Lingnan solvent.[86] With almost a quarter of a century's experience in the Chinese version of an American liberal arts college, he was no stranger to the demands of a college presidency in America in the late 1920s.

Edmunds took pride in his achievements at Canton Christian College and often expressed great appreciation of his experience there—an experience which boosted his career back in America. As he noted in his induction speech at Pomona, "one of my greatest sources of satisfaction is the remembrance that the Chinese for and with whom I worked soon came to speak of our college as 'The Man Factory of Canton.'"[87] His years at Canton and Pomona demonstrated his objectivity, open-mindedness, and eclecticism in dealing with higher education in very different religious and cultural environments. To Edmunds, Lingnan and Pomona connected the East and the West, and indeed the world. His two presidencies presented him with the task of "building up an adequate and beautiful physical plant, of directing the development of educational aims and techniques in keeping with the times, and of maintaining a wise connection with the great world of affairs."[88] Both Lingnan and Pomona gained their national and international prominence in very similar ways—both represented innovation, adjustment, strength, and promise, rather than giving way to despair and helplessness, in their distinctive sociocultural and political contexts.

The third concluding point I want to make is that Edmunds' continuing "China project" during his years back home in the United States gives us an insight into the ongoing American "construction" of China, particularly after the escalation of Japanese aggression there in 1937. The publicizing of war-torn China and its urgent needs by Sino-American campaigners elicited the sympathy of Americans. In the nationwide crusade in America for the China cause led by people—such as Henry R. Luce, the publisher of *Life*, *Time*, and *Fortune*—who were concerned deeply about China,[89] Charles K. Edmunds became very much a "wanted" man. Having been invited to join the National Emergency Committee[90] and the Associated Boards for the Christian Colleges in China,[91] Edmunds helped run the emergency fund campaigns, assuming the chairmanship of Southern California committee on the China College Emergency Campaign.[92] To help achieve the campaign's financial goals, Edmunds even held a concert in his home on March 29, 1939, which raised a total of US$277.[93] On February 21, 1941, Edmunds organized a fundraiser in Los Angeles at the Bovard Auditorium on the University of Southern California campus. Two days before the big rally in Los Angeles, Henry R. Luce, chairman of finance committee of the Christian Colleges in China, wrote to Edmunds enthusiastically:

You meet at a time when the whole world is turning eagerly to America for leadership. One vital area for such leadership is that of providing help wherever the need is greatest. Perhaps nowhere in the world today is the need so urgent, or the results of our assistance so potent, as in China. Our Christian universities and colleges there occupy strategic positions, and are rendering most significant service. Their adequate support is an imperative we all must heed. We most earnestly hope that the activities on their behalf which you and your colleagues are leading so admirably will result in a wide extension of acquaintance with, and support of, these Colleges which so worthily symbolize America's friendship for China.

All of you who attend the meeting in Bovard Auditorium have a wide interest in all that concerns China. So you will be glad to know that throughout the United States those who have been most active in support of the Christian Colleges are joining heartily with other friends of China in organizing a single, nation-wide appeal for funds to meet the whole range of China's urgent needs. You will be hearing more of this undertaking in the weeks which lie just ahead. I am confident that you will enthusiastically join in that effort.

These are times that stir us not so much because of the problems they present as because of the opportunities they offer, in terms both of the present and of the future, [which] call out to us from China. I know that the message which will be given at your meeting will help to make that call not only clear but impelling.[94]

Finally, I wish to conclude this chapter with a statement made by Edmunds at the dinner held in his honor in New York City on March 2, 1922—a statement that holds lessons for our own time. In response to praise from many of the guests at the dinner, representing a variety of constituencies, Edmunds remarked that:

[O]ne of my surprises as well as disappointments, when I came home just before this time, was to find that when we were talking so much in the newspapers and on the platform about "making the world safe for democracy," we had forgotten one of the fundamental facts of geography, namely, that the earth is round and that there are people on the other side of it. And when I have seen the wooden ocean-going sailing vessels that lie off of our college campus, twenty or fifty strong any day, I have been reminded that when Columbus crossed the Atlantic he was not looking for us so to speak; he was looking for the Chinese, and he died believing he had reached islands off the coast of Cathay; and perhaps the influence of China in the discovery of America may suggest some obligation on our part in the present time to help China find herself in establishing that form of government which we have so long advocated before the world.[95]

NOTES

1. Charles K. Edmunds, "Pomona and Lingnan," *The News Bulletin of Lingnan University*, June 1928.

2. Examples of works in Chinese are Jin Yilin, *Jindai Zhongguo daxue yanjiu* [Studies of universities in modern China] (Beijing: Zhongyang wenxian chubanshe, 2000). Peter Ng (Wu Ziming), ed., *Jidujiao daxue huaren xiaozhang yanjiu* [Studies of the Chinese presidents of Christian universities.] (Fuzhou: Fujian jiaoyü chubanshe, 2001). Zhang Kaiyuan, ed., *Shehui zhuangxing yü jiaohui daxue* [Social transformation and Christian universities] (Wuhan: Hubei jaioyü chubanshe, 1999).

3. My formulation of these questions was partially inspired by Lamin Sanneh, "Concluding Remarks at 'Conversion and Converts,' the Yale-Edinburgh Group on the History of the Missionary Movement and Non-Western Christianity," (New Haven, CT: Yale University, 2003).

4. Xi Lian, *The Conversion of Missionaries: Liberalism in American Protestant Missions in China, 1907–1932* (University Park, PA: Pennsylvania State University Press, 1997).

5. Charles Hodge Corbett, *Lingnan University: A Short History Based Primarily on the Records of the University's American Trustees* (New York, NY: The Trustees of Lingnan University, 1963), p. 79.

6. John S. Brubacher, and Willis Rudy, *Higher Education in Transition: A History of American Colleges and Universities*, 4th ed. (New Brunswick, NJ: Transaction Publishers, 1997), pp. 174–97. See also Christopher J. Lucas, *American Higher Education: A History* (New York, NY: St. Martin's Press, 1994), pp. 170–74.

7. Charles K. Edmunds, "A Half-Century of Johns Hopkins: A Fruitful Fifty Years at the Baltimore University," *The American Review of Reviews*, November (1926), p. 525.

8. Elizabeth Edmunds Wheaton, "I Remember Prexy Charles Keyser Edmunds: President, Pomona College, 1928–1941, from the Eve of the Stock Market Crash to the Eve of Pearl Harbor," *Pomona Today* 1988.

9. Ibid. p. 8.

10. See chapter 1 for the arrangements for the turnover of Lingnan to the Chinese.

11. "Memo from Yorke Allen to the Trustees of Lingnan University, February 15, 1956," Trustees of Lingnan University Archives, Group 14, Box 1, Folder 9 (Yorke Allen), Yale Divinity School Library.

12. Based on the information in "Canton Christian College Catalogue, 1906–1907," Trustees of Lingnan University, microfilm roll 25. Sili Lingnan daxue (Lingnan Private University), *Sili Lingnan daxue yilan* [Overview of Lingnan University] (Guangzhou: Lingnan University, 1932). These figures are taken from Dong Wang, "Circulating American Higher Education: The Case of Lingnan University (1888–1951)," *Journal of American-East Asian Relations* 9, no. 3–4 (2006): 147–67.

13. Henry Grant's letter to Herbert Parsons (president of the trustees of the Canton Christian College), May 7, 1913. Trustees of Lingnan University, microfilm roll 5.

14. Henry Grant's letter to Herbert Parsons, May 7, 1913. Trustees of Lingnan University, microfilm roll 5.

15. Henry Grant's letter to Friends of the College, April 14, 1907 from Honglok, Canton. Trustees of Lingnan University, microfilm roll 3.

16. *Canton Christian College Bulletin: President's Report, 1909–1910* (New York, NY: Trustees of Canton Christian College, 1911), p. 22.

17. "Present Christian Activity on the Lingnan University Campus," December 16, 1949. Trustees of Lingnan University, microfilm roll 26.

18. "Extracts from a Letter Written by a Distinguished Minister after a Visit to Lingnan University in the Spring of 1936," Charles Thomas Walkley's letter to James M. Henry. Folder 322, Box 22, Group 14, Yale Divinity School Library.

19. The United Board for Christian Higher Education in Asia was founded in 1922 when three Christian colleges in China formed a joint office in New York City. http://www.unitedboard.org/about/history.htm, accessed on February 11, 2006. Discussions of its relations with the United Board and church groups are found throughout the Lingnan archives, e.g., "Report on the First Phase, Lingnan University Planning Survey," Group 8, Box 107, Folder Mr. and Mrs. J. S. Kunkle, Yale Divinity School Library, p. 1.

20. Henry Grant's letter to Herbert Parsons (president of the trustees of the Canton Christian College), May 7, 1913. Trustees of Lingnan University, microfilm roll 5.

21. Charles K. Edmunds' letter to Henry Grant declining his appointment as president, May 9, 1906. Trustees of Lingnan University, microfilm roll 3.

22. Ibid.

23. Edmunds, "Pomona and Lingnan."

24. William W. Cadbury, "History of the Medical Work of Lingnan University," Group 8, Box 107, Folder Mr. and Mrs. J. S. Kunkle, Yale Divinity School Library.

25. "Kidnapping of Staff and Students," *Ling Naam: the News Bulletin of Canton Christian College* 1, no. 3 (1925).

26. James M. Henry's letter to Edmunds concerning local support and land, August 9, 1920. Records of the Trustees of Lingnan University, Harvard-Yenching Library, Box 36, microfilm roll 6.

27. "Canton Christian College Catalogue, 1906–1907," p. 35. Trustees of Lingnan University, microfilm roll 25. There are discrepancies between the individual course hours and the total hours required for all subjects per semester. Here I have added the hours required for each course in calculating total credit hours.

28. Charles K. Edmunds, "President Report, 1919–1924." Trustees of Lingnan University, microfilm roll 26.

29. Canton Christian College Catalogue, 1906–1907, pp. 4–5. Trustees of Lingnan University, microfilm roll 25. Also see appendix.

30. Charles K. Edmunds, "President Reports, 1919–1924," p. 66. Trustees of Lingnan University, microfilm roll 26.

31. Brubacher, *Higher Education in Transition: A History of American Colleges and Universities*, p. 71.

32. In appreciation of the beauty and strength of Chinese civilization, Groff also compiled a calendar booklet on South China. G. Weidman Groff, *Glimpse of China 1939* (Canton: Lingnan University, 1939).

33. James M. Henry, "Letter to Edmunds Concerning Sericulture, May 22, 1922." Records of the Trustees of Lingnan University, Harvard-Yenching Library, Box 38, microfilm roll 7.

34. K. C. Griggs' letter to Edmunds on silk research, July 20, 1923. Records of the Trustees of Lingnan University, Harvard-Yenching Library, Box 39, microfilm roll 7.

35. K. C. Griggs' letter to Edmunds on silk research, July 20, 1923. Records of the Trustees of Lingnan University, Harvard-Yenching Library, Box 39, microfilm roll 7.

36. "College and Staff Publications," in Charles K. Edmunds, "President Reports, 1919–1924," p. 61. Trustees of Lingnan University, microfilm roll 26.

37. Ibid.

38. Charles K. Edmunds, "President Reports, 1919–1924." Trustees of Lingnan University, microfilm roll 26.

39. Y. K. Chu, "The Academic Life of Lingnan," 1941, p. 120. Trustees of Lingnan University, microfilm roll 26.

40. *Canton Christian College Bulletin: President's Report, 1909–1910* (New York, NY: Trustees of Canton Christian College, 1911), p. 14.

41. E. Wilson Lyon, *History of Pomona College, 1887–1969* (Claremont, CA: Pomona College, 1977).

42. *The Group Plan of the Claremont Colleges* (Claremont, CA: Claremont University Center, 1993), p. 10, 18.

43. Ibid.

44. Lucas, *American Higher Education: A History*, p. 188.

45. Elizabeth Edmunds Wheaton, "I Remember Prexy: Charles Keyser Edmunds, President, Pomona College, 1928–1941," p. 7, Edmunds Papers, Folder 1, year unknown, Honnold/Mudd Library, Claremont Colleges.

46. Lucas, *American Higher Education: A History*, pp. 187–91.

47. Charles K. Edmunds' letter to James M. Henry, December 12, 1922. Records of the Trustees of Lingnan University, Harvard-Yenching Library, Box 38, microfilm roll 7.

48. Elizabeth Edmunds Wheaton, "I Remember Prexy: Charles Keyser Edmunds, President, Pomona College, 1928–1941," p. 5, Edmunds Papers, Folder 1, year unknown, Honnold/Mudd Library, Claremont Colleges.

49. Warren Powers Laird, "Letter to Herbert Parsons, President of Trustees of C.C.C., Praising Edmunds, dated October 19, 1922," Records of the Trustees of Lingnan University, Harvard-Yenching Library, Box 38, microfilm roll 7.

50. Elizabeth Edmunds 'Wheaton, "I Remember Prexy: Charles Keyser Edmunds, President, Pomona College, 1928–1941," p. 10. Edmunds Papers, Folder 1, year unknown, Honnold/Mudd Library, Claremont Colleges.

51. *An Invitation, Pomona College Pamphlet*, 1931, Widener Library, Harvard University, p. 60.

52. E. Wilson Lyon, "Report of the President of Pomona College, 1941–42," (Claremont, CA: Pomona College, 1942), pp. 59, 286. *An Invitation, Pomona College Pamphlet*, 1931, p. 59.

53. The *Student Life*, editorial, May 12, 1928.

54. Charles K. Edmunds' letter to the Trustees of C.C.C., sent from Hong Kong, October 5, 1922. Records of the Trustees of Lingnan University, Harvard-Yenching Library, Box 38, microfilm roll 7.

55. Lyon, *History of Pomona College, 1887–1969*, p. 263.

56. Ibid. pp. 264–75. Elizabeth Edmunds Wheaton, "I Remember Prexy: Charles Keyser Edmunds, President, Pomona College, 1928–1941," p. 9. Edmunds Papers, Folder 1, year unknown, Honnold/Mudd Library at the Claremont Colleges.

57. Ibid., p. 299–300.

58. Charles K. Edmunds, "Edmunds to Speak," *The Student Life*, November 16 1934.

59. Charles K. Edmunds, "Out of the Midst of the Fire—Ye Heard a Voice: An Address by Charles K. Edmunds at Pomona College," 1941. Edmunds Papers, Honnold/Mudd Library, Claremont Colleges.

60. Charles K. Edmunds, "Thinking with the Heart," year unknown. Edmunds Papers, Honnold/Mudd Library, Claremont Colleges.

61. Elizabeth Edmunds Wheaton, "I Remember Prexy: Charles Keyser Edmunds, President, Pomona College, 1928–1941," p. 30. Edmunds Papers, Folder 1, year unknown, Honnold/Mudd Library, Claremont Colleges.

62. Charles K. Edmunds, "Prexy's Greeting," *The Student Life*, September 25, 1928.

63. Unknown, "Party Will Depart for China Soon," *The Student Life*, October 2, 1929.

64. Unknown, "Students to Take Year in Orient Study," *The Student Life*, May 21, 1929.

65. Charles K. Edmunds, "Report of President," (Claremont, CA: Pomona College, 1935), p. 9.

66. "'Lady Precious Stream' English Translation Plays in Bridges Auditorium," Pomona College, *The Student Life*, January 18, 1938, p. 1. Honnold/Mudd Library, Claremont Colleges.

67. C. B. Sumner, *A Pivotal Era in the Life of Pomona College* (Claremont, CA: Pomona College, 1919), p. 9.

68. Unknown, "Pomona to Honor Mei Lan-Fang," *The Student Life*, May 27, 1930.

69. Unknown, "China Talk for Chapel: Special Chapel by Julean Arnold on Consular Service," *The Student Life*, 1929.

70. Samuel Hideo Yamashita, "Asian Studies at American Private Colleges, 1808–1990," in *Asia in the Undergraduate Curriculum*, ed. Susan Wilson Barnett, and Van Jay Symons (Armonk, NY: M.E. Sharpe, 2000), p. 30. Lyon, *History of Pomona College, 1887–1969*, pp. 342–43. Wheaton, "I Remember Prexy Charles Keyser Edmunds: President, Pomona College, 1928–1941, from the Eve of the Stock Market Crash to the Eve of Pearl Harbor," p. 10.

71. Unknown, "Instructional Staff," *Oriental Studies* 19, no. 5 (1948).

72. Lyon, *History of Pomona College, 1887–1969*, p. 343.

73. Lyon, "Report of the President of Pomona College, 1941–42," p. 32. Chen Shou-yi Papers, Honnold/Mudd Library, Claremont Colleges.

74. "Asian Studies in the Claremont Graduate School, Claremont, California," *Claremont Oriental Studies*, June, no. 4 (1942). Pomona, "'Accident Takes Life of Charles Keyser Edmunds' 'Lingnan Mourns Edmunds,'" *The Pomona College Bulletin Newsletter*, January 1949, p. 2. Claremont College Library, *Materials on the Pacific Area in the Oriental Library of Claremont College Library and in the Libraries of Pomona College and Scripps College* (Claremont, CA: Claremont Colleges Library, 1939). This volume lists 141 pages of books, periodicals, and serials.

75. Edmunds' writings on China include "Weights and Measures among the Chinese," year unknown, Charles K. Edmunds Papers, Honnold/Mudd Library, Claremont Colleges. "Irrigation of Chengtu Plain or [and] beyond," perhaps circa 1903, Charles K. Edmunds Papers, Honnold/Mudd Library at the Claremont Colleges. Charles K. Edmunds, *The Challenge in Crisis: Commencement Address, Dec. 18, 1942, Pomona College, Claremont, Ca*, 5 vols., vol. XL, *Pomona College Bulletin* (Claremont, CA: Pomona College, 1943). Charles K. Edmunds, "Geography as a Factor in the Determination of Foreign Policy" (paper presented at the 16th Annual meeting of The Institute of World Affairs, Riverside, CA, 1938). Charles K. Edmunds, *The Purpose and Spirit of Research*, Reprint from Pomona College Magazine, March 1929 ed. (Claremont, CA: Pomona College). Charles K. Edmunds, "Permanent Relief from Famine in China: Yellow River, 'China's Great Sorrow,' Would Be Great Blessing If Properly Utilized," *The Trans-Pacific*, no. July (1921). Charles K. Edmunds, "Taming the Yellow River," *The Military Engineer* XIII, no. 70 (1921).

76. Shou-yi Chen, "The Influence of China on English Culture During the 18th Century" (University of Chicago, 1928). Shou-yi Chen, "John Webb: A Forgotten Page in the Early History of Sinology in Europe," *The Chinese Social and Political Science Review* XIX, no. 3 (1935). Shou-yi Chen, "Thomas Percy and His Chinese Studies," *The Chinese Social and Political Science Review* XX, no. 2 (1936). Shou-yi Chen, "Dr. Chen Interprets Far Eastern Situation; Sympathy for Chinese Grows," *The Student Life*, Sept. 27, 1941. Shou-yi Chen, "Higher Education and the Coming World Charter," in *Higher Education and the Coming World Charter. Today's Emergency by James A. Blaisdell* (Claremont, CA: Claremont Colleges Library, 1942). Kenneth E. Foster, *A Handbook of Ancient Chinese Bronzes*, Revised ed. (Claremont, CA: The Art Department of Pomona College, 1949). Charles B. Fahs, *Government in Japan* (New York, NY: Institute of Pacific Relations, 1940).

77. Frederick Osborn and Olin Wannamaker, "Letter from Trustees of Lingnan University," *Lingnan (Canton Christian College)* IX, no. 1 (1936).

78. Charles K. Edmunds, "Statement Regarding Conditions in China with Reference to Danger to Foreigners and General Peace," April 20, 1906. Trustees of Lingnan University, microfilm roll 3.

79. Ibid.

80. Ibid.

81. Edward Yihua Xü, "Liberal Arts Education in English at St. John's University," paper for the conference, "The American Context of China's Christian Colleges," Wesleyan University, September 5–7, 2003.

82. Corbett, *Lingnan University*, p. 8.

83. Andrew Happer's letter to Rev. F. F. Ellingwood, secretary of the Presbyterian Board of Missions, February 1894, Trustees of Lingnan University, microfilm roll 1.

84. Corbett, *Lingnan University*, p. 35.

85. Charles K. Edmunds, "Weights and Measures among the Chinese," year unknown, Charles K. Edmunds Papers, Honnold/Mudd Library at the Claremont Colleges.

86. Charles Edmunds' letter to W. Henry Grant, secretary-treasurer of the trustees of Canton Christian College, March 12, 1918. Trustees of Lingnan University, microfilm roll 6.

87. Elizabeth Edmunds Wheaton, "I Remember Prexy: Charles Keyser Edmunds, President, Pomona College, 1928–1941," p. 7. Edmunds Papers, Folder 1, year unknown, Honnold/Mudd Library, Claremont Colleges.

88. "Three Anniversaries." Edmunds Papers, Folder 5, Honnold/Mudd Library, Claremont Colleges, 1931, page no. unavailable.

89. Terrill E. Lautz, "The Mirror and the Wall: American Images of China," in *Chinese Images of the United States*, ed. Carola McGiffert (Washington, D.C.: The CSIS Press, 2005), pp. 127–33. Terrill E. Lautz, "Hopes and Fears of 60 Years: American Images of China, 1911–1972," in *China in the American Political Imagination*, ed. Carola McGiffert (Washington, D.C.: The CSIC Press, 2003), pp. 31–37. T. Christopher Jespersen, *American Images of China 1931–1949* (Stanford, CA: Stanford University Press, 1996).

90. The National Emergency Committee for the Christian Colleges in China

was located in New York City. Charles K. Edmunds' note and pledge on behalf of Pomona College to the National Emergency Committee on March 12, 1938. Archives of the United Board for Christian Higher Education in Asia, Box 7, Folder 167, Yale Divinity School Library.

91. Those colleges include Cheeloo University (Shantung), Furien Christian University, Ginling College, Hangchow Christian College, Hua Chung College, Hwa Nan College, Lingnan University, University of Nanking, University of Shanghai, Soochow University, West China Union University, and Yenching University.

92. Letter to Charles K. Edmunds from the Associated Boards for the Christian Colleges in China (my inference) on December 10, 1937. Archives of the United Board for Christian Higher Education in Asia, Box 7, Folder 167, Yale Divinity School Library.

93. Letter to Charles K. Edmunds from the Associated Boards for the Christian Colleges in China (my inference) on April 6, 1939. Archives of the United Board for Christian Higher Education in Asia, Box 7, Folder 167, Yale Divinity School Library.

94. Archives of the United Board for Christian Higher Education in Asia, Box 7, Folder 167, Yale Divinity School Library.

95. Record of the Testimonial Dinner for Dr. Charles K. Edmunds, New York, March 2, 1922, pp. 14–15. Trustees of Lingnan University, microfilm roll 39.

Conclusion

Memories and Legacies of Lingnan University

In this book, I have given a thematic account of a significant Sino-American higher educational institution in Canton (Guangzhou), while recognizing that this approach does not cover—nor does it intend to cover—all aspects of Lingnan University's history. In the hope of prompting further research on the subject, in this monograph I have confined myself to a particular historical topic—the formation of mutual ties between China and America in the sphere of tertiary education.[1] In other words, given the limitations of a case study, I should like to say that my aim is to throw out a minnow to catch a whale (*paozhuan yinyü*).

Sketched out in broad strokes, this book represents my rethinking of the Christian presence in China, particularly of the profound influence of China's Christian colleges in forming the evolving character of Sino-American exchanges, a role that still holds relevance to both sides today. The story of Lingnan connects South China to the outside world and the outside world to South China. The world of South China and the U.S.-China cultural encounter which took place there during the late nineteenth and the first half of the twentieth centuries are revealed to us through the prism of Lingnan, in a way comparable to Norman F. Cantor's depiction of the world of John of Gaunt in fourteenth century England.[2] Having nurtured for itself a relatively privileged life and environment for higher learning, Lingnan had become a modern college by the standards of its own historical moment. As an episode in the history of the U.S.-China relationship—a relationship not begun until the late eighteenth century—the Lingnan story leaves us with much to reflect upon.[3]

153

MEMORIES OF LINGNAN

The ties between China and America are many and close across time, space, and culture. One example will suffice here to give the flavor of the relationship. In 1957, an agreement was reached between the Pennsylvania State University and the Trustees of Lingnan University for the funding of a graduate assistantship in the Department of Agricultural Education of Pennsylvania State's College of Agriculture in honor of G. Weidman Groff, who had taught at Lingnan for thirty-four years as a field representative of the Penn State Mission to China. It was dedicated teachers and messengers like Groff who linked the two sides of the Pacific and their legacies continue still.

In what follows I offer some concluding thoughts on the legacy of Lingnan University, the adaptability of Christianity in China, encounters between China and the West, cultural migration, and multiculturalism in a globalizing world. But before turning to these matters, I want to start with two perceptions of Lingnan's self-image, one recorded in 1924 and the other in the late 1940s in the aftermath of the Sino-Japanese war.

On December 29, 1924, G. Weidman Groff wrote a newsletter to Penn State College describing the development of agricultural education at Canton Christian College:

I know how you like to hear the exciting events of our China experience. Here at Ling Nan [Lingnan]—the Canton Christian College—we have very little to offer in this respect, for our college has grown to be a modern college with a beautiful campus, and with the air of peace, protection and happiness that usually characterize the joyful college life . . .

The most interesting and inspiring part of our life and work is tied up in the details of the constructive side of our college program. I can truly have a very honest enthusiasm for our agricultural work, for I believe with all my heart that it has a very definite place in a peaceful China and a prosperous world. . . . The ultimate aim of an agricultural college is to formulate, direct and develop a practical service for the rural population of the region which it serves. Our college has made a substantial beginning in the field of agricultural education . . .

It has been the policy of our college to project our work in definite fields, as sericulture, horticulture, canning and preserving, and animal husbandry, into those regions needing help in these specific lines of agricultural development . . .

Our research in the botanical fields, study of stocks and varieties, methods of propagation, and our relationship with western plant and seed introduction agencies, will enable us to project a most helpful service in special fruit-producing regions like Lokong, easily accessible from Canton where, in a well-favored valley, thirty-six country villages, all with inhabitants with the surname Chung, await leadership in cooperative nursery, fruit production, and marketing projects, and in the organization of schools fitted for their needs. These are but a few of the opportunities awaiting us in rural reconstruction.[4]

Sometime in the late 1940s, an official document of Lingnan University provided a rather more ambitious self-portrait:

> We believe that Lingnan is in a special position to promote international relations in general and international trade in particular. . . . We recommend that ASAP [sic] Lingnan engage specialists in international relations and trade to do research and to make known to the public the result of such research. The Overseas Chinese have done so much for Lingnan. It is time now that Lingnan should do something for them. . . . A third type of special work done by the Lingnan faculty was that of plant introduction and exchange, begun in 1912. In that year the perfect [sic] flowered dessert papaya was introduced by Professor G. W. Groff to Lingnan from the Hawaiian Islands.[5]

Today, the Lingnan logo, designed by Sz-to Wai (Situ Wei), an artist, a fundraiser, and the founder and a former principal of the Lingnan middle schools, is displayed not only on the lush Sun Yat-sen University campus in Guangzhou, but also in Lingnan kindergartens, middle schools, and universities in Hong Kong, Shanghai, Seattle, San Francisco, and Atlanta, as well as in Australia, Indonesia, Malaysia, Singapore, and Vietnam. How is Lingnan University perceived today? Why do Lingnan's loyal alumni all over the world feel so much nostalgia for their college days fifty-five years after its forced merger with Sun Yat-sen University?

First, memories of Lingnan continue to evoke emotions akin to those associated with home and childhood. In November 1940, Lingnan's Agricultural College was forced to temporarily relocate to Pingshek (Pingshi), Guangdong during the Japanese occupation. Thirty years afterward, one alumnus, in a memoir entitled "Panoramic View of Pingshek" (*Pingshi fengqing hua*), reflected on his years in Pingshek in evocative language: "May the floating cloud carry me back to the beautiful land so like my home, where the verdant hills remain and the stream flows on ceaselessly."[6]

Second, remembering Lingnan involves an emotional attachment to the physical campus and shared residential life. Again, this attachment has its historical roots. In 1916, Helen H. Cassidy (faculty, 1916–1917) assisted Fung Hin Liu to develop the Women's Department at Canton Christian College. In a letter sent on her first visit to the college, she enthused:

> I am delighted with the situation of the College. Its buildings scattered upon the hill facing the river, with their combination of Chinese and western architecture, are an imposing and attractive group, and the residences with their

sloping green tiled roofs, deep verandas and many windows are spacious and inviting. From the hill are to be seen here and there, groves of the graceful bamboo, and towering pine trees, and green rice fields stretch away on every side. The Girls' School building is the one nearest the river. The view of this stream from our windows is enchanting, its surface reflecting the glories of sunset and moonrise.[7]

The ambiance of Lingnan left strong imprints on the minds of staff and students alike, regardless of their length of stay. In December 1970, at the Lingnan University Alumni Day dinner in San Francisco, alumnus Tsang Chiu-sam (Zeng Zhaosen) reminisced about the Lingnan past (*Lingnan wangshi*), associating it in particular with three college songs: the "Alma Mater Song," the "Lingnan Evening Song," and "Lingnan University: One Family."[8] While the music of all three songs resembled typical American alma mater songs, Tsang noted that the lyrics were all original Lingnanian productions, authentic and local. Written by Henry Blair Graybill, the lyrics of the "Alma Mater Song" read:

> Broad the plain before us reaches,
> Calm the tides in flow;
> Far the mountains ever guard us,
> On in strength we go.
> College, mother, calm thou standest,
> Wond'rous land our fathers gave us,
> True to both we are . . .
> In the years and strife before us,
> Never shall we fail.
> Courage, then, as joy thou give us,
> Alma Mater, Hail![9]

Tsang notes that the "Alma Mater Song" captures the undefeatable optimism and confidence of Lingnanians in the college cause. He continues by pointing out that the red and grey Lingnan logo (*xiaohui*) symbolizes the campus scene, portraying the White Cloud Mountain, lychee trees, and the Pearl River as seen from one of the college's main buildings, Swasey Hall (Huaishi Tang).[10]

Remembrance of a revered alma mater also takes the form of open discussions of the "Lingnan ethos" (*Lingnan jingshen*) among alumni through the circulation of print and visual media such as the noncommercial *Lingnan Alumni* (*Lingnan xueyou*) issued by the Guangzhou Lingnan Alumni Association and the *Lingnan Newsletter* (*Lingnan tongxun*) published by the Hong Kong Lingnan Alumni Association. One alumnus concludes that the Lingnan ethos embraces six chief qualities: a feeling of patriotism, support for democracy, the will to serve, courage, friendship, and the pursuit of a healthy lifestyle. These components of the Lingnan ethos give it distinctiveness (*dutexing*), universality (*pubianxing*), and a specific cultural context (*shidaixing*):

> Its distinctiveness originates in our national way of life and thinking. In an age of cultural and ideological exchanges between East and West, the Lingnan ethos also bears some relation to China's exposure to Western values and ideas. It therefore reflects a universal love of humanity. Our shared human inheritance, however, is to a certain extent adaptable to different lifestyles in different circumstances. This is the so-called contextuality [of the Lingnan ethos].[11]

Finally, memories of Lingnan take the form of a nostalgic attachment to an extinct educational establishment and an episode in the propagation of American higher education, American values, and business management in China that has yet to run its full course. Such memories have given rise to a unique Lingnan lexicon. Phrases such as "Kangle yuan," (Honglok campus), "nanda yijiaqin" (Lingnan as one family), "weishen, weiguo, wei Lingnan" (For God, for country, for Lingnan), "Lingnan niu" (the Lingnan cow), "Lingnan shizi" (the Lingnan lion) and "honghui ernü" (Children of red and grey) have drawn together Lingnanians from all over the world.[12] Such sayings have formed a channel through which Chinese elements have merged with "external homogenizing forces."[13] These shared memories of Lingnan are strongly focused on the Lingnan identity, avoiding any divisive political elements.

THE ADAPTABILITY OF CHRISTIANITY IN CHINA? A FEW THOUGHTS ON THE LINGNAN EXPERIENCE

What position did Christianity enjoy at Lingnan which, like many other tertiary institutions, owed its origins to Christian missions as well as to Christian ideas of learning? What did secularization mean in the Lingnan context?

The college's link to Christianity cannot be assessed without considering three major factors that impacted Lingnan, each with important historical, financial, political, and social implications. First, there is the question of Lingnan's place within the Christian colleges in China, founded as it was as a Christian institution of higher learning. Second, the Christian link needs to be understood against the worldwide trend of secularization infiltrating universities and colleges at that time. Third, the impact of the Chinese nationalist movements of the twentieth century must be considered. Against the background of these three major factors, the Christian connection remained present but complex throughout the Lingnan story.

Two conflicting but concurrent tendencies in relation to Christianity are suggested in the post-1925 Lingnan sources. One was Chinese national-ism and the impact of anti-Christianity and secularization movements on Christianity in China. In the upsurge of violence experienced in 1925 (dis-cussed in various chapters above), Lingnan's faculty made some changes to the college's religious policies and practices. As a result, attendance at Christian congregations became voluntary, courses on Christianity were no longer required, and "the daily chapel service would be changed into a morning assembly."[14] However, it would be a mistake to assume that the Christian link was severed at Lingnan. On the contrary, what emerged from troubled times was an adapted version of the college's religious tra-dition.

To make sense of the adaptability of Christianity at Lingnan, we need to examine the figure of Chung Wing Kwong, Lingnan's first Chinese president. A pious Christian baptized in Hong Kong in 1899,[15] Chung strongly believed that theological education, as an essential supplement to the study of law, was necessary to rectify people's intuitive selfishness and greed, and to enhance the conscience (*zijue xing*) of the national citi-zenry (*guomin*) by imparting the spirit of Christ to students.[16] Records show that, even after 1925, some board meetings of the board of Chinese directors started with prayers.[17] In 1937–1938, half of the religion depart-ment's courses—although not prescribed by the Ministry of Education of the Chinese Nationalist government in Nanjing—were on Christianity. Courses offered included Christian Ethics, the Social Teachings of the Bible, the Person of Jesus Christ, Creative Personalities in Christian His-tory, Old Testament Introduction, New Testament Introduction, Chris-tianity and Chinese Culture, Modern Christian Thought, and Christianity and Modern Problems.[18]

What was most interesting was the affiliation of Canton Union Theo-logical College with Lingnan University in the 1940s, in spite of the "unof-ficial" status of the former institution.

On August 1, 1941, representatives of Lingnan University and the Union Theological College met in the tea room of the Student Union at Hong Kong University to discuss the forming of a special relationship.[19] Present were Lingnan's president Lee Ying Lam, dean Chu Yau-kwong, and Henry S. Frank; the Theological College was represented by presi-dent John S. Kunkle, Rev. R. O. Hall (retired), Rev. Frank Short, and Rev. Alton. Amalgamation was the express wish of both parties. Lee Ying Lam welcomed the prospect of affiliation because a similar question "had been considered by Lingnan University ten years ago."[20] Henry Frank noted that "such affiliation would make a contribution to the religious leadership in the university which would be difficult to provide in any other way."[21]

In the end, a general agreement was reached to move the Theological College to the Lingnan campus while letting the former retain a high degree of independence. John Kunkle cited the example of Chicago University and its Divinity School as a precedent for such a special relationship. Following the Sino-Japanese war, in 1945 the Union Theological College officially moved to the Lingnan campus.[22] In the second semester of the academic year 1945–1946, there were sixteen students (twelve men and four women) enrolled in the theological college.[23] In Lingnan's 1948 Planning Survey, information on the Theological College was not disclosed—an omission which in the present author's speculation stemmed from its problematic status as an educational institution that could not be registered with the Guomindang government, and as an organization that, while part of Lingnan, retained its separate leadership and structure. The Union Theological College was administered by the American Presbyterian Church, the United Brethren, the Church of England, the English Wesleyans, the London Missionary Society, the United Church of Canada, and the New Zealand Presbyterian missions. In December 1949, a new building for the theological college was dedicated on the Lingnan campus.

A variety of other sources likewise demonstrate the complex Christian presence at Lingnan.[24] For instance, during the Sino-Japanese war religious work at Lingnan was described as "very active," according to Lee Ying Lam.[25]

Two further examples may be cited here. Historically, the major catchment area for Lingnan's students was Guangdong Province, more than 90 percent of students coming from Guangdong and one-fourth from Hong Kong.[26] In the late 1940s, in an attempt to broaden its pool of candidates, Lingnan was eager to strengthen its Christian ties both inside and outside China by admitting those who had completed their secondary education in Christian middle schools in places such as Hunan, Guangxi, and Fujian, or graduates of government-sponsored schools who "have become or are aspiring to become Christians."[27]

In June 1949 Henry S. Frank, then Lingnan's Provost, filed a confidential report with the Trustees of Lingnan University in New York. In the report, commenting on the achievements of Ch'en Su-ching, then Lingnan's president, Frank noted that "although not a professing Christian, [Ch'en] gained [the] confidence of the various mission bodies in Canton, to an extent not equaled for decades."[28] Frank also noted that, amidst political uncertainty about the looming Communist takeover, the regular Wednesday prayer meetings had been "useful occasions for arriving at a consensus (as opposed to a policy) without calling special meetings which would themselves have created a certain emergency atmosphere."[29]

These examples suggest that, at Lingnan, ways were found to adapt and "layer" a Christian presence at a time when the nationalization and secularization of higher education were making rapid headway on the national and international scene. As researchers shift their attention to the expression of local versions of the Christian tradition in indigenous societies and cultures,[30] the Lingnan story represents one such native voice.

LINGNAN AS A REGIONAL, NATIONAL, AND INTERNATIONAL UNIVERSITY: A LEGACY

As a self-financed institution of higher learning, Lingnan deserves pride of place in any account of the U.S.-China cultural encounter and of Chinese education. As I have noted throughout the book, Lingnan's growth, resilience, and success were partly accounted for by entrepreneurial management. Other aspects of the Lingnan legacy are also worthy of acknowledgement here.

The May 1948 "Report on the First Phase: Lingnan University Planning Survey" shows that plans were in progress to further "build the university as rapidly as practicable into a national or international institution."[31] As a regional, national, and ultimately international university, Lingnan had to balance a number of different tracks of strategic development. One plan, for instance, called for the acceptance of "a relatively greater proportion of students from provinces in other regions of China [than Guangdong Province]."[32] Emphasizing programs of local importance, in the words of a Lingnanian, might be a good idea politically, "since the attitude of provincial leaders might be more favorable toward schools with strong local significance."[33] A document drafted in late 1947 underlined "to make Lingnan more national or [sic] less provincial" as one of the three principles that would guide the future educational policy of the college.[34] The other two principles were "to maintain quality first" and to develop projects suitable to Lingnan in its local setting. Yet another plan proposed a special school, "possibly in Hong Kong, to cater to the children of the Chinese abroad." The justifications for the latter plan were put forward by James Henry in financial terms:[35]

> A school which would take care of several hundred youngsters from all over the world and offer what their parents want for them more than anything else—a sound training in written Chinese—would create no financial worries for the Chinese Board of Directors. It would build up a grateful constitu-

ency which, with the increasing group of regular ex-students, could be depended upon for almost unlimited support.

Despite the different plans made to express different priorities, there was a consensus that "Lingnan can concentrate to a great extent on local needs and yet remain a diversified and balanced university." The college's 1948 Planning Survey explained the reasoning behind this: "Lingnan is in a position to play a role of outstanding importance in the region. . . . [E]ven if it concentrated on playing a national or international role, it might most effectively do so by stressing regionalism, as did the University of North Carolina in this country."[36]

Another aspect of Lingnan's legacy had to do with its efforts to maintain its political neutrality and to fight off its "foreignness" and elitism. After the Sino-Japanese war, at a time when Lingnan was seeking ways to expand its sources of funding, it proceeded gingerly to guard against the possible danger of being viewed as an "instrument" of "American policy." In a letter to J. Leighton Stuart in 1947, American Ambassador to China, Henry F. Frank, then Lingnan's provost, voiced such a concern:[37]

> In their own interests, therefore, the Embassy and the Department [of State] should do everything possible to avoid thinking, or letting others think, of possible grants to these institutions as being made for the purpose of cultivating friendship toward the United States, or of extending American influence. . . . As you know we would have . . . to disavow these as being among the purpose for which either Lingnan or Yenching was founded or is being operated.

Archives reveal that providing education to students from less well-to-do families was also under serious considerations in Lingnan's planning at a time when Lingnan was hard pressed financially. Lingnan had explored possible sources of scholarships for academically deserving but economically disadvantaged students. Making education—and higher education in particular—accessible to ordinary Chinese is an issue very relevant in China today.[38] As the Chinese government works increasingly hard to build a "harmonious society"[39] and to scrap the image of poverty, it is setting its sights on the rural areas. Seeing agriculture as the "key to China's growth,"[40] China recently launched its "building a new countryside" campaign, with one of its major targets being education—something which is still a privilege inaccessible to the majority of peasants.[41]

CULTURAL ENCOUNTER AND MIGRATION

In detailing the clash between academic liberalism and the control exercised by the Guomindang (Nationalist Party) at the National Southwest

Associated University (Xinan Lianda, Lianda)—an amalgam of Beijing University, Qinghua University, and Nankai University in exile during the Japanese occupation of 1937 to 1945—John Israel comments that "[f]oreign educational models had been borrowed, often without modification to suit Chinese conditions."[42] By contrast, as we have seen, the Lingnan model suggests a different paradigm.

The story of Lingnan reflects some patterns in the cultural encounter between the United States and China which constituted a set of mutual interchanges between the two sides of the Pacific. (See photo 1; photo 2.) The result of this encounter was a two-way migration of religions, ideas, higher education, and cultures, hinging on the cultural, political, and social context of both nations at specific times and places. Thus, current U.S.–China cultural exchanges are built upon historical patterns. As the work of Qian Nian has shown, the experience of mainland Chinese students studying and working in America since the opening-up of China in 1978 demonstrates the power of history to dictate the nature of such interactions.[43] The Lingnan enterprise, as one episode in the complex story of Sino-American relations, ought to be placed against a broad historical backdrop: the arrival of Europeans and Americans in South China, particularly from the late eighteenth century, swept the once indomitable Qing empire—which itself had devoured vast Eurasian territories in the eighteenth century[44]—off its feet.

In discussing the Western impact on higher education in Asia, Philip G. Altbach identified the changed Asian relationship with the West in the post–World War II era as a movement from a relationship of inequality to one of conscious selection.[45] In the case of Lingnan, the evidence indicates

Photo 1. *"The Gift Which Traveled 12,000 Miles from Penn State to Lingnan."* Lingnan *(Canton Christian College), vol. VI, no. 4, November 1930.*

Photo 2. *"Our Soccer Team."* Lingnan *(Canton Christian College),*
vol. VI, no. 4, November 1930.

that the interplay between the United States model and the Chinese educational system was more measured and layered, involving more adaptation than imposition, and more conscious selection than blind adoption. Lingnan's flexibility and its rapid growth originated in its pluralist attitude in general, while importing into Chinese education the American ideal of a liberal arts education with its emphasis on the pursuit of truth and the Christian concept of education of the whole person.

Several points are worth considering here. First, Lingnan reflected the inner dynamics and flexibility of the American model of higher learning. Various actors including American and Chinese educators and administrators, overseas Chinese pupils, and United States exchange students brought America to the Chinese campus. The parallels between the formation and development of American and Chinese higher learning institutions are amply illustrated by the emergence of Christian colleges in China in the later nineteenth and early twentieth centuries. "Most [American] private colleges," Thomas B. Coburn observes, "were founded by Christian educators, and most of their presidents and many of their faculty were clergymen."[46] Given Christianity's formidable presence on American college campuses in the nineteenth century, "the educational mission of these [institutions] was fundamentally Christian, and administrators and faculty sought not only to instill in their students Christian values but also to educate them for the ministry."[47] This dual process of Christian character-building and the broad pursuit of humane learning were transferred to the China scene, particularly at the outset. In Paul Davis' words, "[t]hose dedicated people who did such a constructive job in developing the Christian Colleges in China were manifesting Christianity in the most intelligent and effective way possible."[48]

There were also parallels between the growth of Lingnan and general trends in higher education in the United States, such as the increase in enrollments and the expansion of the curriculum. In contrast to English, French, and German traditions of higher learning, Philip G. Altbach argues that the American university is characterized by

> [a] willingness of academic institutions to serve quite specific employment needs, the relative flexibility of the departmental structure, an academic governance process that permits rapid changes in the curriculum, and a tradition in the academic profession itself that encourages rapid adjustments all contribute to the ability of the American university to respond to societal needs.[49]

In Robert Nisbet's view, this adaptability to societal needs has led higher education in the American mold to subject itself to external demands and thus to "give up the idea of liberal education."[50] The place of social and political considerations in higher education has long exercised Lingnanians in their discussions of vocational learning; the value of medical, agricultural, sericultural, and engineering majors; the differentiation of educational levels; and the meeting of local needs. In this sense, in addition to its dual mandate of liberal learning and Christian formation, the Lingnan system brought together a combination of local and international elements.

A second general point that can be made is that, standing as it did "in the very forefront of the higher institutions of learning in China,"[51] Lingnan diversified modern Chinese education and became a successful alternative to traditional Chinese models. "A system that was willing to adjust itself to the changes in the demand for different types of education," Joseph Ben-David argues, "was in a better position to expand than one that resisted change and adjustment."[52] Lingnan's integration into the Chinese educational scene was achieved through involvement in local problems, sometimes against the resistance of the local establishment, sometimes in collaboration with it. This achievement has given Lingnan an enduring place in the history of Chinese education.

Third, the Lingnan experience played an important role in efforts by many types of participants to compel both Chinese and foreign actors to look beyond their own traditions to find ways to tackle educational reform. In this process of interaction and mutual influence, many issues of biculturalism and multiculturalism arose. Advanced in modern China studies by Philip Huang, the concept of biculturalism refers to "the simultaneous participation by one person in two different cultures." Regarding China's contact with Western culture, Huang argues that historians should move beyond "the polarized world of imperialism and anti-imperialist nationalism," which insists on "the necessary triumph of one or the other." He suggests that historians emphasize rather "the coexistential over the conflictual side of biculturality." In response, Prasenjit Duara has pushed the discussion forward by pointing to the complex role played by nation-states in regulating both indigenous and transnational cultural affiliations.[53]

Finally, I wish to finish with a contemporary example. A recent visit I made to Japan (November 20–26, 2005) has provided further validation for this line of thinking. My room in the Osaka Hilton, part of an American hotel chain, contained the following items: Kimono bath robes, green tea, a toilet equipped with a bidet, the *New Testament*, the *Buddhist Scriptures*, a piece of Kimono painting, and Japanese wooden sliding windows—all exemplifying the myriad patterns of adaptation, interaction, and modification involved in the process of fitting together indigenous and foreign elements in both a local setting and a global context.

NOTES

1. I am grateful to Stein Haugom Olsen for alerting me to the character of Lingnan primarily as an American-Chinese venture and to the fact that the kind of exchange exemplified by Lingnan may have had parallels elsewhere, or may have taken place in a different way. Likewise, my gratitude is expressed to John Fitzgerald who reminded me of the role of Chinese-Australian businessmen, such as Ma Ying-Piu (Ma Yingbiao), in funding Lingnan and serving on its board.

2. Norman F. Cantor, *The Last Knight: The Twilight of the Middle Ages and the Birth of the Modern Era* (New York: Harper Perennial, 2005), introduction.

3. Jonathan D. Spence, "The Once and Future China," *Foreign Policy*, no. 146 (2005): 44–46. In this article, Spence reflects on the connection between China's history and its future.

4. "A Review of the Publications and Unpublished Written Works of the Late Professor G. Weidman Groff, Lingnan University, Canton China (Covering the Period 1918–1953)," prepared by John Hsueh-Ming Chen, The Pennsylvania State University, November 1957. Archives of the Trustees of Lingnan University, Group 14, Box 18, Folder 258, Yale Divinity School Library.

5. Guangdongsheng dang'an'guan [Guangdong provincial archives], Untitled and undated document [possibly 1947, my inference], file # 38-4-58.

6. Mi Shi, "Pingshi fengqing hua," (Panoramic view of Pingshek) *Lingnan tongxun* [Lingnan Newsletter], Lingnan Alumni Association in Hong Kong, vol. 69 (October 15, 1972): 16–17.

7. Letter from Helen H. Cassidy, dated October 10, 1916. Trustees of Lingnan University, microfilm roll 37.

8. Tsang Chiu-sam (Zeng Zhaosen), *Muxiao sanshou geqü yishu* [Reminiscences of the three songs about the Alma Mater] (Hong Kong: Hong Kong Progressive Educational Press, 1971).

9. Ibid, pp. 4–5.

10. For relevant information, see the respective websites of the Lingnan Foundation at Yale University, Sun Yat-sen University, and Lingnan University in Hong Kong, at http://www.lingnanfoundation.org/, http://www.lingnan.org, and http://www.ln.edu.hk.

11. He Tiehua, "Lingnan jingshen zhi fayang guangda" [Maintaining the Lingnan Ethos], *Lingnan tongxun* [Lingnan newsletter], vol. 9 (September 1, 1965): 14.

12. Zheng Shurong, "Tan Lingnan niu" [On the Lingnan cow], *Lingnan xiaoyou jianxun* [Newsletter of Lingnan Alumni], issue 3 (November 1981): 27.

13. T. N. Harper, "Empire, Diaspora, and the Languages of Globalism, 1850–1914," ed. by A. G. Hopkins, *Globalization in World History* (New York, N.Y.: W. W. Norton, 2002), p. 155.

14. Edward J. M. Rhoads, "Lingnan's Response to the Rise of Chinese Nationalism: The Shakee Incident (1925)," in *American Missionaries in China: Papers from Harvard Seminars*, ed. Kwang-Ching Liu (Cambridge, MA: Harvard University Press, 1966), 203.

15. "Lingnan daxue xiaozhang Zhong Rongguang boshi xingshu" [The life of Lingnan University President Dr. Chung Wing Kwong], Sili Lingnan daxue jiaozhiyuan lüli [Resumes of faculty and staff at Lingnan University], 1931–1948, Guangdongsheng dang'an'guan, file # 38-1-83.

16. "Zhong Rongguang zhuan" [Biography of Chung Wing Kwong], Guangdongsheng dang'an'guan, file # 38-4-70.

17. "Xiaodonghui di shisan ci huiyi jilu" [Minutes of the 13th meeting of the Board of Directors], December 5, 1929, "Sili Lingnan daxue xiaodonghui huiyi jilu" [Minutes of the Board of Directors of Lingnan University], Guangdongsheng dang'an'guan, file # 38-1-18.

18. Charles Hodge Corbett, *Lingnan University: A Short History Based Primarily on the Records of the University's American Trustees* (New York, NY: The Trustees of Lingnan University, 1963), p. 197.

19. "Proposed Affiliation of Canton Union Theological College and Lingnan University," Group R: 8, Box 107, Mr. and Mrs. J. S. Kunkle, Yale Divinity School Library.

20. Ibid.

21. Ibid.

22. Corbett, *Lingnan University*, p. 148.

23. Academic Year, Semester II, 1945–1946, Lingnan University, Guangdongsheng dang'an'guang, file # 38-4-59.

24. "Present Christian Activities on the Lingnan University Campus," December 16, 1949. Trustees of Lingnan University, microfilm roll 26.

25. Lee Ying Lam's letter to Henry S. Frank (in Berkeley, CA) on May 30, 1944, Guangdongsheng dang'an'guan, "Lingda xiaozhang Li Yinglin xinjian" [Correspondence of Li Yinglin, president of Lingnan University], file # 38-4-8 (2).

26. The statistics obviously included Hong Kong as part of Guangdong.

27. Untitled and undated [late 1947, my inference] document, "Renshi cailiao" [Personnel files], Guangdongsheng dang'an'guan, file # 38-4-58.

28. Henry S. Frank, "Confidential Report to the Trustees of Lingnan University," June 1, 1949, Trustees of Lingnan University, microfilm roll 24.

29. Ibid.

30. Two examples are Kim-Kwong Chan, *Towards a Contextual Ecclesiology: The Catholic Church in the People's Repubic of China (1979–1983): Its Life and Theological Implications* (Hong Kong: Phototech System Ltd, 1987). Mark R. Mullins, *Christianity Made in Japan: A Study of Indigenous Movements* (Honolulu, HI: University of Hawai'i Press, 1998).

31. "Report on the First Phase, Lingnan University Planning Survey," prepared by Raymond Rich & William Cherin Associates, in New York City in May 1948. Group R: 8, Box 107, Folder Mr. and Mrs. J. S. Kunkle, Yale Divinity School Library.

32. Ibid.

33. Ibid.

34. Untitled and undated [late 1947, my inference] document, "Renshi cailiao" [Personnel files], Guangdongsheng dang'an'guan, file # 38-4-58.

35. "Report on the First Phase, Lingnan University Planning Survey," prepared by Raymond Rich & William Cherin Associates, in New York City in May 1948. Group R: 8, Box 107, Folder Mr. and Mrs. J. S. Kunkle, Yale Divinity School Library.

36. Ibid.

37. Henry S. Frank to J. Leighton Stuart, June 10, 1947, Guangdongsheng dang'an'guan, file # 38-4-8 (2).

38. Gerard A. Postiglione, ed., *Education and Social Change in China: Inequality in a Market Economy* (Armonk, NY: M. E. Sharpe, 2006).

39. Tiejun Wen, "Tackling Rural Issues," *Beijing Review*, October 6 2005, pp. 22–24.

40. Xinzhen Lan, "Agriculture: The Key to China's Growth," *Beijing Review*, October 6, 2005, pp. 18–21.

41. Jianhua Feng, "Rural Education: Struggling with Bare Essentials," *Beijing Review*, October 6, 2005, pp. 31–33.

42. John Israel, *Lianda: A Chinese University in War and Revolution* (Stanford, CA: Stanford University Press, 1998), p. 95.

43. Ning Qian (Translated by T. K. Chu from Chinese), *Chinese Students Encounter America* (Seattle, WA: University of Washington Press, 2002). Richard and Ross H. Munro Bernstein, *The Coming Conflict with China* (New York: Vintage Books, 1998).

44. Peter C. Perdue, *China Marches West: The Qing Conquest of Central Eurasia* (Cambridge, MA: The Belknap Press of Harvard University Press, 2005).

45. Philip G. Altbach, *Comparative Higher Education: Knowledge, the University, and Development* (Greenwich, Conn.: Ablex Publishing, 1998), p. 56.

46. Thomas B. Coburn, "Asia and the Undergraduate Curriculum," in Suzanne Wilson Barnett and Van Jay Symons, eds., *Asia in the Undergraduate Curriculum: A Case for Asian Studies in Liberal Arts Education* (Armonk, N.Y.: M.E. Sharpe, 2000), p. 25.

47. Ibid.

48. Letter from Paul Davis to Yorke Allen Jr., president of the Board of Trustees of Lingnan University, dated June 28, 1960. Group 14, box 14, Folder 178, Yale Divinity School Library.

49. Philip G. Altbach, *Comparative Higher Education: Knowledge, the University, and Development*. (Greenwich, Conn.: Ablex Publishing, 1998), p. 93.

50. Robert Nisbet, *The Degradation of the Academic Dogma: The University in America, 1945–70* (New Brunswick, NJ: 1997). Edward Shils, *The American Ethic* (Chicago: University of Chicago Press, 1984).

51. Letter from W. W. Willoughby to Charles Edmunds, Constitutional Advisor to the Chinese Government, dated April 15, 1917. Trustees of Lingnan University, microfilm roll 39.

52. Joseph Ben-David, *American Higher Education* (New York: McGraw-Hill, 1972), p. 5.

53. Philip Huang, "Biculturality in Modern China and in Chinese Studies," *Modern China* 26, no. 1 (January 2000): 3–31. Presenjit Duara, "Response to Philip Huang's 'Biculturality in Modern China and in Chinese Studies,'" *Modern China* 26, no. 1 (January 2000): 32–37.

Glossary

Bao 包

Bund (changdi) 長堤

Cen Bozhu 岑伯著

Chang Pi-shih (Zhang Bishi) 張弼士

chedi de xiandai hua 徹底的現代化

Chen Ce 陳策

Chen Guofu 陳果夫

Chen Jiwu 陳輯五

Chen Jiongming 陳炯明

Chen Lifu 陳立夫

Chen Lianbo 陳廉伯

Chen Shou-yi 陳受頤

Ch'en Su-ching (Chen Xujing) 陳序經

Chen Yinque 陳寅恪

Cheng Tiangu 程天固

Chu Yau-kwong (Zhu You-guang) 朱有光

Chung Wing Kwong (Zhong Rongguang) 鐘榮光

danmin 蛋民

dutexing 獨特性

duoyuan hua 多元化

Fu Lun (Henry S. Frank) 富倫

fugu 復古

gaodeng xiaoxue (elementary or primary school) 高等小學

Gao Lufu (George Weidman Groff) 高魯甫

Ge Peili (Henry B. Graybill) 葛佩理

Gezhi shuyuan 格致書院

gonghan 公函

Guangdong hesheng shenqi 廣東閤省紳耆

guobao 國寶

guoji de Lingnan daxue 國際的嶺南大學

haiwai huaqiao 海外華僑

Hanlin yuan 翰林院

Ho-kow (Hekou) 河口

Honam 河南

honghui ernu 紅灰兒女

Honglok (Kangle) 康樂

Huacheng 花城

Huaqiao xuexiao 華僑學校

169

Huaishi tang 懷士堂

Huang Nianmei (Olin Wannamaker) 黃念美

Jianshe ting 建設廳

jiaohui xuexiao 教會學校

jiaoyu shehuihua 教育社會化

jisu 寄宿

jinri jiaoyu de jichu shi zai chan-
ye 今日教育的基礎是在產業

Kangle yuan 康樂園

Kukong (Qujiang) 曲江

Law Yau-tsit (Agnes, Luo
Youjie) 羅有節

Lee Ying Lam (Li Yinglin) 李應
林

Lei Fuk-lam (Li Fulin) 李福林

Leung Tsau Ming (Liang
Jiuming) 梁就明

Lianda 聯大

Liang Cheng 梁誠

Liang Jingdun (Clinton N.
Laird) 梁敬敦

Lin Liru 林礪儒

Lingnan daxue 嶺南大學

Lingnan jingshen 嶺南精神

Lingnan kexue zazhi 嶺南科學雜
誌

Lingnan niu 嶺南牛

Lingnan shizi 嶺南獅子

Lingnan tongxun 嶺南通訊

Lingnan xiaoyou 嶺南校友

Lingnan xuetang 嶺南學堂

Lingnan xuexiao 嶺南學校

Lingnan xueyuan 嶺南學院

Liu Fung Hin (Liao Fengxian) 廖
奉獻

Liu Fung Yan (Liao Fengen) 廖
奉恩

Lu You tang (Luk Yau Hall) 陸
祐堂

Ma Ying-Piu 馬應彪

Mading tang (Martin Hall)
馬丁堂

Mei Shanda (Edmund W.
Meisenhelder, III) 梅善達

meiguo de xuewen 美國的學問

Meihsien (Meixian) 梅縣

minzhong hua 民眾化

Nanda gongren gongji hui
南大工人共濟會

nanda yijiaqin 南大一家親

Nonggong ting 農工廳

nuxue 女學

paozhuan yinyu 拋磚引玉

pixiang qianbo 皮相淺薄

Pingshek (Pingshi) 坪石

Pingshi fengqing hua 坪石風情
畫

pubianxing 普遍性

quanpan xihua 全盤西化

quanqiu Lingnanren Xianggang
datuanju 全球嶺南人香港大團
聚

Sanshui xian 三水縣

Shanam (Shanan) 沙南

Shanghai College (Hujiang
daxue) 滬江大學

Shen Zengtong (Shum Cheng
Tung) 沈曾桐

shengming xian 生命線

Shibo si 市泊司

Shidafu 士大夫

shidaixing 時代性

shihe Zhongguo zhi xuyao 適合中國之需要

shixing renge zhi jiaoyu 施行人格之教育

shiying Zhongguo shehui 適應中國社會

Sili Lingnan daxue 私立嶺南大學

Sun Foh (Sun Fo, Sun Ke) 孫科

Sun Yat-sen University (Zhongshan daxue) 中山大學

Sz-to Wai (Situ Wei) 司徒衛

Taitsuen (Lingda cun) 嶺大村 (韶關仙人廟)

Tam Lai-Ting (Tan Liting) 譚禮庭

Tsang Chiu-sam (Zeng Zhaosen) 曾昭森

Wanguo gongbao 萬國公報

Wang Li 王力

weishen, weiguo, wei Lingnan 爲神、爲國、爲嶺南

Wu Hon Man (Hu Hanmin) 胡漢民

Wu Yuey Len (Wu Ruilin) 伍銳麟

Wu Zhande (James T. Wu) 伍沾德

Xiguan 西關

Xinan Lianda 西南聯大

Xinan shehui jingji yanjiusuo 西南社會經濟研究所

xiandai hua 現代化

Xiang Bianwen (Benjamin C. Henry) 香便文

Xiang Yage (James McClure Henry) 香雅各

xiaohui 校徽

Xin fenghuang cun 新鳳凰村

Xu Chongqing 許崇清

xueshu 學術

xunzhao yitiao chulu 尋找一條出路

Yantai (Dengzhou) 煙臺 (登州)

Yan Wenshi (Charles K. Edmunds) 晏文士

Yangcheng 羊城

yangcheng kexue zhi rencai 養成科學之人才

yitiaolong jiaoyu 一條龍教育

Yin Shijia (Oscar F. Wisner) 尹士嘉

yingyong 應用

Zhaowa tang (Java Hall) 爪窪堂

Zhongguo jiaohui daxue yanjiu zhongxin 中國教會大學研究中心

Zhongshan daxue Lingnan xueyuan 中山大學嶺南學院

zhongxue 中學

Zhujiang sanjiaozhou (Pearl River Delta) 珠江三角洲

Zou Haibin 鄒海濱

zuoyu yingcai, fuwu shehui 作育英才, 服務社會

CHRISTIAN COLLEGES AND UNIVERSITIES IN CHINA

Protestant Institutions

1. Dongwu daxue (Soochow University, in Soochow) 東吳大學
2. Fujian xiehe daxue (Fukien Christian University, in Foochow) 福建協和大學
3. Huanan nu wenli xueyuan (Hwa Nan College, in Foochow) 華南女文理學院
4. Huaxi xiehe daxue (West China Union University, in Chengdu, founded in 1911) 華西協和大學
5. Huazhong daxue (Huachung University, in Wuchang) 華中大學
6. Hujiang daxue (University of Shanghai, or Shanghai College) 滬江大學
7. Jiling daxue (University of Nanking, in Nanking) 金陵大學
8. Jinling nu wenli xueyuan (Ginling College in Nanking) 金陵女文理學院
9. Lingnan daxue (Canton Christian College, Lingnan University) 嶺南大學
10. Qilu daxue (Shantung Christian University, also Cheeloo University, in Jinan) 齊魯大學
11. Shanghai nuzi yixueyuan (Women's Christian Medical College, in Shanghai) 上海女子醫學院
12. Sheng yuehan daxue (St. John's University, in Shanghai) 聖約翰大學
13. Xiangya yixueyuan (Hsiang-Ya Medical College, also Yale-in-China, in Changsha) 湘雅醫學院
14. Yanjing daxue (Yenching University, in Peiking) 燕京大學
15. Zhejiang daxue (Hangchou University) 浙江大學

Roman Catholic Institutions

16. Furen daxue (Catholic University, in Peking) 輔仁大學
17. Jingu daxue (Tsinku University, in Tientsin) 津沽大學
18. Zhendan daxue (Aurora University, in Shanghai) 震旦大學

Selected Bibliography

"Accident Takes Life of Charles Keyser Edmunds." "Lingnan Mourns Edmunds." *The Pomona College Bulletin Newsletter*, January 1949, 1–2.

A Romantic Achievement of Chinese and American Cooperation: Illustrated Historical Sketch. New York: Trustees of Lingnan University, 1941.

Aikman, David. *Jesus in Beijing: How Christianity Is Transforming China and Changing the Global Balance of Power*. D.C.: Regnery Publishing, 2003.

Altbach, Philip G. *Comparative Higher Education: Knowledge, the University, and Development*. Greenwich, Conn.: Ablex Publishing, 1998.

Anderson, Gerald H., ed. *Biographical Dictionary of Christian Missions*. New York: Macmillan Reference, 1998.

Anderson, Mary Raleigh. *A Cycle in the Celestial Kingdom, or Protestant Mission Schools for Girls in South China (1827 to the Japanese Invasion)*. Mobile, Ala.: Heiter-Starke Printing Co., 1943.

Bays, Daniel H., "Chinese Protestant Christianity Today." *The China Quarterly* 174, Special Issue: Religion in China Today (2003): 488–504.

———, ed. *Christianity in China: From the Eighteenth Century to the Present*. Stanford, Calif.: Stanford University Press, 1996.

Bays, Daniel H., and Grant Wacker, eds. *The Foreign Missionary Enterprise at Home: Explorations in North American Cultural History*. Tuscaloosa, Ala.: University of Alabama Press, 2003.

Bays, Daniel H., and Ellen Widmer, eds. *China's Christian Colleges: Transpacific Connections, 1900–1950*. Forthcoming.

173

Beeching, Jack, *The Chinese Opium Wars.* San Diego: Harcourt Brace Jovanovich, Publishers, 1975.

Ben-David, Joseph. *American Higher Education.* New York: McGraw-Hill Book Company, 1972.

Benson, George C. S., et al. *A Brief History of the Group Plan of the Claremont College.* Claremont, Calif.: Claremont University Center, 1993.

Bernard, Robert J. *An Unfinished Dream: A Chronicle of the Group Plan of the Claremont Colleges.* Claremont, Calif.: The Castle Press, 1982.

Bernstein, Richard, and Ross H. Munro. *The Coming Conflict with China.* New York: Vintage Books, 1998.

Bliss, Edwin Munsell. *Encyclopedia of Missions.* New York: Funk and Wagnells, 1891.

Bonk, Jonathan J. *Missions and Money: Affluence as a Western Missionary Problem.* Maryknoll, N.Y.: Orbis Books, 1990.

Brackett, Frank P. *Granite and Sagebrush: Reminiscences of the First Fifty Years of Pomona College.* Los Angeles: The Ward Ritchie Press, 1944.

Britt, Albert. *Ellen Browning Scripps: Journalist and Idealist.* Claremont, Calif.: The University Press, 1960.

Brook, Timothy, and Bob Tadashi Wakabayashi, eds. *Opium Regimes: China, Britain, and Japan, 1839–1952.* Berkeley, Calif.: University of California Press, 2000.

Brown, G. Thompson. *Christianity and the People's Republic of China.* Atlanta: John Knox Press, 1986.

Brubacher, John S., and Willis Rudy. *Higher Education in Transition: A History of American Colleges and Universities.* 4th ed. New Brunswick, N.J.: Transaction Publishers, 1997.

Buhle, Mari Jo, and Paul Buhle, eds. *The Concise History of Woman Suffrage: Selections from History of Woman Suffrage,* by Elizabeth Cady Stanton, Susan B. Anthony, Matilda Joslyn Gage, and the National American Woman Suffrage Association. Urbana: University of Illinois Press, 2005.

Bush, Richard C., Jr. *Religion in Communist China.* New York: Abingdon Press, 1970.

Canton Christian College Bulletin: President's Report, 1909–1910. New York: Trustees Canton Christian College, 1911.

Cantor, Norman F. *The Last Knight: The Twilight of the Middle Ages and the Birth of the Modern Era.* New York: Harper Perennial, 2005.

Carter, Susan Graybill, ed. *Gladly as This Song.* Huntington, W.Va.: University Editions, 1991.

Chan, Kim-kwong. "Missiological Implications of Chinese Christianity in a Global Context." An East-West Lecture given at Gordon College, October 27, 2004.

———. "Religion in China in the Twenty-First Century: Some Scenarios." *Religion, State & Society* 33, no. 2 (2005): 87–119.

———. *Towards a Contextual Ecclesiology: The Catholic Church in the People's Republic of China: Its Life and Theological Implications.* Hong Kong: Phototech System, 1987.

Chan, Kim-kwong, and Alan Hunter. *Prayers and Thoughts of Chinese Christians.* London: Mowbray, 1991.

Chan, Kim-kwong, and Tetsunao Yamamori. *Holistic Entrepreneurs in China: A Handbook on the World Trade Organization and New Opportunities for Christians.* Pasadena, Calif.: William Carey International University Press, 2002.

Chen, Li-fu. *Chinese Education during the War (1937–42).* Chongqing: Ministry of Education, 1943.

———. "War and Education in China." *China Forum* 4, no. 6 (1939): 161.

——— (陳立夫). *Zhanshi jiaoyu xingzheng huiyi* [《戰時教育行政回憶》 Memoirs of wartime educational administration]. Taibei: Shangwu yinshuguan, 1970.

Chen, Qijin (陳其津). "Chen Xujing xiaozhang zhuchi Lingnan daxue" [陳序經校長主持嶺南大學 President Ch'en took the helm of Lingnan University]. *Lingnan tongxun* [《嶺南通訊》Lingnan newsletter], no. 151 (September 15, 2001): 15–17.

Chen, Qingzhi (陳青之). *Zhongguo jiaoyu shi* [《中國教育史》 Chinese educational history]. Shanghai: Shangwu yinshuguan, 1936.

Chen, Shou-yi. "Dr. Chen Interprets Far Eastern Situation; Sympathy for Chinese Grows." *The Student Life*, September 27, 1941: 1.

———. "Higher Education and the Coming World Charter." In *Today's Emergency*, edited by James A. Blaisdell, 2–11. Claremont, Calif.: Claremont Colleges Library, 1942.

———. "John Webb: A Forgotten Page in the Early History of Sinology in Europe." *The Chinese Social and Political Science Review* XIX, no. 3 (1935).

———. "Sino-European Cultural Contacts since the Discovery of the Sea Route: A Bibliography Note." *Nankai Social and Economic Quarterly* III, no. 1 (1935).

———. "The Influence of China on English Culture during the 18th Century." Chicago: University of Chicago, 1928.

———. "Thomas Percy and His Chinese Studies." *The Chinese Social and Political Science Review* XX, no. 2 (1936): 202–30.

Ch'en, Su-ching (陳序經 Chen Xujing). *Dongxi wenhua guan* [《東西文化觀》 My view on Eastern and Western cultures], 3 vols., *Lingnan xuebao* [《嶺南學報》 Lingnan Journal], vol. 5, no. 1–4 (July, August and December 1936).

———. "Duiyu xiandai daxue jiaoyu fangzhen de shangque" [對於現代大學教育方針的商榷 Discussion of the principles of modern university education]. In Ch'en Su-ching, *Daxue jiaoyu lunji* [《大學教育論輯》 Selected works on university education]. Guangzhou: Southwest Economy Institute of Lingnan University, 1949.

———. "Jiaoyu de Zhongguo hua he xiandai hua" [教育的中國化和現代化 Sinicification and modernization in education]. *Duli pinglun* [《獨立評論》 Independent commentaries], March 26, 1933, no. 43.

———. "Xinan wenhua yanjiu de yiyi" [西南文化研究的意義 The significance of doing research on Southwestern culture]. In *Lingnan daxue xinan shehui jingji yanjiusuogaikuang* [《嶺南大學西南社會經濟研究概況》 The South West Social and Economics Institute Lingnan University: A Review of Its Activities—sic]. Guangzhou: Lingnan daxue, 1949.

———. *Zhongguo wenhua de chulu* [《中國文化的出路》 The future of Chinese culture]. Shanghai: Commercial Press, 1934.

Chen, Yung-fa (陳永發 Chen Yongfa). *Zhongguo gongchan geming qishi nian* [《中國共產革命七十年》 The seventy years of the Chinese Communist revolutions]. Taibei: Lianjing, 2001.

"China Talk for Chapel: Special Chapel by Julean Arnold on Consular Service." *The Student Life* (Pomona College), 1929: 1.

Christian, William A., Jr. *Local Religion in Sixteenth-Century Spain*. 1981,

1st ed. Princeton: Princeton University, 1989.

————. *Visionaries: The Spanish Republic and the Reign of Christ.* Berkeley, Calif.: University of California Press, 1996.

Chung, Wing Kwong (鍾榮光 Zhong Rongguang). "Guoji de Lingnan," [國際的嶺南 International Lingnan University]. Reprinted, Guangzhou, *Lingnan xiaoyou* [《嶺南校友》 Lingnan alumni] 16 (1988): 15–16.

Clary, William W. *The Claremont Colleges: A History of the Development of the Claremont Group Plan.* Claremont, Calif.: The Castle Press, 1970.

Coburn, Thomas B. "Asia and the Undergraduate Curriculum." In *Asia in the Undergraduate Curriculum: A Case for Asian Studies in Liberal Arts Education,* edited by Suzanne Wilson Barnett and Van Jay Symons. Armonk, N.Y.: M.E. Sharpe, 2000.

Cody, Jeffrey W. *Building in China: Henry K. Murphy's Adaptive Architecture.* Hong Kong: Chinese University Press, 2001.

————. *Exporting American Architecture.* London: Routledge, 2003.

Cohen, Warren I. *America's Response to China: A History of Sino-American Relations.* 4th ed. New York: Columbia University Press, 2000.

Collis, Maurice. *Foreign Mud: Being an Account of the Opium Imbroglio at Canton in the 1830s and the Anglo-Chinese War That Followed.* Reprinted ed. of 1946. New York: New Directions Publishing Corporation, 2002.

Committee of Reference and Counsel of the Foreign Missions Conference of North America. *Christian Education in China: A Study Made by an Educational Commission Representing the Mission Boards and Societies Conducting Work in China.* New York: Committee of Reference and Counsel of the Foreign Missions Conference of North America, 1922.

Corbett, Charles Hodge. *Lingnan University: A Short History Based Primarily on the Records of the University's American Trustees.* New York: The Trustees of Lingnan University, 1963.

Couchman, Sophie, John Fitzgerald, and Paul Macgregor, eds. *After the Rush: Regulations, Participation, and Chinese Communities in Australia 1860–1940.* Kingsbury, Australia: Otherland Literary Journal, 2004.

Crouch, Archie R., et al., ed. *Christianity in China: A Scholar's Guide to Resources in the Libraries and Archives of the United States.* Armonk, N.Y.: M. E. Sharpe, 1989.

Deng, Kaisong (鄧開頌), and Lu Xiaomin (陸曉敏), eds. *Yuegang'ao jindan guangxi shi* [《粵港澳近代關係史》 The history of Canton-Hong Kong-Macao relations]. Guangzhou: Guangdong renmin chubanshe, 1996.

Department of Education and Science, Her Majesty's Inspectorate of Schools. *1839–1989: Public Education in England 150th Anniversary.* London: Elizabeth House, 1990.

Ding, Shenzun (丁身尊), et al., eds. *Guangdong minguoshi* [《廣東民國史》 The history of Guangdong in the Republic of China]. Guangzhou: Guangdong renmin chubanshe, 2004, 2 vols.

Dr. Kerr. *A Guide to the City and Suburbs of Canton.* Reprint of the 1918 edition by Kelly & Walsh, Printers in Hong Kong. San Francisco: Chinese Materials Center, 1974

Duara, Presenjit. "Response to Philip Huang's 'Biculturality in Modern China and in Chinese Studies.'" *Modern China* 26, no. 1 (January 2000): 32–37.

Dunch, Ryan. "Mission Schools and Modernity: The Anglo-Chinese College, Fuzhou." In *Education, Culture, and Identity in Twentieth-Century China*, edited by Glen Peterson, et al. Hong Kong: Hong Kong University Press, 2001.

———. "Protestant Christianity in China Today: Fragile, Fragmented, Flourishing." In *China and Christianity: Burdened Past, Hopeful Future*, edited by Stephen Uhalley Jr. and Xiaoxin Wu, 195–217. Armonk, N.Y.: M.E. Sharpe, 2001.

Edmunds, Charles K. "A Half-Century of John Hopkins: A Fruitful Fifty Years at the Baltimore University." *The American Review of Reviews* November (1926): 525–33.

———. "Permanent Relief from Famine in China: Yellow River, 'China's Great Sorrow,' Would Be Great Blessing If Properly Utilized." *The Trans-Pacific*, July (1921).

———. "Pomona and Lingnan." *The News Bulletin of Lingnan University*, June 1928.

———. "Prexy's Greetings." *The Student Life* (Pomona College), September 25, 1928, 2.

———. "Report of President." Claremont, CA: Pomona College, 1935.

"Edmunds to Speak." *The Student Life* (Pomona College), November 16, 1934.

———. "Taming the Yellow River." *The Military Engineer* XIII, no. 70 (1921): 336–37.

———. *The Challenge in Crisis: Commencement Address, December 18, 1942. Pomona College, Claremont, California.* 5 vols. Vol. XL, *Pomona College Bulletin.* Claremont, Calif.: Pomona College, 1943.

———. *The Purpose and Spirit of Research.* Claremont, Calif.: Pomona College, reprint from Pomona College Magazine, March 1929.

Esherick, Joseph W., ed. *Remaking the Chinese Cities: Modernity and National Identity, 1900–1950.* Honolulu, Hawaii: University of Hawai'i Press, 2000.

Fahs, Charles B. *Government in Japan.* New York: Institute of Pacific Relations, 1940.

Fairbank, John K., ed. "The Creation of the Treaty System." In *The Cambridge History of China,* edited by Denis Twitchett and John K. Fairbank. Cambridge: Cambridge University Press, 1976.

———. *The Missionary Enterprise in China and America.* Cambridge, Mass.: Harvard University Press, 1974.

Fay, Peter Ward. *The Opium War, 1840–1842: Barbarians in the Celestial Empire in the Early Part of the Nineteenth Century and the War by Which They Forced Her Gates Ajar.* Chapel Hill, N.C.: University of North Carolina Press, 1997, 2nd ed., 1st ed. in 1975.

Feng, Jianhua. "Rural Education: Struggling with Bare Essentials." *Beijing Review.* October 6, 2005, 31–33.

Fenn, William Purviance. *Christian Higher Education in Changing China, 1880–1950.* Grand Rapids, Mich.: William B. Eerdmans Publishing Co., 1976.

———. *Ever New Horizons: The Story of the United Board for Christian Higher Education in Asia, 1922–1975.* New York: The United Board for Christian Higher Education in Asia, 1980.

Fitzgerald, John, ed. *Rethinking China's Provinces.* London: Routledge, 2002.

Foster, Kenneth E. *A Handbook of Ancient Chinese Bronzes.* Revised ed. Claremont, CA: The Art Department of Pomona College, 1949.

Fukuzawa, Yukichi. *The Autobiography of Yukichi Fukuzawa*. New York: Columbia University Press, 1980.

Fuson, Chester. "Brief Report on Social Service in the Canton Christian College." *Chinese Recorder* 47 (March 1916): 209-211.

Gao, Guantian (高冠天), compiler. *Lingnan daxue jiehui guoren ziban zhi jingguo ji fazhan zhi jihua* [《嶺南大學接回國人自辦之經過及發展之計畫》 The process of Lingnan's return to the Chinese and its development plan]. Guangzhou: Lingnan daxue, 1928.

Garrett, Valery M. *Heaven Is High, the Emperor Far Away: Merchants and Mandarins in Old Canton*. Oxford: Oxford University Press, 2002.

Gillespie, Miln. "Lingnan Exchange Student Tells of Rising Japanese Standards." *The Student Life* (Pomona College), October 20, 1936, 1.

Goring, Georgia. "East-West Fusion Is Hope." *The Student Life* (Pomona College), October 6, 1936, 1.

Graham, Gael. *Gender, Culture, and Christianity: American Protestant Mission Schools in China, 1880–1930*. New York: Peter Lang, 1995.

Grant, Henry W. *Educational Requisitions for the Church in China*. New York: Trustees of Canton Christian College, 1924.

———. "Is It Worth While to Educate Chinese Girls?" in *Ling Naam: The News Bulletin of Canton Christian College*, New York, vol. 1, no. 1 (August 1924).

Graybill, Henry B. "Looking Back in C.C.C." *Ling Naam: the News Bulletin of Canton Christian College* 1, no. 3 (1925): 2.

———. *The Educational Reform in China*. Hong Kong: Kelly and Walsh, 1911.

Gregg, Alice H. *China and Educational Autonomy: The Changing Role of the Protestant Educational Missionary in China, 1807–1937*. Syracuse, N.Y.: Syracuse University Press, 1946.

Gregory, Martyn, ed. *Canton to the West: Historical Pictures by Chinese and Western Artists 1770–1870 (Catalogue 77)*. London: Martyn Gregory Gallery, 2001.

Griggs, John C. "What South China Is Fighting For." *Current History* XV, no. 4 (January 1922): 637–43.

Groff, Weidman G. *Glimpse of China 1939*. Canton: Lingnan University, 1939.

The Group Plan of the Claremont Colleges. Claremont, Calif.: Claremont

University Center, 1993.

Guangdongsheng dang'an'guan (廣東省檔案館 Guangdong provincial archives), Lingnan University archives. "Academic Year Semester II, 1945–46, Lingnan University." Renshi cailiao [人事材料 Personnel files]. File # 38-4-59.

———. Kung-Hsiang Lin, Associate Professor, Plant Pathology Laboratory, Agricultural College, Lingnan University. "An Opportunity for Pioneering Phytopathological Work in South China." File # 38-4-17.

———. Lee Ying Lam (李應林 Li Yinglin). "Sili Lingnan daxue yu cici yubei shibian zhong chuli zhi jingguo" [私立嶺南大學於此次粵北事變中處理之經過 The process of Lingnan's handling of the recent northern Guangdong Incident]. June 1945 at Meixian. Li Yuanhong yu Lingda laiwang hanjian, 1916-1918 [黎元洪等與嶺大來往函件 The correspondence between Li Yuanhong, et al. (President of Republic of China, 1916–17 and 1922–23) and Lingnan University—This document appears to have been misfiled]. File # 38-1-23.

———. Liao Chongzhen (廖崇真). "Guangdong cansi fuxing zhi tu" [廣東蠶絲復興之途 A road map for the revival of Guangdong's silk industry]. May 1933, a report for the celebration week held by the Guangdong Construction Bureau (建設廳 Jianshe ting). File # 38-1-11.

———. *Lingnan daxue gongchao yunniang ji jiejue shimo ji* [嶺南大學工潮醞釀及解決始末記 A record of the origins and resolution of the labor unrest at Lingnan University]. File # 38-1-27.

———. Lingnan daxue Chen Xujing cailiao [嶺南大學陳序經材料 Lingnan University files on Ch'en Su-ching]. File # 38-4-5.

———. "Lingnnan daxue gongxueyuan gaikuang" [嶺南大學工學院概況 General situation of the College of Engineering at Lingnan University], Lingnan daxue gongnong liang xueyuan gaikuang [General situation of the engineering and agricultural colleges at Lingnan University 嶺南大學工、農兩學院概況]. 1929–34, File # 38-1-6.

———. "Lingnan daxue jiaozhiyuan yilanbiao [List of staff, Lingnan University, sic], 1933–34." File # 38-4-224.

———. "Lingnnan daxue nongxueyuan chengli jingguo ji gaikuang"

[嶺南大學農學院成立經過及概況 The formation and general situation of the College of Agriculture at Lingnan University]. Lingnan daxue gongnong liang xueyuan gaikuang [General situation of the engineering and agricultural colleges at Lingnan University 嶺南大學工、農兩學院概況]. May 1934, File # 38-1-6.

————. "Lingnnan daxue nongxueyuan fushe nongchang zuzhi jianzhang" [嶺南大學農學院附設農場組織簡章 By-laws of the College of Agriculture farms at Lingnan University]. Sili Lingnan daxue nongke yanjiu jihua zhangcheng deng cailiao [Agricultural scientific research plans and regulations at Lingnan University 私立嶺南大學農科研究計畫、章程等材料]. 1930, File # 38-1-12.

————. "Lingnan daxue xiaozhang Zhong Rongguang boshi xingshu" [嶺南大學鐘榮光博士行書 The life of Lingnan University President Dr. Chung Wing Kwong]. Sili Lingnan daxue jiaozhiyuan luli [私立嶺南大學教職員履歷 Resumes of faculty and staff at Lingnan University]. 1931–48, File # 38-1-83.

————. "Minutes of Advisory Committee (Session 28) held at President S. C. Chen's residence, November 9, 1949." File # 38-4-59.

————. "Minutes of Meeting of Hookworm Committee held at Dr. Cadbury's residence, Friday, February 29, 1934." File # 38-4-17.

————. "Program approved by Horkworm [sic] Investigation Committee and sent to Dr. Grant by Dr. Oldt in May, 1923." File # 38-4-17.

————. "Proposed revised By-laws of the Board of Managers of the College of Agriculture of the Canton Christian College as Amended and Adopted November 12, 1922" [in English]. "Lingda Nongxueyuan huiyi jilu he yuanzhang Li Peiwen cailiao, 1922–49" [嶺大農學院會議記錄和院長李沛文材料 Minutes of the College of Agriculture meetings at Lingnan University and Dean Li Peiwen files]. File # 38-4-17.

————. "Renshi cailiao" [人事材料 Personnel files] (n.d.). [End of 1947, my inference]. File # 38-4-58.

————. "Sili Lingnan daxue Tang Liting jijinghui baoguan weiyuanhui banli jiguo ji xiaochan xianzhuang" [私立嶺南大學譚禮庭基金保管委員會辦理經過及校產現狀 A report of the Committee of Lingnan University charged with oversight of the Tan Liting funds and the status of associated properties]. File # 38-1-68, 1945–50.

———. "Sili Lingnan daxue min ershi nian canbing yanjiu gongzuo baogao" [私立嶺南大學民二十年蠶病研究工作報告 Report on the research on the silk worm disease by Lingnan University in 1931]. File # 38-1-11.

———. Situ Wei cailiao [司徒衛材料 the Sz-to Wai files]. File # 38-4-6.

———. "The South West Social and Economics Institute, Lingnan University—A Review of Its Activities," Chen Xüjing cailiao [嶺南大學陳序經材料 Lingnan University files on Ch'en Su-ching]. File # 38-4-5.

———. "Xiaodonghui di shibaci huiyi jilu" [校董會第十八次會議記錄 Minutes of No. 18th meeting of the Chinese Board of Directors]. March 29, 1930 in Macao. File # 38-1-18.

———. "Zhong Rongguang zhuan" [鐘榮光傳 Biography of Chung Wing Kwong]. File # 38-4-70.

Guangdong dang'an'guan *Shenbao* Guangdong ziliao xuanji bianjizu (廣東省檔案館《申報》廣東資料選輯編輯組 Editorial team of Guangdong related sources appearing in *Shenbao*, Guangdong provincial archives), *Shenbao Guangdong ziliao xuanji* [《申報》廣東資料選輯 Selected sources on Guangdong in *Shenbao*]. Guangzhou: Guangdong sheng gongxiao xuexiao yinshuachang, 1995.

Guangdongsheng difang shizhi bianzuan weiyuanhui (廣東省地方史志編纂委員會 Committee on the local history of Guangdong Province), ed. *Guangdong shengzhi* [《廣東省志》History of Guangdong]. Guangzhou: Guangdong renmin chubanshe, 1993–present.

Guangzhou shi difangzhi bianzuan weiyuanhui (廣州市地方誌編纂委員會), ed., *Guangzhou shizhi* [《廣州市志》History of Guangzhou]. Guangzhou: Guangzhou chubanshe, 1995–2000, 19 vols.

Guangzhou Social Sciences Research Institute, compiler. *Handbook of Investment and Tourism in Guangzhou*. Beijing: Beijing Review, 1986.

Guo, Deyan (郭德焱). *Qingdai Guangzhou de Basi shangren* [《清代廣州的巴斯商人》Parsee Merchants in Canton during the Qing period. sic]. Beijing: Zhonghua shuju, 2005.

Harper, T. N. "Empire, Diaspora, and the Languages of Globalism, 1850–1914." In *Globalization in World History*, edited by A. G. Hopkins. New York: W. W. Norton, 2002.

Harvard-Yenching Library, Records of Trustees of Lingnan University. Alex Baxter. "Letter to Edmunds Re. Sericulture, 1923." Box 40, Roll 7.

————. Alex Baxter. "Letter to W. H. Grant, Secretary of the Trustees of Canton Christian College Re. Revised Statutes, 1923." Lingnan University archives, Harvard-Yenching Library, Box 40, Roll 7.

————. Alex Baxter. "Letter to J. M. Henry, Vice President then re- siding in New York, 1923." Box 40, Roll 7.

————. Alex Baxter. "Letter to W. Henry Grant, Secretary Re. The Proposed Agreement between the Agricultural College and the Local Government Drawn up in Chinese by W. K. Chung and Civil Governor Liao, 1923." Box 40, Roll 7.

————. C. H. Parkhurst. "Letter from Rev. Parkhurst to Edmunds Concerning the Report of the Educational Commission, 1922." Box 38, Roll 7.

————. Charles K. Edmunds. "Letter of Appointment of Dr. Tsin Shue Fan as Trustee of C.C.C. Making the College a Joint Undertaking with the Chinese, 1923." Box 39, Roll 7.

————. Charles K. Edmunds. "Letter to Trustees of C.C.C., September 16, 1922." Box 38, Roll 7.

————. Charles K. Edmunds. "Letter to the Trustees of C.C.C. Sent from Hong Kong, October 5, 1922." Box 38, Roll 7.

————. Charles K. Edmunds. "Letter to James M. Henry, December 12, 1922." Box 38, Roll 7.

————. Charles K. Edmunds. "Letter to Herbert Parsons and 20 All Trustees, 1920." Box 36, Roll 7.

————. Charles K. Edmunds. "Letter to H. B. Graybill, 1922." Box 38, Roll 7.

————. Charles K. Edmunds. "Letter Sent the Trustees of Canton Christian College from Shanghai, 1922." Box 38, Roll 7.

————. Charles K. Edmunds. "Letter to Herbert Parsons, President of the Trustees of C.C.C., November 18, 1922." Box 38, Roll 7.

————. Charles K. Edmunds. "Fund-Raising Efforts by Edmunds, 1922 and 1923." Box 38, Roll 7.

————. Charles K. Edmunds. "Letter to James M. Henry, Vice-Presi- dent of C.C.C. Re. Newark Museum, 1923." Box 39, Roll 7.

————. Clinton N. Laird (Dean). "Letter to Edmunds Concerning Personnel, 1923." Box 40, Roll 7.

———. "Exhibit of Detail of Staff Maintenance Canton Christian College, 1923." Box 39, Roll 7.

———. "Extract from Dr. Edmunds' Letter to Dr. Jackson, July 9, 1908." Honglok, Box 15.

———. Henry B. Graybill. "Letter to Edmunds Expressing Concerns, 1920." Box 38, Roll 7.

———. Henry B. Graybill. "Personal Letter to an Unknown Person [Perhaps to Edmunds While He Was Doing His Lecture Tour to the Pacific Coast] from Canton, 1922." Box 38, Roll 7.

———. Henry B. Graybill. "Letter to Parsons, Copied to Edmunds etc., 1922." Box 38, Roll 7.

———. Henry B. Graybill. "Letter to Edmunds Concerning Personnel, 1922." Box 38, Roll 7.

———. Henry B. Graybill. "Letter to Henry Grant, November 20, 1908." Box 15.

———. Herbert Parsons (President of the Trustees of the Canton Christian College). "Parson's Letter to Warren Powers Laird (Professor at University of Pennsylvania), 1922." Box 38, Roll 7.

———. James M. Henry (Secretary and Treasurer of the Trustees of Lingnan University in New York). "C.C.C. Publicity and Cultivation Brief." Box 202, 1914.

———. James M. Henry (Executive Secretary of C.C.C.). "Letter to C. K. Edmunds Concerning Language School, 1920." Box 36, Roll 6.

———. James M. Henry (Executive Secretary of C.C.C.). "Letter to Edmunds, 1922." Box 38, Roll 7.

———. James M. Henry, "Letter to Edmunds, 1923." Box 39, Roll 7.

———. James M. Henry. "Letter to Edmunds Concerning Canton Medical Missionary Union, 1920." Box 36, Roll 6.

———. James M. Henry. "Letter to Edmunds Concerning Funding, 1920." Box 36, Roll 6.

———. James M. Henry. "Letter to Edmunds Concerning Fund-Raising and Dormitory, 1920." Box 36, Roll 6.

———. James M. Henry. "Letter to Edmunds Concerning Local Support and Land, August 9, 1920." Box 36, Roll 6.

———. James M. Henry. "Letter to Edmunds Concerning the Medical Situation, 1920." Box 36, Roll 6.

———. James M. Henry. "Letter to Edmunds Concerning the Political Situation in South China, 1920." Box 36, Roll 6.

———. James M. Henry. "Letter to Edmunds Concerning the Presbyterian Mission, 1920." Box 36, Roll 6.

———. James M. Henry. "Letter to Edmunds Concerning Sericulture, Dated May 22, 1922." Box 38, Roll 7.

———. James M. Henry. "Letter to Edmunds in New York Re. The Language School, 1923." Box 39, Roll 7.

———. James M. Henry. "Letter to Edmunds Re. The Presbyterian Mission, 1920." Box 36, Roll 6.

———. James M. Henry. "Letter to Edmunds (Who Might Be on Furlough in the Later Half of 1920) Re. Language School and C.C.C. Relation to Missions, 1920." Box 36, Roll 6.

———. James M. Henry (Provost). "Letter to Olin D. Wannamaker (American Director of the Trustees of Lingnan University), 1938." Box 217, Rolls 42 and 43.

———. James M. Henry. "Letter to W. H. Grant (Trustees of Canton Christian College), 1920." Box 36, Roll 6.

———. Katherine C. Griggs. "Letter to Edmunds Concerning the Silk Work, July 20, 1923." Box 38, Roll 7.

———. Katherine C. Griggs. "Letter to David Eugene Smith (Teachers College, Columbia University; New York), 1923." Box 39, Roll 7.

———. Katherine C. Griggs. "Letter to W. Henry Grant, 1922." Box 38, Roll 7.

———. Katherine C. Griggs. "Letter to Mr. F. H. Hawkins, Secretary of London Missionary Society, 1922." Box 38, Roll 7.

———. "Lingnan University Harvard-Yenching Income, 1938." Box 217, Rolls 42 and 43.

———. Olin D. Wannamaker. "Letter to Serge Elisseeff (Director of the Harvard-Yenching Institute, Harvard University), 1938." Box 217, Rolls 42 and 43.

———. Olin D. Wannamaker. "Letter to James M. Henry (Provost of Lingnan University), 1938." Box 217, Rolls 42 and 43.

———. Olin D. Wannamaker. "Letter to Serge Elisseeff (Director of Harvard-Yenching Institute), in response to Elisseeff's letter dated December 6, 1939." Box 217, Rolls 42 and 43.

———. Olin D. Wannamaker. "Letter to Harold B. Hoskins (President of the Board of the Trustees of Lingnan University), 1940." Box 217, Rolls 42 and 43.

———. Serge Elisseeff. "Letter to Olin D. Wannamaker, American Director of Lingnan University in Reply to Wannamaker's Letter on December 1, 1939." Box 217, Rolls 42 and 43.

———. Serge Elisseeff. "Letter to Wannamaker, American Director of Lingnan University, 1940." Box 217, Rolls 42 and 43.

———. "Sericulture Items Taken from the Minutes of Executive Committee, 1923." Box 39, Roll 7.

———. Sue Graybill (Mrs. Henry Graybill). "Personal Letter Concerning American Minister Schurman's Visit to Canton, 1922." Box 38, Roll 7.

———. Warren Powers Laird. "Letter to Herbert Parsons, President of Trustees of C.C.C., Praising Edmunds, October 19, 1922." Box 38, Roll 7.

Hayford, Charles W. "Andrew P. Happer and the Founding of Canton Christian College: A Problem in Missionary Strategy." Unpublished manuscript, Harvard University, 1966.

Hayhoe, Ruth. *China's University, 1895–1995: A Century of Cultural Conflict.* New York: Garland Publishing. 1996.

He, Tiehua (何鐵華). "Lingnan jingshen zhi fayang guangda" [嶺南精神之發揚光大Maintaining the Lingnan Ethos]. *Lingnan tongxun* [《嶺南通訊》 Lingnan newsletter], vol. 9 (September 1, 1965): 14.

Hershatter, Gail. "State of the Field: Women in China's Long Twentieth Century." *The Journal of Asian Studies* 63, no. 4 (2004): 991–1065.

Hofstadter, Richard, et al., eds. *American Higher Education: A Documentary History.* 3 vols. Chicago: University of Chicago Press, 1961.

Holden, Reuben Andrus. *Yale-in-China: The Mainland, 1901–1951.* New Haven, Conn.: Yale-in-China Association, 1964.

Honnold/Mudd Library, Claremont Colleges. Charles K. Edmunds Papers. "Three Anniversaries." Claremont, Calif.: Claremont Colleges, 1931. Folder 5.

———. Charles K. Edmunds Papers. "Geography as a Factor in the Determination of Foreign Policy." Paper presented at the 16th Annual meeting of The Institute of World Affairs, Riverside, California, 1938.

————. Charles K. Edmunds Papers. "Out of the Midst of the Fire—Ye Heard a Voice: An Address by Charles K. Edmunds at Pomona College." 1941.

————. Charles K. Edmunds Papers. "Weights and Measures among the Chinese." Folder of Notes on Weights and Measures among the Chinese (n.d.).

————. Charles K. Edmunds Papers. "Thinking with the Heart." (n.d.)

————. Charles K. Edmunds Papers. "Irrigation of Chengtu Plain or Beyond." Circa 1903.

————. Charles K. Edmunds Papers. Judith Bland. "Charles Keyser Edmunds: President Pomona College, 1928–1941." Folder 2.

————. Charles K. Edmunds Papers. E. Wilson Lyon. "Tribute to Edmunds." In *Charles Keyser Edmunds: In Memoriam*. Claremont, Calif.: 1949.

————. Charles K. Edmunds Papers. Elizabeth Edmunds Wheaton. "I Remember Prexy: Charles Keyser Edmunds, President, Pomona College, 1928-1941." Folder 1 (n.d.)

————. Chen Shou-yi Papers. "Students' Essays." Box 1.

————. Chen Shou-yi Papers. "Notes on China History." Box 2.

————. Chen Shou-yi Papers. "Notes on Asia." Box 3.

————. Chen Shou-yi Papers. "Notes and Essays on History and Literature (Chinese and Western)." Box 4.

————. Chen Shou-yi Papers. "Chen's Student Years' Class Syllabi." Box 5.

————. Chen Shou-yi Papers. "Letter to President E. Wilson Lyon." Unsorted Chen's Writings and Notes, 1954, Box 6.

Huang, Juyan (黃菊豔), ed. *Jindai Guangdong jiaoyu yu Lingnan daxue* [《近代廣東教育與嶺南大學》 Modern education in Guangdong and Lingnan University]. Hong Kong: The Commercial Press, 1995.

Huang, Philip. "Biculturality in Modern China and in Chinese Studies." *Modern China* 26, no. 1 (January 2000): 3–31.

Hunter, Alan and Kim-kwong Chan. *Protestantism in Contemporary China*. Cambridge: Cambridge University Press, 1993.

Hunter, Jane. *The Gospel of Gentility: American Women Missionaries in Turn-of-the-Century*. New Haven, Conn.: Yale University Press, 1984.

Hunter, William C. *The "Fan Kwae" at Canton before Treaty Days: 1825–1844.* Reprint ed. Taipei: Ch'eng-wen Pub. Co., 1965.

Huntington, Samuel P. *The Clash of Civilizations and the Remaking of World Order.* New York: Simon & Schuster, 1996.

Israel, John. *Lianda: A Chinese University in War and Revolution.* Stanford, Calif.: Stanford University Press, 1998.

Jespersen, T. Christopher. *American Images of China 1931–1949.* Stanford, Calif.: Stanford University Press, 1996.

Jian, Youwen (簡又文). "Lingnan, wo Lingnan"[《嶺南我嶺南》 Lingnan, My Lingnan]. *Lingnan tongxun* [《嶺南通訊》Lingnan newsletter], vol. 60.

Jiang, Zuyuan (蔣祖緣), and Fang Zhiqin (方志欽), eds. *Jianming Guangdong shi* [《簡明廣東史》A concise history of Guangdong]. Guangzhou: Guangdong renmin chubanshe, 1993.

Jin, Yilin (金以林). *Jindai Zhongguo daxue yanjiu* [《近代中國大學研究》 Studies of universities in modern China]. Beijing: Zhongyang wenxian chubanshe, 2000.

Johnson, Graham E., and Glen D. Peterson. *Historical Dictionary of Guangzhou (Canton) and Guangdong.* Lanham, MD: The Scarecrow Press, Inc., 1999.

Kerr, Phyllis Forbes, ed. *Letters from China: The Canton-Boston Correspondence of Robert Bennet Forbes, 1838–1840.* Mystic, Conn.: Mystic Seaport Museum, 1996.

"Kidnapping of Staff and Students." *Ling Naam: the News Bulletin of Canton Christian College* 1, no. 3 (1925): 1, 3, and 8.

Kuo, Ping-Chia. *Canton and Salem.* [n.p.] Southworth Press, 1930.

Kuo, Ping Wen. *The Chinese System of Public Education.* New York: Columbia University, 1914.

Kwok, Pui-lan. *Chinese Women and Christianity, 1860–1927.* Atlanta: Scholars Press, 1992.

———. "Chinese Women and Protestant Christianity at the Turn of the Twentieth Century." In *Christianity in China: From the Eighteenth Century to the Present,* edited by Daniel H. Bays. Stanford, Calif.: Stanford University Press, 1996.

"'Lady Precious Stream' English Translation Plays in Bridges Auditorium." *The Student Life* (Pomona College), January 18, 1938, 1.

Lan, Xinzhen. "Agriculture: The Key to China's Growth." *Beijing Review*, October 6, 2005, 18–21.

Latourette, Kenneth. *A History of Christian Missions in China*. New York: MacMillan, 1929.

———. *A History of Christian Missions in China*. Reprint ed. New York: Russell & Russell, 1967.

Lautz, Terrill E. "Hopes and Fears of 60 Years: American Images of China, 1911–1972." In *China in the American Political Imagination*, edited by Carola McGiffert. D.C.: The CSIS Press, 2005, 31–37.

———. "The Mirror and the Wall: American Images of China." In *Chinese Images of the United States*, edited by Carola McGiffert. D.C.: The CSIS Press, 2005, 127–33.

Lee, Edward Bing-Shuey. *Modern Canton*. Shanghai: The Mercury Press, 1936.

Lee, Sui-ming (李瑞明 Li Ruiming), transl. and comp. *Lingnan daxue* [《嶺南大學》 Lingnan University]. Hong Kong: The Lingnan (University) Development Fund, Ltd., 1997.

———. ed. *Lingnan daxue wenxian mulu: Guangzhou Lingnan daxue lishi dang'an ziliao* [《嶺南大學文獻目錄: 廣州嶺南大學歷史檔案資料》 Index of the Lingnan University archives]. Hong Kong: Lingnan University, 2000.

———. *Nanguo fenghuang: Zhongshan daxue Lingnan xueyuan* [《南方鳳凰: 中山大學嶺南(大學)學院》 A Phoenix of South China: The Story of Lingnan (University) College, Sun Yat-sen University-sic]. Hong Kong: The Commercial Press, 2005.

Lee, Ying Lam (李應林 Li Yinglin). "Tan Liting xiansheng xianchan xingxue ji" [譚禮庭先生獻產興學記 An account of Mr. Tan Liting's donating his property to education]. *Guangdong jiaoyu* [《廣東教育 Education in Guangdong》], (n.d.): 40.

Li, Cheng, ed. *Bridging Minds across the Pacific: U.S.-China Educational Exchange*. Lanham, Md.: Lexington Books, 2005.

Li, Xiaobi (李小璧), and Li Xiaoqiong (李小瓊). "'Lingnan niu' yü 'Niulin: huainian fuqin Li Yinglin'" ["嶺南牛"與"牛林": 懷念父親李應林 "Lingnan Cow" and "Cow Lin": Remembering our father Lee Ying Lam]. *Lingnan xiaoyou* [《嶺南校友》 Lingnan alumni], Guangzhou, 16 (1988): 20–21.

Li, Youning (李又甯), and Zhang Yufa (張玉法). *Jindai Zhongguo nu-quan yundong shiliao, 1842–1911* [《近代中國女權運動史料, 1842–1911》]. Taibei: Zhuanji wenxueshe, 1975.

Lian, Xi. *The Conversion of Missionaries: Liberalism in American Protestant Missions in China, 1907–1932.* University Park, Pa.: Pennsylvania State University Press, 1997.

Lin, Liru (林礪儒), *Lin Liru wenji* [《林礪儒文集》Collected works of Lin Liru]. Guangzhou: Guangdong jiaoyü chubanshe, 1994.

Ling Naam: The News Bulletin of Canton Christian College, vol. 1, no. 3 (April 1925).

Lingnan (Canton Christian College)

Lingnan: The News Bulletin of Lingnan University, vol. 5, no. 4 (November 1928), Canton.

Lingnan daxue Sanfan shi tongxuehui jianbao [《嶺南大學三藩市同學會簡報》Bulletin of Lingnan University Alumni Association in San Francisco], May–August 2006, Alumni Day Special Edition.

Lingnan daxue xinan shehui jingji yanjiusuo gaikuang [《嶺南大學西南社會經濟研究所概況》The South West Social and Economics Institute Lingnan University: A Review of Its Activities—sic]. Guangzhou: Lingnan daxue, 1949.

Lingnan daxue xiaobao [嶺南大學校報 Lingnan University newspaper], April 1, 1943.

Lingnan daxue Xianggang tongxuehui [嶺南大學香港同學會 Lingnan University Hong Kong Alumni Association], ed. *Zhong Rongguang xiansheng zhuan* [《鍾榮光先生傳》Biography of Chung Wing Kwong]. Hong Kong: Lingnan daxue Xianggang tongxuehui, 1996.

Lingnan tongxun [《嶺南通訊》Lingnan Bulletin]. Published by Zhongshan daxue Lingnan (daxue) xueyuan, no. 17 (April 2006): 1.

Lingnan xiaoyou [《嶺南校友》Lingnan alumni]. Guangzhou: Guangzhou Lingnan University Alumni Association, 1988, vol. 16.

Lingnan (University) College of Sun Yat-sen University, brochure, Guangzhou, January 2003.

Liu, Cunkuan (劉存寬). *Xianggang shi luncun* [《香港史論叢》Collected works on the history of Hong Kong]. Hong Kong: Qilin shuye youxian gongsi, 1998.

Liu, Fung Ling. "The Epic Woman of China." *Ling Naam: The News*

Bulletin of Canton Christian College, vol. 1, no. 1 (August 1924).

Liu, Jiafeng (劉家峰). "Qilu daxue jingfei laiyuan yü xuexiao fazhan: 1904–1952" [齊魯大學經費來源與學校發展: 1904–1952 Qilu University—Income sources and development: 1904–1952]. Zhang Kaiyuan (章開沅), and Ma Min (馬敏), eds. *Jidujiao yü Zhongguo wenhua congkan* [《基督教與中國文化叢刊》 Christianity and Chinese culture series]. Wuhan: Hubei jiaoyu chubanshe, 1999, vol. 3, 81–130.

Liu, Judith, and Donald P. Kelly. "'An Oasis in a Heathen Land': St. Hilda's School for Girls, Wuchang, 1928–1936." In *Christianity in China: From the Eighteenth Century to the Present*, edited by Daniel H. Bays. Stanford, Calif.: Stanford University Press, 1996.

Lozada, Eriberto P., Jr. "Civil Society Redux: Rural Catholicism and State-Society Relations in Postsocialist China." Cambridge, MA: Fairbank Center for East Asian Research, Harvard University, October 7, 2005.

———. *God Aboveground: Catholic Church, Postsocialist State, and Transnational Processes in a Chinese Village.* Stanford, Calif.: Stanford University Press, 2001.

Lu, Hanchao. "Book Review of Kristin Stapleton's *Civilizing Chengdu: Chinese Urban Reform* and Michael Tsin's *Nation, Governance, and Modernity in China: Canton, 1900–1927.*" *American Historical Review* 106, no. 3 (2001): 949-50.

Lucas, Christopher J. *American Higher Education: A History.* New York: St. Martin's Press, 1994.

Lutz, Jessie Gregory. *China and Christian Colleges, 1850–1950.* Ithaca, N.Y.: Cornell University Press, 1971.

———. *Chinese Politics and Christian Missions: The Anti-Christian Movements of 1920–28.* Notre Dame, Ind.: Cross Cultural Publications, Cross Roads Books, 1988.

Lyon, E. Wilson. *History of Pomona College, 1887-1969.* Claremont, Calif.: Pomona College, 1977.

———. "Report of the President of Pomona College, 1941–42." Claremont, Calif.: Pomona College, 1942.

Madsen, Richard. "Catholic Revival During the Reform Era." *China Quarterly* 174 (June 2003): 469-74.

————. *China and the American Dream: A Moral Inquiry.* Berkeley, Calif.: University of California Press, 1995.

————. *China's Catholics: Tragedy and Hope in an Emerging Civil Society.* Berkeley, Calif.: University of California Press, 1998.

Manning, Patrick. *Migration in World History.* London: Routledge, 2005.

Materials on the Pacific Area in the Oriental Library of Claremont College Library and in the Libraries of Pomona College and Scripps College. Claremont, Calif.: Claremont Colleges Library, 1939.

McKeown, Adam. "Chapter 1: Introduction: The Continuing Reformulation of Chinese Australians." In *After the Rush: Regulations, Participation, and Chinese Communities in Australia 1860–1940*, edited by Sophie Couchman, John Fitzgerald, and Paul Macgregor. Fitzroy, Australia: Arena Printing and Publishing, 2004.

Meisenhelder, Edmund W., III. *The Dragon Smiles.* New York: Pageant Press, 1968.

Menegon, Eugenio. "Child Bodies, Blessed Bodies: The Contest between Christian Virginity and Confucian Chastity." *Nan Nu* 6, no. 2 (2004): 177–240.

Mi Shi (采時). "Pingshi fengqing hua" [坪石風情畫 panoramic view of Pingshek]. *Lingnan tongxun* [《嶺南通訊》 Lingnan Newsletter]. Lingnan Alumni Association in Hong Kong, vol. 69 (October 15, 1972): 16–17.

Minden, Karen. *Bamboo Stone: The Evolution of a Chinese Medical Elite.* Toronto: University of Toronto Press, 1994.

Mullins, Mark R. *Christianity Made in Japan: A Study of Indigenous Movements.* Honolulu, Hawaii: University of Hawaii Press, 1998.

Murdock, Michael G. "Whose Modernity? Anti-Christianity and Educational Policy in Revolutionary China, 1924–1926." *Twentieth-Century China* 31, no. 1 (2005): 33–75.

"The New Plans at Pomona College." *Harvard Alumni Bulletin* January (1926): 393–95.

Ng, Peter, ed. *Changing Paradigms of Christian Higher Education.* Lewiston, N.Y.: The Edwin Mellen Press, 2002.

————. (吳梓明 Wu Ziming), ed. *Jidujiao daxue huaren xiaozhang yanjiu* [《基督教大學華人校長研究》 Studies of the Chinese president of Christian universities]. Fuzhou: Fujian jiaoyu chubanshe, 2001.

———. "Lingnan daxue de diyiwu xuesheng—Cheng Shaobai" [嶺南大學的第一位學生: 陳少白 The first student of Lingnan University: Chen Xiaobai]. Zhongguo lishi xuehui jikan [《中國歷史學會史學集刊》], no. 23 (July 1991): 139–48.

Ng, Yong Sang. *Canton, City of the Rams: A General Description and a Brief Historical Survey.* Canton: M.S. Cheung, 1936.

Nickerson, Bob. "Chinese Girl Refugee Comes Here for Graduate Work." *The Student Life* (Pomona College), October 21, 1937.

Nisbet, Robert. *The Degradation of the Academic Dogma: The University in America, 1945–70.* New Brunswick, N.J.: 1997.

North-China Daily News & Herald. *China's in Chaos: A Brief Outline of the Foreign Concessions with Examples of China's Disruption and Failure to Observe Her Obligations Due to Civil War, Bolshevist Propaganda and Mob Law.* Shanghai: North-China Daily News & Herald, 1927.

Noyes, Harriet Newell. *A Light in the Land of Sinim, Forty-five Years in the True Light Seminary, 1872–1917.* New York: Fleming H. Revell, 1919.

———. *History of the South China Mission of the Presbyterian Church in the United States.* Shanghai: Presbyterian Mission Press, 1927.

Osborn, Frederick, and Olin Wannamaker. "Letter from Trustees of Lingnan University." *Lingnan (Canton Christian College)* IX, no. 1 (1936): 1–2.

Ouyang, Chu (歐陽初). *Minguo shiqi de jiaoyu* [《民國時期的教育》 Education in Republican China]. Guangzhou: Guangdong renmin chubanshe, 1996.

Ouyuan, Huai (歐元懷). "Kangzhan shinian lai Zhongguo de daxue jiaoyu" [抗戰十年來中國的大學教育 China's university education during the past ten years of the War of Resistance]. *Zhonghua jiaoyujie* [《中華教育界》 Chinese education], new ser. I (January 5, 1947): 3–4.

"Party Will Depart for China Soon." *The Student Life* (Pomona College), October 2, 1929: 1.

Perdue, Peter C. *China Marches West: The Qing Conquest of Central Eurasia.* Cambridge, Mass.: Belknap Press of Harvard University Press, 2005.

Perrottet, Tony. "The Glory That Is Rome." *Smithsonian*, October 2005, 88–95.

Pierson, George W. "The Elective System and the Difficulties of College Planning, 1870–1940." *Journal of General Education* IV, (April 1950): 165.

"Pomona to Honor Mei Lan-Fang." *The Student Life* (Pomona College), May 27, 1930: 1.

Pong, David. *A Critical Guide to the Kwangtung Provincial Archives Deposited at the Public Record Office of London* [《清代廣東省檔案指南》 Qingdai Guangdongsheng dang'an zhinan, sic]. Cambridge, Mass.: Harvard University, 1975.

Postiglione, Gerald A., ed. *Education and Social Change in China: Inequality in a Market Economy*. Armonk, N.Y.: M.E. Sharpe, 2006.

Power, Edward J. *A Legacy of Learning: A History of Western Education*. Albany, N.Y.: State University of New York Press, 1991.

"Presidents Edmunds Heads Association." *The Student Life* (Pomona College), May 14, 1929, 1.

Pruitt, Lisa Joy. *A Looking-Glass for Ladies: American Protestant Women and the Orient in the Nineteenth Century*. Maon, Ga.: Mercer University Press, 2005.

Qi, Liang (啓良). "Chongping Chen Xujing" [重評陳序經 Reassess Chen Xujing]. *Zhejiang shehui kexue* [《浙江社會科學》], no. 6 (1998): 111–27.

Qian, Ning. *Chinese Students Encounter America*. Translated by T. K. Chu from Chinese. Seattle: University of Washington Press, 2002.

Qiu, Zhihua (邱志華), ed. *Chen Xujing xueshu lunzhu* [《陳序經學術論著》 Scholarly works of Chen Xujing]. Hangzhou: Zhejiang renmin chubanshe, 1998.

Rabe, Valentin H. *The Home Base of American China Missions*. Cambridge, Mass.: Harvard University Press, 1978.

Records of the General Conference of the Protestant Missionaries of China, held at Shanghai, May 10–24, 1877. Shanghai: Presbyterian Mission Press, 1878.

Rea, Kenneth W., ed. *Canton in Revolution: The Collected Papers of Earl Swisher, 1925–1928*. Boulder, Colo.: Westview Press, 1977.

Renshaw, Michelle. *Accommodating the Chinese: The American Hospital in China, 1880–1920.* New York: Routledge, 2005.

Rhoads, Edward J. M. *China's Republican Revolution: The Case of Kwangtung, 1895–1913.* Cambridge, Mass.: Harvard University Press, 1975.

———. "Lingnan's Response to the Rise of Chinese Nationalism: The Shakee Incident (1925)." In *American Missionaries in China: Papers from Harvard Seminars,* edited by Kwang-Ching Liu, 183–214. Cambridge, Mass.: East Asian Research Center of Harvard University, 1966.

Ross, Heidi A. "'Cradle of Female Talent': The McTyeire Home and School for Girls, 1892–1937." In *Christianity in China: From the Eighteenth Century to the Present,* edited by Daniel H. Bays. Stanford, Calif.: Stanford University Press, 1996.

Rubinstein, Murray A. *The Origins of the Anglo-American Missionary Enterprise in China, 1807–1840.* Lanham, Md.: Scarecrow Press, 1996.

Rudolph, Frederick. *The American College and University: A History.* 2nd ed. Athens, Ga.: University of Georgia Press, 1990. 1st ed. 1962.

Sanneh, Lamin. "Concluding Remarks at 'Conversion and Converts,' the Yale-Edinburgh Group on the History of the Missionary Movement and Non-Western Christianity." New Haven, Conn.: Yale University, July 2003.

Shanghaishi lishi bowuguan [上海歷史博物館 Shanghai historical museum], et al., eds. *Zhongguo de zujie* [《中國的租界》 The Foreign concessions in China, sic]. Shanghai: Shanghai guji chubanshe, 2004.

Sheehan, James. "The Varieties of History." *Perspective,* vol. 43, no. 9 (December 2005): 2. www.historians.org/Perspectives/issues/2005/0512/0512pre1.cfm, accessed on December 11, 2005.

Shending, Yingfu (深町英夫 Fukamachi Hideo). *Jindai Guangdong de zhengdang shehui guojia: Zhongguo guomindng jiqi dangguo tizhi de xingcheng guocheng* [《近代廣東的政黨.社會.國家: 中國國民黨及其黨國體制的形成過程》 Political parties, society, and state in modern Guangdong: the Nationalist Party and the formation process of its party-state system]. Beijing: Shehui wenxian chubanshe, 2003.

Shi, Jiashun (施家順). *Chen Jitang yu Guangdong junzheng, 1928–1936*

[《陳濟棠與廣東軍政》 Chen Jitang and the military and politics of Guangdong, 1928–1936]. Pingdong: Ruiyu chubanshe, 1999.

Shils, Edward. *The American Ethic*. Chicago: University of Chicago Press, 1984.

Sili Lingnan daxue [私立嶺南大學 Lingnan University]. *Sili Lingnan Daxue yilan* [《私立嶺南大學一覽》Overview of Lingnan University]. Guangzhou: Lingnan University, 1932.

Smalley, Martha Lund, and Joan R. Duffy. "Guides to the Archives of the Trustees of Lingnan University." Special Collections, Yale Divinity School Library, 1986.

Snow, Edgar. *Red Star over China*. First revised and enlarged ed. New York: Grove Press, 1973.

Solomon, Barbara Miller. *In the Company of Educated Women: A History of Women and Higher Education in America*. New Haven, Conn.: Yale University Press, 1985.

Spence, Jonathan D. *The China Helpers: Western Advisers in China, 1620–1960*. London: The Bodley Head, 1969.

———. "The Once and Future China." *Foreign Policy*, no. 146 (2005): 44–46.

Standaert, Nicolas, ed. *Handbook of Christianity in China*. Leiden: Brill, 2001.

Stauffer, Milton. *The Christian Occupation of China*. Shanghai: China Continuation Committee, 1922.

"Students to Take Year in Orient Study." *The Student Life* (Pomona College), May 21, 1929: 1 and 4.

Sumner, C. B. *A Pivotal Era in the Life of Pomona College*. Claremont, Calif. Pomona College, 1919.

Sun, Banghua (孫邦華). *Furen daxue: Huiyou Beilefu* [《輔仁大學: 會友貝勒府》 Furen University]. Shijiazhuang: Hebei jiaoyu chubanshe, 2004.

Sun, Haiying (孫海英). *Jinling nuzi daxue: Jinling baiwufang* [《金陵女子大學：金陵百屋房》 Ginling college in Nanking]. Shijiazhuang: Hebei jiaoyu chubanshe, 2004.

Sutter, Robert. "Asia in the Balance: America and China's 'Peaceful Rise'." *Current History* 103, no. 674 (2004): 284–89.

Swisher, Earl. *Today's World in Focus: China*. Boston, Mass.: Ginn and

Company, 1964.

Tao, Feiya (陶飛亞), and Wu Ziming (吳梓明 Peter Ng). *Jidujiao daoxue yu guoxue yanjiu* [《基督教大學與國學研究》Christian universities and China studies]. Fuzhou: Fujian jiaoyu chubanshe, 1998.

Tao, Feiya (陶飛亞). "Taian jiaoqu Mazhuang zhen Beixinzhuang jiaohui de ge'an yanjiu," [泰安郊區馬莊鎮北新莊教會的個案研究 A case study of the Beixinzhuang church in the town of Mazhuang in the suburbs of Taian]. In *Shengshan jiaoxia de shizijia: Zongjiao yü shehui hudong ge'an yanjiu* [《聖山腳下的十字架: 宗教與社會互動個案研究》Christianity at the foot of Mount Tai: A study of the interplay between religion and society, sic], by Wu Ziming (Peter Ng), et al. 97–157. Hong Kong: Hanyü Jidujiao wenhua yanjiusuo, 2005.

Tomlinson, John. *Cultural Imperialism: A Critical Introduction*. Baltimore, Md.: John Hopkins University Press, 1991.

Trustees of Lingnan University. "Anonymous Letter to James M. Henry, October 15, 1945." Roll 19.

———. "Answers of the Canton Mission to the Questions Asked in the Letter from the Board of Trustees of the Canton Christian College of November 19th, 1889." Roll 1.

———. "Canton Christian College Catalogue, 1906–1907." Roll 25.

———. Charles Edmunds. "Letter to Clinton N. Laird, April 3, 1918." Roll 6.

———. Charles K. Edmunds. "Letter to Henry Grant, March 12, 1918." Roll 6.

———. Charles K. Edmunds. "Letter to Henry Grant Declining the Appointment of President of Lingnan, May 19, 1906." Roll 3.

———. Charles K. Edmunds. "President Reports, 1919–1924." Roll 26.

———. Charles K. Edmunds. "Statement Regarding Conditions in China with Reference to Danger to Foreigners and General Peace, April 20, 1906." Roll 3.

———. Chu, Y. K. "The Academic Life of Lingnan, 1941." Roll 26.

———. Chung Wing Kwong. "Letter to Henry Grant, September 21, 1917." Roll 6.

———. Fung Hin Liu. "Letters to Henry Grant, and others, 1910s." Roll 37.

———. Fung Hin Liu. "Samples of English Work by Chinese Girls." (n.d.). Roll 37.

———. Henry S. Frank. "Confidential Report to the Trustees of Lingnan University." Roll 24.

———. "History and Present Status of Lingnan University." Roll 26.

———. "Informal Notes Regarding Lingnan Women Students." Roll 37.

———. Henry W. Grant. "Letter to Charles K. Edmunds, February 2, 1906." Roll 3.

———. Henry W. Grant. "Letter to Friends, April 14, 1907 from Honglok, Canton." Roll 3.

———. Henry W. Grant. "Letter to Parsons, President of Trustees of the Canton Christian College), May 7, 1913." Roll 5.

———. Miscellaneous files on education for women. Roll 37.

———. "Present Christian Activities on the Lingnan University Campus, December 16, 1949." Roll 26.

———. "President's Report by Charles K. Edmunds, 1919–1924." Roll 26.

———. "Proposed Budget—Girls' School, 1917–18." Roll 37.

———. "Record of the Testimonial Dinner for Dr. Charles K. Edmunds, New York, March 2, 1922." Roll 39.

———. "Report of the Dean of Women." Roll 37.

———. Summary of Income and Expenditure of Lingnan, 1897–1944. Roll 26.

———. "W. E. Hoffmann's Letter to Olin Wannamaker, October 2, 1945." Roll 19.

———. "Women's Departments, Canton Christian College." Roll 37.

———. Y. L. Lee. "President's Report to the Members of the Board of Directors of Lingnan University for the Year 1943–44." Roll 19.

Tsang, Chiu-sam (曾昭森 Zeng Zhaosen). "Lingnan daxue yuanxun Zhong Rongguang xiansheng xingzhuan" [嶺南大學元勳鍾榮光先生行傳 Biography of Chung Wing Kwong: Lingnan University's pioneer]. *Lingnan tongxun* [《嶺南通訊》 Lingnan newsletter], March 25, 1972: 8.

———. *Muxiao sanshou gequ yishu* [《母校三首歌曲憶述》 Reminiscences of the three songs about the Alma Mater]. Hong Kong: Hong Kong

Progressive Educational Press, 1971.

———. *A Tribute to Henry Blair Graybill (1888–1951)*. Hong Kong: Chung Chi College, Chinese University of Hong Kong, 1960.

Tsin, Michael. *Nation, Governance, and Modernity in China: Canton, 1900–1927*. Stanford, Calif.: Stanford University Press, 1999.

Tsutsui, William. *Godzilla on My Mind: Fifty Years of the King of Monsters*. New York: Palgrave Macmillan, 2004.

Vogel, Ezra F. *Canton under Communism: Programs and Politics in a Provincial Capital, 1949–1968*. Cambridge, Mass.: Harvard University Press, 1969.

Waley, Arthur. *The Opium War through Chinese Eyes*. Paperback ed. Stanford, Calif.: Stanford University Press, 1968. 1st ed. 1958.

Walls, Andrew. "The Nineteenth-Century Missionary as Scholar." In *The Missionary Movement in Christian History: Studies in Transmissions of Faith*, edited by Andrew Walls. Maryknoll, N.Y.: Orbis Books, 1996.

Wallace, Ethel L. *Hwa Nan College: The Woman's College of South China*. New York: United Board for Christian Colleges in China, 1956.

Wang, Dong. *China's Unequal Treaties: Narrating National History*. Lanham, Md.: Rowman & Littlefield, Lexington Books, 2005.

———. "Circulating American Higher Education: The Case of Lingnan University (1888–1951)." *Journal of American East-Asian Relations* 9, no. 3–4 (delayed 2000, appeared in 2006): 147–67.

———. "From Lingnan to Pomona: Charles K. Edmunds and His Chinese-American Career." In *China's Christian Colleges: Transpacific Connections, 1900–1950*. Edited by Daniel Bays and Ellen Widmer. Forthcoming.

Wang, Guoping (王國平). *Dongwu daxue: boxi tiancizhuang* [《東吳大學: 博習天賜莊》Soochou university]. Shijiazhuang: Hebei jiaoyu chubanshe, 2003.

Wang, Licheng (王立誠). *Meiguo wenhua shentou yu jindai Zhongguo jiaoyu: Hujiang daxue de lishi* [《美國文化滲透與近代中國教育: 滬江大學的歷史》American cultural penetration and the modern education of China: a history of the University of Shanghai, sic]. Shanghai: Fudan daxue chubanshe, 2001.

Watson, James L., ed. *Golden Arches East: McDonald's in East Asia*.

Stanford, Calif.: Stanford University Press, 1997. 2nd ed. 2006.

Wen, Tiejun. "Tackling Rural Issues." *Beijing Review*, October 6, 2005, 18–21.

West, Philip. *Yenching University and Sino-Western Relations, 1916–1952.* Cambridge, Mass.: Harvard University Press, 1976.

Wheaton, Elizabeth Edmunds. "I Remember Prexy Charles Keyser Edmunds: President, Pomona College, 1928–1941, from the Eve of the Stock Market Crash to the Eve of Pearl Harbor." *Pomona Today* 1988, 7–11.

Wiest, Jean-Paul. "Religious Studies and Research in Chinese Academia: Prospects, Challenges, and Hindrances." *International Bulletin* 29, no. 1 (2005): 21–26.

Wilbur, Martin C. *Forging the Weapons: Sun Yat-Sen and the Kuomintang in Canton, 1924.* New York: East Asian Institute of Columbia University, 1966.

———. *The Nationalist Revolution in China, 1923–1928.* Cambridge: Cambridge University Press, 1983.

———. "Problems of Starting a Revolutionary Base: Sun Yat-Sen and Canton, 1923." *Bulletin of the Institute of Modern History, Academia Sinica* 4, no. 2 (1974): 665–727.

Woody, Thomas. *A History of Women's Education in the United States.* 2 vols. New York: Octagon Books, 1974. 2nd ed. 1st ed. by Science Press 1929.

Wu, Yixiong (吳義雄). *Zai zongjiao yu shisu zhijian: Jidujiao Xinjiao chuanjiaoshizai huanan yanhai de zaoqi huodong yanjiu* [《在宗教與世俗之間: 基督教新教傳教士在華南沿海的早期活動研究》Between religion and secularism: a study of the earlier activities of Protestant missionaries on the coast of South China]. Guangzhou: Guangdong jiaoyü chubanshe, 2000.

Wu, Zhande (伍沾德 James T. Wu). "Lingnan jiaoyü chongxian Kangle de jingguo" [嶺南教育重現康樂的經過 The process of restoring Lingnan education in the spirit of Honglok]. Manuscript provided by Lee Sui-ming.

Xianggang lishi bowuguan [香港歷史博物館 Hong Kong Museum of History], compiler. *Xuehai wuya: Jindai Zhongguo liuxuesheng zhan* [《學海無涯: 近代中國留學生展》Boundless learning: Foreign-educated students of modern China-sic]. Hong Kong: Government Logistics Department, 2003.

Xiao, Chaoran (蕭超然). *Beijing Daxue yu jindai Zhongguo* [《北京大學與近代中國》Peking University and modern China, sic]. Beijing: Zhongguo shehui kexue chubanshe, 2005.

Xie, Bizhen (謝必震). *Fujian xiehe daxue: xiangpiao Weiqi cun* [《福建協和大學: 香飄魏歧村》Fukien Christian University]. Shijiazhuang: Hebei jiaoyu chubanshe, 2004.

Xu, Chongqing (許崇清). *Xu Chongqing wenji* [《許崇清文集》Collected works of Xu Chongqing]. Edited by Xu Xihui. Guangzhou: Guangdong jiaoyu chubanshe, 2004.

Xu, Yihua (徐以驊). "Liberal Arts Education in English at St. John's University." Paper for "The American Context of China's Christian Colleges" conference, Wesleyan University, September 5–7, 2003.

———. *Sheng Yuehan daxue: Haishang fanwang du* [《聖約翰大學: 海上梵王渡》St. John's university]. Shijiazhuang: Hebei jiaoyu chubanshe, 2003.

Yale Divinity School Library. "Andrew Happer's Correspondence from 1845 to 1889." Group R: 8, Box 107, Folder Mr. and Mrs. J. S. Kunkle.

———. Barron H. Lerner. "The University of Pennsylvania in China: Medical Missionary Work, 1905–1914." Senior thesis presented to the Department of History of the University of Pennsylvania, April 16, 1982.

———. Charles K. Edmunds. "Authoritative Statements Regarding Lingnan University, 1941." Group 14, Box 14, Folder 178.

———. "English Version of Proposed by-Laws of the Board of Directors of Lingnan University, January 11, 1927." Group 14, Box 1, Folder 4.

———. "Extracts from a Letter Written by a Distinguished Minister after a Visit to Lingnan University in the Spring of 1936." Charles Thomas Walkley's letter to James M. Henry. Group 14, Box 22, Folder 322.

———. "Letter of C. K. Edmunds, March 12, 1941." Archives of the United Board for Christian Higher Education in Asia. Box 7, Folder 167.

———. "Letter from Foreign Claims Settlement Commission of the United States to Trustees of Lingnan University, February 24, 1971." Box 37, Folder 439.

———. "Letter from Yorke Allen, Jr., President of the Board of Trustees of Lingnan University, to John J. Stiglmeier, Dated April 26, 1965; to C.T. Young, President of Chung Chi College." Group 14, Box 18, Folders 241 and 251.

———. "Memo from Yorke Allen to the Trustees of Lingnan University, February 15, 1956." Group 14, Box 1, Folder 9 (Yorke Allen).

———. "Memorandum re.: Lingnan University," Office of the Trustees, New York City.

———. Olin D. Wannamaker (American Board of Directors). "Lingnan University, Agriculture and Rural Reconstruction: Immediate Needs for Which No Funds Are Available, May 29, 1941." Group 14, Box 22, Folder 328.

———. "Proposed Affiliation of Canton Union Theological College and Lingnan University." Group R: 8, Box 107, Folder Mr. and Mrs. J. S. Kunkle.

———. "A Review of the Publications and Unpublished Written Works of the Late Professor G. Weidman Groff, Lingnan University, Canton China (Covering the Period 1918–1953)." Prepared by John Hsueh-Ming Chen, The Pennsylvania State University, November 1957. Group 14, Box 18, Folder 258.

———. "Report on the First Phase, Lingnan University Planning Survey, 1948." Group R: 8, Box 107, Folder Mr. and Mrs. J. S. Kunkle.

———. "Trustees of Lingnan University, Annual Meeting of Trustees, Brief Report on Conditions at the University and Prospects, May 21, 1946." Box 25, Folder 372.

———. William W. Cadbury. "History of the Medical Work of Lingnan University." Group R: 8, Box 107, Folder Mr. and Mrs. J. S. Kunkle.

Yamamori, Tetsunao, and Kim-kwong Chan. *Witnesses to Power: Stories of God's Quiet Work in a Changing China*. Waynesboro, Ga.: Paternoster Publishing, 2000.

Yamashita, Samuel Hideo. "Asian Studies at American Private Colleges, 1808–1990." In *Asia in the Undergraduate Curriculum*, edited

Index

About the Author

Dong Wang is associate professor of History and executive director of the East-West Institute of International Studies at Gordon College (Wenham, Mass.). As research associate, she is also affiliated with the Fairbank Center for East Asian Research at Harvard University. She is the author of *China's Unequal Treaties: Narrating National History* (Lexington Books, 2005), among other publications. Her two ongoing book projects examine the history of United States-China relations and the social transformation of Luoyang, China, from antiquity to the present, respectively.